This book aims at reconciling emerging conceptions of mind and their contents that have, in recent years, come to seem irreconcilable. Post-Cartesian philosophers face the challenge of comprehending minds as natural objects possessing apparently non-natural powers of thought. The difficulty is to understand how our mental capacities, no less than our biological or chemical characteristics, might ultimately be products of our fundamental physical constituents, and to do so in a way that preserves the phenomena. Externalists argue that the significance of thought turns on the circumstances of thinkers; reductionists hold that mental characteristics are physical; eliminativists contend that the concept of thought belongs to an outmoded folk theory of behaviour.

John Heil explores these topics and points the way to a naturalistic synthesis, one that accords the mental a place in the physical world alongside the nonmental. Providing a lucid account of complex technical matters, this book will prove suitable to upper-division undergraduate or graduate courses in the philosophy of the mind.

CAMBRIDGE STUDIES IN PHILOSOPHY

# The Nature of True Minds

# CAMBRIDGE STUDIES IN PHILOSOPHY

*General editor* ERNEST SOSA

*Advisory editors* J.E.J. ALTHAM, SIMON BLACKBURN,
GILBERT HARMAN, MARTIN HOLLIS, FRANK JACKSON
WILLIAM G. LYCAN, JOHN PERRY, BARRY STROUD,
SYDNEY SHOEMAKER

## RECENT TITLES

# The Nature of
# True Minds

## John Heil
### Davidson College

CAMBRIDGE
UNIVERSITY PRESS

Published by the Press Syndicate of the University of Cambridge
The Pitt Building, Trumpington Street, Cambridge CB2 1RP
40 West 20th Street, New York, NY 10011-4211, USA
10 Stamford Road, Oakleigh, Victoria 3166, Australia

First published 1992

Printed in the United States of America

*Library of Congress Cataloging-in-Publication Data*
Heil, John.
The nature of true minds / John Heil.
p.      cm. – (Cambridge studies in philosophy)
Includes bibliographical references and index.
ISBN 0-521-41337-0. – ISBN 0-521-42400-3 (pb.)
1. Philosophy of mind.   I. Title.   II. Series.
BD418.3.H45      1992
128'.2 – dc20            91–44335
CIP

A catalog record for this book is available from the British Library.

ISBN 0-521-41337-0 hardback
ISBN 0-521-42400-3 paperback

*For the two Lucys – Lucy F. and Lucy P.*

The origin of action – its efficient, not its final cause – is choice, and that of choice is desire and reasoning with a view to an end.

– Aristotle, *Nicomachean Ethics*

# Contents

# Preface

Wittgenstein remarks that philosophy leaves everything as it is. This book is, in that respect at least, Wittgensteinian. I do not advance a new programme of research in the philosophy of mind nor promote any startling views as to the character of mental states and episodes. There are quite enough new programmes and startling views in circulation already. My aim, rather, is to reconcile emerging conceptions of the mind and its contents that have, in recent years, come to seem irreconcilable. Post-Cartesian philosophers face the challenge of comprehending minds as natural objects possessing apparently nonnatural powers of thought. The difficulty is to understand how our mental capacities, no less than our biological or chemical characteristics, might ultimately be products of our fundamental physical constituents, and to do so in a way that preserves the phenomena. Having abandoned Cartesian dualism, we confront a dilemma. On the one hand, we could opt for an out-and-out *eliminativism*, according to which minds and their contents are taken to be, like Ptolemaic epicycles, discredited posits of outmoded theories. On the other hand, we might suppose that mental properties or kinds are, in one way or another, *reducible* to physical properties or kinds. Since reductionism is often taken to be a species of implicit, *back-door* eliminativism, and since naturalism gives rise to the dilemma, it may seem that we must choose between eliminativism and some nonnaturalistic conception of mind.

My suggestion is that there is nothing to prevent us from allowing that mental characteristics, while distinctive, have a place in the physical world alongside familiar nonmental characteristics. This puts me at odds with the spirit of aggressive versions of eliminativism. I shall remain neutral, however, on the question of reduction. If there are strong nomological or metaphysical dependencies of mental characteristics on nonmental characteristics of agents, and if these dependencies count as reductive for some people, I do not regard that as necessarily a bad thing – a threat to the integrity of the mental world.

I set out to write a book on the philosophy of mind that would be accessible to nonphilosophers without being too breezy for philosophers concerned with topics that only a philosopher could love: externalism, supervenience, mental causation, privileged access. Although I have attempted, in Chapter 2, to sketch a picture of externalism – the view that states of mind depend for their character on conditions external to agents – for the benefit of readers unfamiliar with the territory, most of the remaining chapters contain discussions that are more intricate than I should have liked. I have tried to be clear and to minimise off-putting technical jargon. At the same time, I have sought to avoid oversimplification. The result is perhaps something on the challenging side of accessible.

I am grateful to various editors and publishers for allowing me to use parts of previously published papers, although in most cases the original has been utterly transformed. In at least one instance, I now defend *p* where earlier I had urged not-*p*. Those papers are 'Intentionality Speaks for Itself', in Stuart Silvers, ed., *Rerepresentation: Readings in the Philosophy of Mental Representation* (© 1989 by Kluwer Academic Publishers): 345–68; 'Mental Causes' (written with Alfred Mele), *American Philosophical Quarterly*, 28 (1991): 61–71; 'Privileged Access', *Mind*, 97 (1988): 238–51; and 'Talk and Thought', *Philosophical Papers*, 17 (1988): 153–70.

A version of this book was composed in 1987 while I was a visitor in the Department of Psychology at the University of California, Berkeley. I am grateful to members of the department, especially to Ervin Hafter and Donald A. Riley, for their hospitality. Bruce Vermazen kindly read and commented on that first draft of the manuscript. Material in several chapters was incorporated in three Hoernle lectures presented at the University of the Witwatersrand in July 1988 and in papers delivered at Rutgers University, the University of North Carolina at Chapel Hill, and the University of Idaho. I benefited from comments and suggestions received on those occasions. Those comments and suggestions, the subsequent comments of others who agreed to read parts of the manuscript, and my own rethinking of a number of issues led me to rewrite everything from the ground up twice more. At various stages the project was facilitated by support from the Davidson

College Faculty Research Fund and the National Endowment for the Humanities (NEH Fellowship FB-24078-86, and NEH Summer Stipend FT-35411-91).

I am indebted to many people for their comments and suggestions. The list is embarrassingly long (and doubtless incomplete): Frederick Adams, Robert Audi, Kent Bach, Lynne Rudder Baker, William Bechtel, Jonathan Bennett, James Beran, Simon Blackburn, Roman Bonzon, Jack Boyce, Anthony Dardis, Michael Devitt, Hubert Dreyfus, Fred Dretske, Steven Hales, Barbara Hannan, Hilary Kornblith, Mark Leon, Kirk Ludwig, Penelope Mackie, Christopher Maloney, Dugald Owen, Michael Pendlebury, John Post, Piers Rawling, Irma Reyna, Eleanor Rosch, David Sapire, John Searle, Ernest Sosa, James Van Cleve, Stephen Yablo. I am particularly grateful to Jaegwon Kim and Brian McLaughlin for detailed advice on supervenience and related metaphysical topics. I owe my sense of the territory to an unlikely duo, Donald Davidson and C. B. Martin, philosophers of depth, integrity, and good sense. It is no longer possible for me to separate certain of my own ideas from those of my colleague Alfred Mele, a philosopher's philosopher. Two people, Mark Overrold and Harrison Hagan Heil, have influenced everything I have written or thought since 1979.

# 1

# *Introduction*

## 1. AGENCY AND THE SCIENTIFIC IMAGE

It has long been supposed that the intentional attitudes – beliefs, desires, intentions, and the like – have a central place in the aetiology of intelligent behaviour. Actions are most naturally seen as bodily movements induced – or, in the case of refrainings, inhibited – in part by appropriate constellations of beliefs and desires.[1] Aristotle puts it succinctly: 'The origin of action – its efficient, not its final cause – is choice, and that of choice is desire and reasoning with a view to an end' (*Nicomachean Ethics* VI, ii, 1139a). This conception of action incorporates two distinct components, one intentional, one causal: Actions are performed in light of agents' reasons, and reasons influence agents' trajectories through the world. Beliefs, for instance, encompass both a particular intentional or propositional content and a measure of somatic efficacy. What one *does* depends in some measure on what one *believes*. Further, the effects of a belief within an agent's psychological economy vary with its content. If Clara wants some soup and believes that this bowl contains soup, then, other things being equal, she will take steps to consume the bowl's contents. Were she to believe that the bowl contained dishwater, she would behave differently.

This is familiar territory. We share, it seems, a conception of agency, one that informs our institutions, our relations with one another, even our self-image. That conception has, on the whole, been taken over into psychology, where it underlies our most rigorous attempts to understand ourselves qua intelligent beings. Significantly, the commonsense conception has proved remarkably

---

1 I do not intend this as an analysis or definition of 'action', only as a characterisation of one commonsense notion. Mental acts, for instance, need not issue in a bodily motion.

adaptive. For millennia it has enabled human beings to make sense of, to manipulate, and, within limits, to predict the behaviour of their fellows. It encompasses an outlook we self-consciously share, and without which the simplest sorts of intelligent interaction would be chancy at best. Our conception of agency is not one to be taken lightly.

Difficulties arise, however, when we endeavour to reconcile common sense and science – or, rather, when we juxtapose common sense and particular philosophical *reconstructions* of science. We have a picture of what science requires and how it operates. We are troubled when it proves difficult to square that picture with what we hold dear. When this happens, theorists divide into camps, some rejecting the universality of science, some arguing that we are better off leaving everyday ideas behind, some insisting that it is (or *must be*) possible somehow to render those ideas scientifically respectable.

Common sense is notoriously fickle, but no more so than favoured reconstructions of science. It would be putting the cart before the horse to suppose that the success science has historically enjoyed vindicates the latest philosophical accounts of the enterprise. These ride science's coattails, informed, most often, by aspects of empirical inquiry that, at historical moments, are made salient by the circumstances. Today we find philosophers proclaiming themselves cognitive scientists, beating the drum of progress, and encouraging us to move beyond traditional categories of agency to something more respectable. Talk about belief, desire, intention, and action should be replaced, eliminated, or, at the very least, beefed up (or pared down) to accord with an image of a polished science of mind. The proposal evokes a sense of déjà vu. The character of psychology seems fated always to be linked to emerging images of science. In the earliest days, in the writings of Wundt, James, and Titchner, this linkage was explicit; and the behaviourist revolution was occasioned in part by evolving views on the nature of science. Psychologists insist on *being scientific*. When they look to philosophers to tell them what that is, we are happy to oblige. We have absorbed a view of the territory and acquired the knack of pronouncing endeavours scientifically admissible or not. Meanwhile, science charts its own course, mostly oblivious to philosophical skirmishes waged in its wake.

Of course, attempts to resolve philosophical issues by reference to some preferred image of scientific acceptability face the risk of being outrun, like behaviourism, by scientific practice. So it is with the current debate on the status and future of 'folk psychology', the label nowadays wielded to indicate a complex and ungainly canon that includes what I have described as the commonsense conception of agency. My suspicion is that philosophers who tie the fate of agency to advances in neuroscience simultaneously underestimate the tenacity of that conception and overestimate their ability to divine the course of empirical inquiry. Suppose we grant that current ideas concerning the scientific vindication of folk psychology are apt, however. Where, exactly, does this leave the ordinary notion of agency and, in particular, our commonsense picture of intentional causation? There is reason to think that these notions survive intact. It is a long story, one best begun at the beginning.

## 2. FROM DESCARTES TO NATURALISM

Philosophers have generally followed Descartes in lumping together heterogeneous collections of episodes, dispositions, and conditions and assigning them to the mind. 'But what then am I? A thing that thinks. What is that? A thing that doubts, understands, affirms, denies, is willing, is unwilling, and also imagines and has sensory perceptions' (*Meditation* II). Attempts to find a common element, that in virtue of which each of these items could count as a *thought*, or a mental mode, have not been notably successful. Gradually it is becoming clear that we should be seeking, not similarities, but differences and distinctions. Perceptual experiences have little in common with pains, hopes, or images. Believing, feeling regret, and understanding move in different circles.

I am doubtful, then, that there is anything useful to be said about mental states and episodes taken as a whole. My target will be the intentional attitudes, or more particularly, those intentional characteristics of agents commonly taken to underlie intelligent behaviour. I shall use the expressions *intentional content* and *representational content* interchangeably to designate whatever it is about the intentional attitudes or, for that matter, about images, dreams, and other 'contentful' states of mind that leads us to speak of them as being *of* or *about* objects or states of affairs. In telling you what I dreamed last night, what I think about the designated hitter rule, or how I imagine it feels to walk on the moon, I am describing the

3

content, respectively, of a dream, a thought, and an image. We can, I think, allow that psychological states and episodes possess content without thereby committing ourselves to the notion that contents are kinds of intentional *entity* or that, in reporting the contents of my thoughts, I am describing features of peculiar sorts of *object* of which I am introspectively aware. Introspecting, at least in the sense of knowing the contents of one's thoughts, is not to be modelled on observation. In setting out to consider the status of contentful psychological states or events, then, we need not imagine that our quarry is a special class of entities, *contents*. Such things are creatures of philosophical theorising about thinking.

All of this takes for granted that the notion of intentional content is an essential ingredient in our conception of agency, but why, exactly, might content be thought important to a science of the mind? Two reasons suggest themselves at once.

First, the capacity to construct and employ meaningful artifacts – symbols, utterances, inscriptions, labels, and the like – evidently constitutes a significant human capacity, one on a par with ambulating and perceiving. At an early age children master an intentional repertoire. They discover that gestures, sounds, and pictures possess significance; and they learn to produce and manipulate significant items themselves. Considered in this light, representing is on all fours with a host of psychologically noteworthy phenomena.

There is, however, a second, rather different slant on the status of intentional states and events: The intentional aspect of intelligent agency is what renders it distinctively *psychological*. Psychological explanations of behaviour differ from physiological or biological accounts in appealing to intentional characteristics of agents. To turn one's back on such characteristics is, it seems, to turn one's back on psychology. This is not to say that intentional goings–on exhaust the subject matter of psychology, only that they occupy a central place in the conceptual web that distinguishes psychology from other systematic attempts to understand behaviour.

In continuing to take the intentional attitudes seriously, and thus to countenance traditional intentional psychology, we evince our conviction that a naturalistic account of intentional goings–on, an account of mentality that does not itself presuppose an intentional basis, has a reasonable prospect of success. Naturalism in the philosophy of mind is the view that mental characteristics are determined by or *supervene* on features of agents comprehended by the natural sciences. Agents possess thoughts *in virtue of* their possession of particular sorts of physical characteristics. This is not to say that intentional concepts are analysable into, and so reducible to, nonintentional concepts. The determination of the intentional by the physical is ontological, not conceptual. Whether determination of this sort implies the possibility of reduction in some weaker sense is, so far as I am concerned, an open question.

Naturalism makes its appearance in this volume in the guise of the *supervenience hypothesis*, the hypothesis that mental characteristics supervene on physical characteristics. Supervenience has been a buzz word in the philosophy of mind since the early seventies (see, e.g., Davidson 1970/1980). More recently, the discussion of supervenience has taken on a life of its own. Journals are brimming with papers with titles like 'Concepts of Supervenience', 'Supervenience Is a Two-Way Street', and, inevitably, 'The Myth of Supervenience'.[2] I must apologise, then, for adding to the heap. I am convinced, however, that supervenience relations are pervasive. We inhabit a *layered* world, the characteristics of which present a hierarchical or sedimented appearance. The dependence of intentional characteristics on characteristics at 'lower levels', I believe, is simply one example of supervenience among countless others.

A commitment to naturalism is a commitment to supervenience, or something like it. If the intentional attitudes depend on the existence of linguistic or social norms, then these norms themselves depend on the obtaining of unexciting physical states of affairs, and ultimately on the sorts of entities and characteristics presided over by physicists: the atoms and the void. I regard naturalism as a substantive metaphysical thesis, though not one for which it is reasonable to expect knock-down arguments. The proof of naturalism lies, not in its self-evidence, or the self-evidence of its supporting doctrines, but in its providing us with a framework that leaves room for, and at the same time affords us the opportunity to make sense of, ourselves, our institutions, and our world.


### 3. ELIMINATIVISM

My fondness for the intentional attitudes evidently puts me at odds with *eliminativists*, theorists who deny, or at least seriously doubt,

2 See, respectively, Kim (1984a), Miller (1990), and Grimes (1988).

that beliefs, desires, intentions, and the rest exist (see, e.g., P. M. Churchland 1979, 1981, 1985; P. S. Churchland 1986; Stich 1983). I am prepared to admit that eliminativists may be right or partly right. That is not something I intend to challenge. Rather, my plan is to set eliminativism to one side and operate as though the intentional attitudes were perfectly respectable investigative targets. Some of the claims I shall advance bear on eliminativism at least indirectly. I hold, for instance, that intentional characteristics are grounded in nonintentional, physical features of agents, and that those features can be seen to have a causal role in the production of behaviour. To the extent that I am right, eliminativism loses some of its allure.

My strategy, then, will be to bracket eliminativism and move ahead to other matters. Before moving on, however, I shall pause to comment briefly on the character of eliminativism, if for no other reason than to make clear what exactly I shall be ignoring. This may have the added benefit of heading off eliminativist considerations that might otherwise intrude in later chapters and threaten to carry the discussion in unproductive directions.

Eliminativists suppose that a proper scientific appreciation of the mind has been hampered by an aggregate of outmoded concepts, the origin of which antedates recorded history. This aggregate – 'folk psychology' – has served us well enough, but the time is ripe to move ahead, as the title of a recent book by Stephen Stich urges, 'from folk psychology to cognitive *science*'. Folk psychology comprises a *theory* of the mind, a *paradigm*, one that has been taken over, embellished, and codified by experimental and clinical psychologists. The upshot is an *intentional psychology*, a theoretical edifice distinguished by its commitment to the intentional attitudes in descriptions, predictions, and explanations of behaviour. Although intentional psychology has enjoyed some success, it is, at this writing, at a point of crisis. Thus, investigators attempting to assimilate the study of cognition and behaviour to thrilling discoveries in the neurosciences have been held in check by an uncritical reliance on an archaic conceptual system rooted in animism and superstition. Because psychology has traditionally cleaved to the aim of extending and refining folk categories, the discipline has failed to keep pace with genetics and nuclear physics. Intentional psychology, then, like astrology, in its day, or phlogistic chemistry, or Aristotelian kinematics, provides a clear-cut example of a 'stagnant or

6

degenerating research programme' (P. M. Churchland 1981). Carried along on the shoulders of bold pioneers in the neurosciences, however, we are gradually working our way free of this theoretical dead end. Once liberated, we shall look back on today's mental science, the psychology of the intentional attitudes, as no less quaint than our ancestors' beliefs about witches, demons, and a flat Earth.

Eliminativists do not, or *need* not, deny that folk psychology serves us well enough in everyday life. Attempts to refine and extend folk categories, however, merely result in a limping theoretical patchwork that 'suffers explanatory failures on an epic scale' (P. M. Churchland 1981, p. 76). Intentional psychology is, for instance, unrevealing about 'the nature and dynamics of mental illness, the faculty of creative imagination, or the ground of intelligence differences between individuals'. We remain ignorant of

the nature and function of sleep, . . . the common ability to catch an outfield fly ball on the run, or hit a moving car with a snowball, . . . the internal construction of a 3-D visual image from the subtle differences in the 2-D array of stimulations in our respective retinas, . . . the rich variety of perceptual illusions, . . . the miracle of memory. (P. M. Churchland 1981, p. 76)

Although investigators who have persisted in framing explanations in intentional terms have made little headway in the enterprise, workers operating outside the intentional domain suspect that important theoretical advances are imminent.

If we approach *homo sapiens* from the perspective of natural history and the physical sciences, we can tell a coherent story of his constitution, development, and behavioural capacities which encompasses particle physics, atomic and molecular theory, biology, physiology, and materialistic neuroscience. That story, though still radically incomplete, is already extremely powerful, outperforming [folk theory] at many points even in its own domain. . . . [T]he greatest theoretical synthesis in the history of the human race is currently in our hands. (P. M. Churchland 1981, p. 75)

Even if none of these approaches to mentality turned out to be correct in detail, one might still wish to draw a general moral. The present direction of neuroscience offers scant comfort to the friends of the intentional attitudes. It seems possible, and to some, inescapable, that our evolving theories of behaviour will have no place for familiar intentional states and processes, that they will leave no room for beliefs, wants, dreams, and images.

7

The conclusion is, as it stands, ambiguous. It might be taken merely to license the thought that a mature science of the mind will feature an intentional vocabulary not smoothly isomorphic with everyday intentional terminology. On such an interpretation we might expect the emergence of theories incorporating, for instance, appeals to *finer-grained* intentional states and processes. Thus construed, the conclusion is, from the point of view of the present volume, innocuous. Indeed, approaches of this sort have long been common in mainstream intentional psychology (see, e.g., Anderson 1985). When we scrutinise considerations advanced against commonsense intentional categories, however, it is clear that, more often than not, something stronger is intended. Problems thought to beset traditional psychology evidently stem from perfectly general features of intentionality. As a result, the eliminativist programme is most naturally regarded as supporting the conclusion that intentional states and goings-on *generally* will be left behind as science marches forward.

In leaving intentional psychology behind, we leave behind its posits, items earlier postulated to account for intelligent behaviour. Belief, intention, desire, and the rest drop out of the picture. This, eliminativists insist, should afford neither surprise nor shock. It is simply a manifestation of a long-acknowledged general feature of theoretical advance. As theories are replaced, ontologies are abandoned. In the early nineteenth century, chemists were forced to concede that, despite widely accepted evidence to the contrary, phlogiston did not after all exist. Early in our own century, the ether met a similar fate. Eventually, perhaps, psychologists will be obliged to admit that there are no intentional attitudes, no beliefs, intentions, or desires.

It is easy to imagine that eliminativism is not merely false, but *incoherent*. One might worry, for instance, that such a doctrine, if true, could neither be taken seriously nor accepted: Takings and acceptings would be mere fictions; and we swoon at the prospect of a theory that, if apt, must be simultaneously unbelievable and indubitable: Belief and doubt must go the way of witches and phlogiston. A doctrine with these remarkable features slips through our fingers whenever we try to grasp it. In setting out to abolish beliefs, it relinquishes its claim to be a doctrine we ought reasonably to believe. In the same way, we may be hard put to see how it could be

8

thought to be *true*: Truth is precisely the sort of semantic artifact the theory apparently leaves behind.

Considerations of this sort suggest that anyone setting out to obtain converts to eliminativism runs a nonnegligible risk of being charged with willful incoherence. Incoherence, however, though troubling, may be a small price to pay for impressive theoretical advance. An apparently incoherent doctrine can turn out to be obliquely perspicuous. The point is explicit in Wittgenstein's *Tractatus*:

My propositions serve as elucidations in the following sense: Anyone who understands me eventually recognises them as nonsensical, when he has used them – as steps – to climb beyond them. (He must, so to speak, throw away the ladder after he has climbed up it.) He must transcend these propositions, and then he will see the world aright. (Wittgenstein 1921/1960, §6.54)

Certain truths may be such that attempts to express them are bound to be frustrated. Theories purporting to express such truths could be called *Tractarian*.

The hypothesis that there are no intentional attitudes is evidently Tractarian. It obliges us to envisage a world, indistinguishable by its human inhabitants from our world, but one bereft of intentionality. In that world, there are no beliefs, wants, or intentions. There are, to be sure, sentences (or sentence-like inscriptions) in which the *words* 'belief', 'want', and 'intention' occur. In such a world it might turn out that nothing is true or false, though, again, the *words* 'true' and 'false' appear from time to time in utterances and inscriptions. A theorist who spurns the intentional attitudes has it that *our* world is *that* world. Were this so, the claim that it *is* so would not be *true*. It would not be false either: *Nothing* would be true or false. This is simply an intriguing, if kinky, consequence of the theory. It cannot be believed or asserted – it cannot even be true – in a world that satisfies it. The difficulty comes, not in imagining a world satisfying the theory, but in making sense of the claim that our world is, or might be, such a world. That claim could *have* a sense only in a world in which it is false. It does not follow, however, that it *is* false, but (at most) that if it has a truth-value, if it is *either* true or false, it is false. Nevertheless, I shall suppose that a theory recommending abandonment of the intentional attitudes, whatever its liabilities, ought not to be rejected solely on the grounds that it is, when advanced, apparently self-defeating. The theory may *show* somehow what it cannot *say*.[3]

A natural response to eliminativist rhetoric is to insist that intentional psychology is in fact in tolerable condition. As long as we consider everyday explanations of everyday actions, this seems right. Opponents of intentional theorising, however, are not inclined to dispute these pedestrian successes. For them, the issue is not whether, at some relatively shallow level, intentional categories suffice, but whether, beneath the surface, they bear any interesting relation to reality. The alleged failure of elaborations of intentional categories, the failure, that is, of traditional intentional psychology to yield a unified and fruitful theory of behaviour, suggests to many that it does not.

It could well turn out that the conceptual framework implicit in intentional psychology is practically indispensable. The price of abandoning that framework might be unreasonably high. An eliminativist, however, could accept this possibility without conceding the argument. One need only distinguish that for which we have evidence – the traditional province of science – from that for which we have good reason to pursue. We might imagine physicists have proved that there are no tables, chairs, and icebergs, that there are only clouds of particles. Nevertheless, and for a variety of reasons, we might continue to speak of tables, chairs, and icebergs and, in general, to *act* as though such things existed. The point is not that eliminativism about tables and icebergs is defensible, only that it could be defensible and, at the same time, it could be reasonable – practically reasonable – for most of us most of the time to continue to talk and act as though tables and icebergs exist.

One might worry, of course, that were we to discover the intentional idiom indispensable, this itself would call for an explanation of some sort. One possibility is that intentional categories are not, after all, inapplicable. Their applicability is explicable, perhaps, by reference to what may turn out to be nonintentional, neurological facts. Classical physicists depicted a world in which rigid objects moved about and collided in the manner of billiard balls. We have

---

3 Lynne Rudder Baker (1987) is less charitable toward theories of this sort. See also Malcolm (1968), and Chapter 4, § 3, below. Of necessity I shall, in common with everyone else, continue to employ an intentional idiom in discussing theories that deny its legitimacy.

left classical physics behind. We no longer conceive of material substances as composed of indivisible, rigid, billiard-ball-like corpuscles. But we have not abandoned the practice of treating *billiard balls* as rigid. Indeed, we regard physics and chemistry as providing an *explanation* of this very feature, rigidity. In the same way, we may come to see advances in neuroscience as providing explanations of intentional goings-on, not evidence for their nonexistence.

These observations are not meant to provide a priori assurance concerning the status of intentional psychology. They are intended, instead, to operate at the same level as the position against which they are directed. That position, eliminativism, holds that intentionality is put at risk by recent trends in neuroscience. I am urging that this is not obviously so. Intentional categories have a broad and varied application that could well remain relatively unscathed by the disappearance of any particular empirical theory, or family of theories, of behaviour.

## 4. LOOKING AHEAD

Having bracketed – without dismissing – one sort of scepticism about the intentional attitudes, I shall henceforth make use of the intentional idiom freely and unselfconsciously. My aspiration in the chapters that follow is to interpret recent work in the philosophy of mind in a way that illuminates intentional psychology, our commonsense conception of agency, and the naturalistic worldview that characterises the modern temperament. Naturalism is suspicious of Cartesian dualism: The mind's place is in, not adjunct to, nature. It is, at the same time, no less suspicious of the reductionist, 'nothing but' impulse to show that minds are really nothing but brains, or nothing but dispositions to behaviour, or nothing but artifacts of our forms of explanation.

When we consider the intentional attitudes, then, what do we find? Wittgenstein, in the *Tractatus*, depicted thought as 'reaching out' to the world, illuminating stretches of reality, rather as a beam of light illuminates features of a surface on which it is directed (see, e.g., Wittgenstein 1921/1960, §§ 2.15–2.1515). This conception affords a pure, uncompromising instance of *internalism*, a doctrine according to which meanings are taken to issue *from* items possessing significance intrinsically. From these, meanings spread to other things, providing them with inherited, *extrinsic* meaning. In the *Tractatus*, sentences are said to express thoughts, and thoughts – internal sentences – to project themselves spontaneously onto states of affairs.

Some years later, in repudiating the Tractarian conception of language and thought, Wittgenstein painted a very different, contextualist or *externalist*, picture of meaning. Meaning was taken to emerge, not from intrinsic features of originally meaningful signs, but from roles signs played in the activities of human beings, the place of signs in *forms of life*. The source of meaning on this view is largely, though not exclusively, social: The words we use mean what they do because they are rooted in shared practices, and the thoughts we entertain inherit their significance from the words we deploy to express them.

Contemporary philosophy of mind has been deeply influenced by this picture. It is now widely suspected that the contents of our thoughts, like the meanings of the words we utter, are fixed, not by the intrinsic features of those thoughts, but by the circumstances of thinkers. The idea is sometimes illustrated by means of thought experiments in which we are called upon to imagine pairs of agents, each pair consisting of 'twins' who are identical with respect to their intrinsic, nonintentional characteristics yet differ linguistically and mentally. When I become thirsty, my thoughts turn to water. Were I to have a 'molecule-for-molecule' twin on a distant planet, a planet indistinguishable from Earth except for the presence of something other than $H_2O$ in its rivers, ponds, and Perrier bottles, my twin's thoughts would concern not *water*, but *twin* water.

Twin Earth examples motivate, but fall short of establishing, externalism. Although a detailed articulation and discussion of externalist doctrine is beyond the scope of this volume, I shall, in much of what follows, operate on the assumption that externalist accounts of the mind must be taken seriously, and, against this background, reflect on the status of intentionality – in the guise of the intentional attitudes. There are at least three reasons for proceeding in this way.

First, whatever its liabilities, externalism captures a range of notable insights into mind and meaning. It may be possible to recast these internalistically, but it is difficult, from our current perspective, to see how that might be done. It is no accident that Searle's

(1983) suggestion that the brain is the source of intentionality has not been widely embraced.[4]

Second, much of today's *angst* concerning the place of intentionality in the natural world is traceable to widespread misgivings about the implications of externalism. It is safe to say, I think, that were we in possession of a remotely plausible internalist theory of mind, many, though by no means all, of these misgivings would evaporate. There is something to be said, then, for externalism as a kind of worst-case possibility. If it could be shown that agents' intentional characteristics might be entirely respectable *even if* those characteristics turned out to depend on agents' extrinsic features, it would seem that there could be no special further problem in finding a place for intentional properties, internalistically construed.

A third reason for scrutinising the intentional attitudes against an externalist backdrop is that a comparison of externalist and more traditional Cartesian or internalist conceptions of mentality along particular dimensions will afford an opportunity of making ingredients of those conceptions explicit. It turns out – perhaps to no one's surprise – that certain philosophical diagnoses underlying the traditional picture of the mind badly miss the mark. It is, for instance, easy to imagine that the evident ease with which we know our own thoughts has something to do with the *proximity* of mental objects to the mind's gaze. As it happens, this mode of explanation is unilluminating. Placing the determinants of thought inside the head, even inside a Cartesian ego, does nothing to advance our understanding of the epistemic privilege we apparently enjoy with respect to particular thoughts.

In Chapter 2, then, I turn to considerations that incline philosophers of mind to embrace some version of externalism, to suppose that states of mind owe their intentional character not solely to the nonrelational, intrinsic features of agents, but to agents' circumstances as well. Two agents might be 'molecule-for-molecule' duplicates, yet, owing to differences in history or environment, might be taken to entertain different thoughts. As I have indicated already, externalist views of this sort have attracted a considerable following among philosophers. Nonphilosophers, in contrast, typically find

4 Not by philosophers, at any rate. Nonphilosophers often imagine that Searle's view, or something like it, is obviously correct; see, e.g., Young (1987). Cf. Sosa (1992).

them next to incomprehensible. In any case, although I shall try to *motivate* externalism, I do so, not for the purpose of defending some particular externalist doctrine, but for the reasons mentioned above, and because externalism represents an important break with our Cartesian heritage, one the consequences of which are only gradually being appreciated.

In Chapter 3, I introduce the supervenience hypothesis – according to which the intentional characteristics of agents supervene on their nonintentional, physical characteristics – and advance a view about what this might mean. I regard the prospect of supervenience not as providing a *solution* to the traditional mind–body problem, but as affording a framework within which it may be possible to sharpen our appreciation of what that problem encompasses. I suggest that externalism and the supervenience hypothesis are perfectly compatible provided we allow the supervenience 'base' of intentional characteristics to be 'broad'. This would mean that agents possess certain of their intentional characteristics partly in virtue of their historical or circumstantial features.

At this point the mind–body problem reasserts itself. It is difficult to see how a 'broadly supervenient' characteristic, one that depends on an agent's extrinsic features, could play anything like a causal role in the production of that agent's behaviour. The prospects of a sensible notion of mental causation are the focus of Chapter 4. I argue that the intentional attitudes can indeed have causal relevance, that mental characteristics can make a difference. If that is so, then intentional psychology and our ordinary conception of agency are partly vindicated. Such results cannot refute eliminativism, of course, any more than naturalistic accounts of knowledge or justified belief refute scepticism. If successful, however, they provide an alternative to scepticism, and perhaps that is all we can ask.

Having defended the notion that mental/physical supervenience and mental causation are consistent with externalism, I turn in Chapter 5 to another potential stumbling block for externalist construals of the intentional attitudes: our notion of privileged access. If anything is clear, it is that we know the contents of our own thoughts directly and with something approaching Cartesian certainty. A thought may be fleeting, and so forgotten, or unconscious. When I consider my own conscious thoughts, however, I experience what feels like an immediate grasp of their intentional

14

character, what those thoughts concern. On the face of it, this feature of our mental lives is impossible to reconcile with externalism. If the intentional content of a thought depends in part on our circumstances or causal histories, then it is hard to see how we could grasp those characteristics directly and immediately. I shall offer an account of privileged access, however, that purports both to make sense of the phenomenon and to mesh with the externalist picture.

Chapter 6 contains a discussion of the relation of language to thought. I spend much of the chapter developing a somewhat speculative reconstruction of Donald Davidson's grounds for regarding language and thought as conceptually linked. Surprisingly, an understanding of this relation is facilitated by our earlier results on privileged access. I take this sort of mutual, though unexpected, support to reinforce both positions.

Although the focal point of this volume is the character of intentionality, I have not set out to provide anything like a theory of mind or meaning. Given my naturalistic bias, I assume that any such theory would require a substantial empirical component. That is not to say that philosophers, qua philosophers, might not have a significant role to play in the articulation of possible constraints on theories of intentionality. Even here, however, I offer only the sketchiest of suggestions, and these are scarcely exciting or original. I make heavy use of a broadly externalist conception of the intentional attitudes, but, as I suggested earlier, this is in part due to my belief that externalism can be used as a foil for the more general topics I treat in some detail. To the extent that my treatment of those topics is successful, perhaps externalism is supported indirectly. The failure of externalism, however, would not affect the main lines of argument pursued here.

## 5. TERMINOLOGICAL PRELIMINARIES

For various reasons, some of which will emerge in subsequent chapters, discussions of the intentional attitudes commonly focus on belief. It is crucial in such discussions to distinguish *states* of belief, *believings*, from *sentences* held true or *propositions* believed. In an everyday conversation, when I refer to Clara's belief that Wayne is a deconstructionist, I may be referring either to what Clara believes, the proposition that Wayne is a deconstructionist, or to a

15

facet of Clara's mental condition. Let me be frank. Although, like everyone else, I find it convenient to speak of propositions in this context, I have no clear understanding of what it might be to stand in a relation of believing to a proposition, or even what propositions might *be*. Perhaps propositions are specialised abstract entities like numbers, or perhaps they are sets of possible worlds, or perhaps they are something else altogether. Sentences, I think, are only slightly less puzzling. Happily we can leave aside such conundrums. In considering belief, I shall be concerned, not with sentences or propositions believed, but with *states* of believing – and with related states of wanting, intending, hoping, dreaming, and the like. That is, I shall be concerned with the character of what are commonly called states of mind, as distinct from the sentences, or propositions, or nonpropositional intentional items associated with the contents of states of mind.

In speaking here of Clara's belief that Wayne is a deconstructionist, then, I mean to be referring to a *state* Clara is in, a component of her *mental condition*, not to a sentence or to the proposition that Wayne is a deconstructionist. I take states to be concrete, dated particulars: states of affairs, conditions. States – Clara's belief, or her believing, that Wayne is a deconstructionist, for instance – are often put into contrast with *events* – Clara's forming, or acquiring, or losing the belief that Wayne is a deconstructionist. The distinction has an undoubted appeal. The occurrence of an event typically, though perhaps not inevitably, is marked by a change. If Clara's forming the belief that Wayne is a deconstructionist is an event, then it occurs at, or during, a particular time, *t*. Before *t* Clara lacks the belief, after *t* she possesses it. In contrast, Clara may be in a particular state, the state of believing that Wayne is a deconstructionist, for some more or less extended period of time, and not change at all, or at any rate not change in any respect relevant to her harbouring this particular belief.

What is not clear to me is whether an event–state distinction is a deep one. We might regard the oscillation of a pendulum as an event or series of events, though, in one sense, so long as the oscillation continues, the pendulum system does not change at all. Indeed, we sometimes speak of continuous alterations of this sort as states: oscillatory states, steady states, states of change. In other cases, the *absence* of change may come to be regarded as an event. Your remaining seated when 'The Star Spangled Banner' is played might be a deliberate action on your part, something you *do*, and doings are ordinarily classified as events. My suspicion is that, at some deeper level, states and events are instances of a single metaphysical kind. The suspicion stems from three notable, though entirely inconclusive, considerations.

First, it is uncontroversial that events may be composed of subevents, and states of substates. But apparent states – the oscillatory state of a pendulum, for instance, or the state of an evaporating liquid – could, it seems, include events. For their part, events seem sometimes to include states as components. Clara's forming the belief that Wayne is a deconstructionist incorporates Clara's believing that Wayne is a deconstructionist, and the pendulum's oscillating includes an instantaneous state indistinguishable from that of the pendulum at rest.

Second, events and states are susceptible in parallel ways to fine-grained and coarse-grained analyses.[5] An event might be characterised in the fine-grained mode as the exemplifying of an event property at a time. Similarly, a state might be said to be the exemplifying of some *state* property at a time. The question then arises whether state properties and event properties are fundamentally distinct kinds of properties.

On a coarse-grained characterisation of events, events are entities – concrete, dated particulars – that satisfy event predicates. A conception of this sort is coarse-grained in the sense that it may count events as the same (only 'differently described') that a fine-grained account distinguishes. One and the same particular may satisfy many different predicates, one and the same thing may fall under many different descriptions. When this is so, a fine-grained account may pick out many different events, a coarse-grained account, just one – under many different descriptions. Wayne's moving his arm and Wayne's signalling, for instance, might be counted as distinct events by a fine-grained theorist, since two distinct event properties are exemplified, but as the same event under different descriptions by a coarse-grained theorist.

Consider a coarse-grained conception of states: A state is a concrete, dated particular, that satisfies a state predicate. On such a conception, the water's being frozen and the water's having a cer-

---

5 Fine-grained accounts of events are associated with Goldman (1970) and Kim (1973); coarse-grained accounts, with Davidson (1963/1980, 1970/1980). See Lombard (1986, chap. 3) for a useful discussion of this distinction.

tain rigid molecular structure might count as two descriptions of a single state. A fine-grained theorist might reckon that the descriptions pick out distinct states.

A third reason for suspecting that events and states belong to the same metaphysical genus is rather more controversial: Prima facie, both events and states occur as constituents of causal transactions. I behave as I do, it seems, in part because of my beliefs. If that is so, certain of my states, my belief states, contribute to the aetiology of my behaviour. A locomotive's moving down a track is caused by certain events. The character of that motion, however, its direction, is due in some measure to the state or condition of the tracks along which the locomotive moves. The trajectory of a ball bounced off a wall is caused partly by its hitting the wall in a certain way, but, in addition, by the condition of the wall: Rigid walls deflect balls differently than walls padded with foam rubber. A ball rolling down an incline rolls as it does in part because of the state of the incline.

No doubt in such cases it is possible to find – or contrive – events that play the causal roles we might otherwise be inclined to assign to states. Perhaps it is just my *acquiring* or my *activating* certain beliefs that affects my behaviour; perhaps it is just the wheels' engaging the tracks that affects the locomotive's course; and perhaps it is just the ball's losing energy to the wall or gaining energy from its trip down the incline that affects its behaviour. Still, these events seem to owe *their* character, in some degree, to the character of the pertinent states. This suggests that it might make sense to allow states a part in our overall conception of causality. Perhaps causal transactions always include events as components. This does not forestall their including, as well, states. Of course, if the state–event distinction is not ultimate, if states and events are instances of a single metaphysical kind, then there is less reason to exclude states as legitimate causal relata.

I intend to remain neutral on such questions. That is, I shall neither endorse nor condemn the notion that states and events are instances of a single metaphysical kind. Nor shall I recommend adoption of any particular conception of events (or states). What I have to say is, so far as I can tell, consistent with both fine-grained and coarse-grained accounts. Finally, nothing I say hinges on acceptance of the idea that states, and not just events, have causal clout. Like most philosophers and all nonphilosophers, I shall sometimes speak *as though* states figured as components in causal transactions. I now stipulate that this way of speaking should be taken literally if and only if states do in fact figure in causal transactions. Otherwise, I should be taken to be referring obliquely to some identifiable event. I remain neutral on these matters not because I lack views on them, but because I do not think that the positions I defend here require commitments one way or the other. It is, I think, important to evaluate those positions independently of issues that do not directly bear on them.

A final terminological point: In discussing intentional states of mind, some philosophers focus on mental *properties*, whereas others prefer to speak of mental *predicates*. Predicates are satisfied or fail to be satisfied, properties are instantiated or exemplified or fail to be instantiated or exemplified. Predicates are linguistic, most properties are not. Although there is a rough correspondence between properties and predicates, there are undoubtedly properties for which there are no predicates – at least there are if there are properties at all – and distinct predicates may not correspond to distinct properties. Should we, then, couch discussions of mentality in terms of properties or predicates? Or does it make a difference?

I am not convinced that it does make a difference. I have a slight preference for thinking of these matters in terms of predicates, largely because I lack a clear conception of what exactly properties are, how they are known, and how they are *individuated*, distinguished one from another. We routinely predicate greenness of grass. But is greenness a property of grass? I am inclined to think that it is, but I admit that I should be hard pressed to say why. Do we rely on science to tell us what are and are not genuine properties? Or is this something we can discover a priori? Because these questions threaten to take us into deep metaphysical waters, I shall try to say what I have to say in a way that does not imply any particular answer to them. To that end, I shall use the term 'property' in a relaxed sense. A property (in this relaxed sense) is exemplified whenever a predicate associated with it is satisfied. Having the belief that Wayne is a deconstructionist, then, is, in my relaxed sense, a property exemplified by Clara when it is true that Clara believes that Wayne is a deconstructionist. Similarly, being green is a property exemplified by grass if it is true that grass is green. Whether having the belief that Wayne is a deconstructionist or being green are genuine properties, I leave for others to discern.

19

# 2

# *The legacy of Cartesianism*

## 1. THE CARTESIAN PICTURE

An important component of our everyday conception of the mind began as a lively philosophical thesis and evolved into common sense. The philosophical thesis was spelled out by Descartes, and, without suggesting that Descartes was its sole author, I shall, for convenience, refer to it as the *Cartesian conception*. According to this conception, minds are *entities*, sentient *organs* on a par with hearts and livers. Whereas the heart circulates blood, and the liver regulates metabolism, the mind *feels* and *thinks*. Minds receive *stimuli* from bodily receptors via impulses born by nerves that connect receptors to the brain. According to official Cartesian doctrine, the mind and the brain are separate entities, and events occurring in the mind are distinct from events occurring in the brain. Descartes believed that the brain operated on exclusively *mechanical* principles, whereas the mind was governed by principles of *reason*. There was, he thought, no prospect of deriving the latter from the former; hence minds must be separate, nonphysical substances, and brains turn out to be physical modes. Even God could not build a sentient robot, a physical device with the capacity to feel or think. Feelings and thoughts require a nonphysical, *mental* basis.

Although Descartes's contemporaries had doubts about the dualistic component of this picture, they accepted the notion that the mind is a receptacle harbouring feelings and thoughts and operating in accord with an identifiable set of mental principles. Some, like Hobbes, lobbied for the identification of minds and brains, and for the reduction of mental principles to mechanical, *computational* principles. Minds, Hobbes thought, were calculators housed inside the skull. Others, leery of Hobbesian materialism, rejected the identity. Few, however, questioned the broader picture. It is this picture that

20

we have inherited and that even today leads our thoughts on mentality down familiar paths.

A second, epistemological, component of the Cartesian notion of mind has been no less influential. According to Descartes, the contents of our minds are always and infallibly present to us. I know my own thoughts – my beliefs, my desires, my choices, my feelings – immediately and with certainty. In its extreme form, this doctrine, too, was attacked by Descartes's contemporaries, and today it finds few advocates. Still, the core of the doctrine survives in the notion of *privileged access*: We are aware of at least some of the contents of our own minds directly and immediately, if not infallibly. Some of our beliefs and desires may be hidden from us, we may misread our own motives, but when we know what we think, we know it in a way not open to others.

Important components of the Cartesian picture, then, have weathered both the demise of dualism and the abandonment of much of Descartes's epistemological project. We continue to think of the mind as an organ, a part of us that houses feelings and thoughts and plays an executive role in the pursuit of our ends. Feelings – sensations and sensory experiences – are presumed to arise in the mind as a result of neural stimulation, and thoughts contained in the mind project outward onto the world. We are still moved by the Cartesian notion that our conception of the world must be built from the inside out: We have only the contents of our minds to go on, and our task is to construct from these an accurate map of the 'external world'. Scepticism and antirealism loom when we recognise that many maps are consistent with our information.

Traditional responses to scepticism work from within the Cartesian picture. Even our instinctive, ground-level belief that *of course* the world is, on the whole, as we think it is, countenances a logical gap between the contents of our minds and the character of our surroundings. We presume a match between what we think and what there is, but we acknowledge this as a presumption the moment we are pressed.

The Cartesian picture informs even our most ambitious systematic efforts at understanding intelligent behaviour. We may think of minds as computing machines realised in the brain, or simply as brains operating in accord with specialised neurobiological principles. In either case we are fleshing out details concerning the operation of a mechanism the general character of which we do not think

21

to question. The mind is a device, a 'black box', that feels and thinks (cf. Hamlyn 1990). It is located inside the head, though it is connected, via a system of nerves, to every part of the body. The mind responds to goings-on beyond the body, but only indirectly, only insofar as these affect the body's sensory surfaces. The mind's contents include sensations and thoughts. The former exhibit a range of 'phenomenal' characteristics, the latter are 'intentional', they are of, or about, or 'directed on' actual or possible objects and states of affairs.

A corollary of this conception is that the thoughts we entertain are self-contained, logically independent of our circumstances. Thoughts may be induced by external occurrences, of course, but their significance – their 'intentionality' – is independent of those external occurrences. We have noted already a sceptical moral that can be drawn from this picture. The world may in fact be very different from the way I think it is. I might one day awaken to discover that my life, until then, had been a seamless dream, and that reality differs wildly from my image of it. I might be the plaything of an evil demon of the sort described by Descartes, or I might be a brain afloat in a vat of nutrients and wired to a computing machine capable of simulating receptor inputs.

## 2. CHALLENGES TO THE CARTESIAN PICTURE

The Cartesian picture is, I submit, a familiar one. Many who would balk at endorsing it explicitly, endorse it implicitly by advancing theses designed to accommodate its quirks. Its seeming naturalness signals that it has found its way into popular consciousness and common sense. The picture is, nevertheless, the historical product of a particular philosophical stance. This does not invalidate it, of course, but it should serve as a reminder that assumptions we make in embarking on inquiry often bring with them unrecognised, and therefore unacknowledged, philosophical baggage.

The Cartesian picture has not gone unchallenged. Behaviourists set out to abolish the 'Cartesian Myth' by attempting, without much success, to reduce mental events to behaviour and 'nonoccurrent' states of mind to behavioural dispositions.[1] In recent years, a number of philosophers have argued in ways that suggest Carte-

---

1 By 'behaviourists' here I mean *philosophical* behaviourists (aka 'analytical' or 'logical' behaviourists). Behaviourist *psychologists*, though methodologically austere,

sianism is largely inappropriate as a model for intentional states of mind – beliefs, desires, imaginings, emotions, and the like. These often encompass attitudes toward particular propositions, and, in keeping with a suggestion of Russell's, they are commonly referred to as propositional attitudes. I may believe, hope, fear, or doubt, that $p$, where $p$ is some proposition (that it is raining, for instance, or that truth is beauty, beauty truth). I prefer the label 'intentional attitudes' for these states of mind, leaving open whether all such attitudes are strictly propositional in character.

According to the Cartesian picture, our attitudes owe their intentional character – their 'of-ness' or 'about-ness' – exclusively to the intrinsic features of agents possessing them (or perhaps to the intrinsic features of the minds of such agents). If we hold these intrinsic features constant and vary the context in which they occur, we may alter the truth-value (or satisfaction-value) of particular attitudes, but we do not thereby alter their satisfaction-conditions or their content. I believe truly that there is a sheet of paper in front of me. Suppose an evil demon causes the paper to vanish while simultaneously inducing me to hallucinate a sheet of paper. I may now believe falsely that there is a sheet of paper in front of me, but the *content* of my belief is unaltered: It is still a belief about a sheet of paper, a belief that is true if and only if there is a sheet of paper in front of me. An evil demon might, in this way, destroy my whole world, without altering in the slightest the contents of my thoughts. Indeed, if his goal is deception, he will succeed only to the extent that I continue to believe what I previously believed. More radically, since, according to the Cartesian, the content of my thoughts depends only on certain of my intrinsic properties, it is at least conceivable that I have *always* been wrong in my beliefs about the material world: There is no paper, no Earth, no sky, no other people, only hallucinations of these things brought on by the evil demon.

The example is an extreme one, but it is intended merely to highlight one important aspect of the Cartesian picture, what I have called its *internalism*: The content of every intentional attitude is determined exclusively by intrinsic features of agents (or minds) harbouring those attitudes. If you like: Intentional characteristics *supervene* on the intrinsic characteristics of agents (or minds). A

seem to me to fall squarely within the Cartesian tradition. Ryle is usually regarded as the arch philosophical behaviourist, but I am not convinced that this characterisation would survive a careful reading of *The Concept of Mind* (1949).

supervenient characteristic is distinct from but dependent on and determined by some other, presumably 'more basic', characteristic or collection of characteristics. I shall have more to say in Chapter 3 about supervenience. A word about intrinsic characteristics or properties is in order, however.

By 'intrinsic' I do not mean 'essential'. An intrinsic property (in my usage) is nonrelational in the sense that its possession by an object does not (logically or conceptually) require the existence of any separate object or the existence of that same object, or a part of that same object, at some other time. An object, $o_1$, is separate from an object, $o_2$, just in case $o_1$ is not identical with $o_2$ or with any part of $o_2$. 'Internal' might be a synonym for 'intrinsic', provided that 'internal' is taken to mean 'logically internal', not 'inside'. I shall speak of relational or extrinsic characteristics meaning thereby characteristics the instantiation of which by an object *does* require the existence of a separate object or the existence of that same object, or a part of that same object, at some distinct time. If my left arm possesses the characteristic of being longer than my right arm, it does so extrinsically. An extrinsic or relational feature in this sense, then, differs from a diadic (or in general an $n$-adic) feature. My right arm's being longer than my left arm is a diadic but, in my sense, nonrelational feature of the complex entity of which these are components – my body. Similarly, instances of relations among neurons could be considered intrinsic to brains.

Although internalists believe that agents' intentional characteristics depend exclusively on intrinsic features of agents, *externalists* hold that mental content is context-dependent: In altering agents' circumstances, we may vary the content of their intentional attitudes. The character of those attitudes depends not solely on the intrinsic features of agents, but also on relations those agents bear to extrinsic states of affairs. Reverting to the technical jargon employed above, externalists hold that the characteristics on which intentional features of ordinary agents depend or supervene include, necessarily, characteristics extrinsic to those agents.

The externalist conception of mind is, I believe, nothing short of revolutionary. It is, arguably, *the* philosophical contribution of the latter half of the twentieth century.[2] Its contemporary source is

2 This proclamation is probably historically naïve. According to Tyler Burge (1979) externalism is implicitly endorsed by Hegel and perhaps by some Hegelians.

Wittgenstein, although versions of externalism have been advanced by philosophers from widely different backgrounds. My aim here is not to defend externalism or to offer new arguments in its support, but to explicate and motivate a version of the doctrine, and to examine certain of its consequences. These seem to me to fall into two broad categories: epistemological and metaphysical. I shall have little here to say about the former. Although externalist theories of mind and meaning are sometimes thought to have monumental antisceptical and antirealist implications, I am not satisfied that this is so (see Heil 1988). Even if I were right about that, however, externalism does indeed mandate a fundamental reordering of our conception of mind, its standing in the natural world, and its relation to behaviour. It is worth asking how much of our traditional conception of agency and intelligent action, how much of our science of psychology could survive such a reordering. Before tackling these matters, however, it may be useful to look briefly at some of the sorts of consideration that have motivated externalism.

## 3. WITTGENSTEIN

In Chapter 1, I noted that Wittgenstein's picture theory of meaning advances an especially pure form of internalism.[3] According to the picture theory, it is part of the nature of a mental sign that it project a definite sense. Interestingly, Wittgenstein seemed unconcerned as to how this might be possible. His argument was Kantian in form: Clearly, the thoughts we think and the sentences we utter have meaning; meaning requires picturing; therefore picturing occurs. How it occurs is not something we are in a position to discover a priori. 'Man possesses the ability to construct languages capable of expressing every sense, without having any idea how each word has meaning or what its meaning is – just as people speak without knowing how the individual sounds are produced' (1921/1960, § 4.002). The mechanism of meaning, no less than the mechanism of speech, is discoverable only a posteriori.

3 This section and the next can be skipped by readers already familiar with the territory. Its purpose is not to offer any new arguments for externalism, but merely to sketch some of the considerations that have historically influenced philosophers' thinking on the topic. For a more exhaustive discussion, see McGinn (1989).

Later, Wittgenstein came to believe that the notion that meanings could be produced by a mechanism of the sort required by the picture theory was deeply confused. Any such mechanism would have to project meanings exclusively by its own internal operations. Meaning is not the sort of thing that could be so produced, however. The concept of a meaning mechanism suffers the sort of incoherence exhibited by the steam roller illustrated in Figure 2.1, and concerning which Wittgenstein remarks:

The following design for the construction of a steam roller was shown to me and seems to be of philosophical interest. The inventor's mistake is akin to a philosophical mistake. The invention consists of a motor inside a hollow roller. The crank-shaft runs through the middle of the roller and is connected at both ends by spokes with the wall of the roller. The cylinder of the petrol-engine is fixed onto the inside of the roller. At first glance this construction looks like a machine. But it is a rigid system and the piston cannot move to and fro in the cylinder. Unwittingly we have deprived it of all possibility of movement. (Wittgenstein 1974, p. 194)

Variations on this theme occupy the early sections of Wittgenstein's *Philosophical Investigations* (1953/1968). I shall not attempt to reproduce the line of argument developed there, however, but take up only a single aspect of that argument that illustrates its character.

Consider Figure 2.2 (see Wittgenstein 1953/1968, p. 54). What does this drawing represent? A man walking up a steep hill? Or a man sliding backwards downhill? Does it depict how a particular person walked on a particular occasion? Or perhaps how one ought – or ought not – to walk? The questions seem odd. The picture might be *used* to represent any of these things, or many other things for that matter. Indeed, you and I might use the picture as part of a secret code to mean anything we pleased. Wittgenstein invites us to conclude that the picture does not represent whatever it represents intrinsically. Its significance depends on something – its being 'given a use', perhaps – extrinsic to it.

It will not help merely to add to the picture or to include the picture in a system of pictures. Thus, suppose we add an arrow to indicate direction of travel (Figure 2.3). Again, the same problem crops up, for we must interpret the arrow. Does it indicate the direction in which the figure is moving, or the direction from which it has moved? Or does it signify something else altogether? The answer is that the arrow, just in itself, means nothing. It must be given a meaning by something outside it. That something, as the

Figure 2.1

Figure 2.2

Figure 2.3

arrow itself illustrates, cannot be an additional pictorial element or system of elements. A representational item, an inscription, depends for its significance neither on its own intrinsic features nor on relations it bears to similar items. If an inscription bears meaning, it does so in virtue of something that is not itself an inscription.[4]

Perhaps inscriptions acquire meaning by relations they bear to the thoughts of inscription makers. This seems on the right track.

4 An inscription might inherit significance from some other inscription – as when I use words to tell you what a certain word means – but this is possible only if some inscriptions have already acquired significance from their relations to noninscriptions.

27

When asked what Figure 2.2 represents, we may be inclined to respond that it represents what its originator intended it to represent. We are thus led to the notion that the source of meaning is ultimately mental.

It might seem that there are certain mental processes bound up with the working of language, processes through which alone language can function. I mean the processes of understanding and meaning. The signs of our language seem dead without these mental processes; and it might seem that the only function of the signs is to induce such processes, and that these are the things we ought really to be interested in. Thus, if you are asked what is the relation between a name and the thing it names, you will be inclined to answer that the relation is a psychological one. (1958, p. 3)

Now, however, we must ask about these mental accompaniments, intentions or, more generally, thoughts. What are these? Suppose that a thought is a mental picture. In drawing Figure 2.2, I have a mental picture of a man walking with difficulty up a steep hill. Or perhaps I say to myself the words, 'Here is a man walking with difficulty up a steep hill'. If I can convey this information to you, you will know what Figure 2.2 represents, what its intended significance is.

At this point, however, our original worry resurfaces. For what is it that gives meaning to my *mental* picture or inscription? Why should pictures or inscriptions inside the mind have an intrinsic, nonderivative meaning when their counterparts outside the mind do not? Once more we are driven to postulate a mechanism of meaning.

We are tempted to think that the action of language consists of two parts; an inorganic part, the handling of signs, and an organic part, which we may call understanding these signs, meaning them, interpreting them, thinking. These latter activities seem to take place in a queer kind of medium, the mind; and the mechanism of the mind, the nature of which, it seems, we don't quite understand, can bring about effects which no material mechanism could. (1958, p. 3)

Explanations of the significance or ordinary inscriptions that simply appeal to mental inscriptions do nothing to advance our understanding. In accepting them, we accept the notion that a mental inscription has a special 'occult' property lacked by an ordinary inscription.

To drive the point home, Wittgenstein suggests that we test appeals to mental mechanisms in explanations of meaning by imagining that these mechanisms are realised outside the mind. If, in so doing, we discover that we are still in the dark as to how meaning is generated, we have exposed the putative explanation as fraudulent.

> If the meaning of the sign . . . is an image built up in our mind when we see or hear the sign, then first let us adopt the method . . . of replacing the mental image by some outward object seen, e.g. a painted or modelled image. Then why should the written sign plus this painted image be alive if written sign alone was dead? – In fact, as soon as you think of replacing the mental image by, say, a painted one, and as soon as the image thereby loses its occult character, it ceases to impart any life to the sentence at all. (1958, p. 5)

Suppose we wonder how Figure 2.2 could represent a man climbing a hill. We appeal to a mental image I have in mind in creating the picture. It is this mental picture that breathes life into the 'inorganic' inscription on the page. You understand what Figure 2.2 represents when you acquire a similar mental image. Now imagine that my mental picture is not inside my head, but that it is inscribed on a sheet of paper I carry with me. I copy the second from the first and place the two pictures side by side. Does the first picture endow the second with meaning? If the second picture lacks meaning by itself, how is meaning created by the addition of a picture, by the addition of *more of the same*?

The example illustrates a point to which Wittgenstein returns repeatedly: No sign or collection of signs possesses meaning intrinsically. Words or pictures – whether realised as physical marks on paper, as impact waves in the air, or as mental inscriptions – owe their significance to something outside themselves. For Wittgenstein, this something concerned their role in the lives of speakers. The meaning of a particular utterance, for instance, is associated with the use utterances of that type – similar utterances – have in a given speech community. We understand an utterance only by grasping the practices or 'forms of life' in which it has a part. The significance of states of mind is equally dependent on their connection to agents' activities and patterns of interaction.

Whether we imagine that Wittgenstein is right in associating meaning and forms of life, we may sympathise with his criticism of internalism. Signs acquire significance only by way of relations they bear to goings-on and states of affairs extrinsic to them. To insist that a thought or a mental image might possess 'original meaning' is to fall prey to what Hilary Putnam, echoing Wittgenstein, dubs a 'magical theory' (1981, pp. 3–5).

Wittgenstein provides a powerful antidote to internalist Cartesian intuitions concerning meaning. Putnam takes up the case against internalism by enlarging and extending Wittgenstein's critique. Because the influence of the sort of approach Putnam takes to meaning has been considerable, I shall consider it briefly here.

## 4. PUTNAM AND BURGE

In 'The Meaning of "Meaning"', Putnam (1975a/1975b) advances an argument to the conclusion that the meaning of certain terms – those designating natural kinds – depends, not merely on the internal states of speakers, but on how things stand in speakers' environments. The argument turns on a simple thought experiment. Imagine a planet elsewhere in our universe that is as similar to Earth as you please, but for one crucial difference. On that planet, Twin Earth, the clear, colourless liquid that fills rivers, lakes, and ice trays, is not water, not $H_2O$, but a complex chemical substance, superficially indistinguishable from water but possessing a distinct chemical composition, XYZ. Some of the inhabitants of Twin Earth speak a language similar to English. These people call the clear, colourless liquid they drink, sail on, and bathe in 'water'. Despite these and other similarities, Putnam argues, the word 'water', in the mouth of a 'Twin Earthian', does not mean water: Water is $H_2O$, and *their* word signifies, not $H_2O$, but XYZ, *twin* water.

We can imagine a resident of Twin Earth who is a 'molecule for molecule' duplicate of an inhabitant of Waynesboro: Wayne.[5] Wayne and Dwayne (who resides in Dwaynesboro) may 'think the same verbalised thoughts', have 'the same sense data, the same dispositions, etc.' Despite these internal similarities, however, Wayne and Dwayne mean different things by utterances of 'water'. Since Wayne and Dwayne are, in all relevant respects, internal duplicates, whatever determines what Wayne and Dwayne mean by 'water' must include factors outside their respective bodies. Putnam

5 Putnam says that two such agents could be identical 'in the sense in which two neckties can be "identical"' (p. 227), though this seems doubtful. Assuming that XYZ replaces $H_2O$ on Twin Earth, then at least the body chemistry of Wayne and his twin must be different. Furthermore, the twins may differ significantly with respect to their *extrinsic*, relational characteristics. The example requires, however, only that we suppose that this difference is not, for an internalist, a *relevant* difference.

concludes: 'Cut the pie any way you like, "meanings" just ain't in the *head*' (p. 227).

The sentiment is echoed by Tyler Burge (see, e.g., Burge 1979, 1986). Burge provides a two-stage thought experiment designed to extend and broaden Putnam's line of attack on internalism. First, imagine that someone, Clara perhaps, who suffers from arthritis in her ankles comes to believe that the condition has spread to her thigh. Clara's doctor assures her that this is impossible: Arthritis is an inflammation of the joints, so one cannot have arthritis in the thigh. Clara's 'incomplete understanding' of the character of arthritis – what Burge might call her 'notion' of arthritis – leads Clara to believe falsely that she has arthritis in her thigh. Note that, despite Clara's confusion, we evidently have no hesitation in saying that she has beliefs *about arthritis*, some true, and some false.

The second stage of Burge's thought experiment requires that we imagine a physical twin of the arthritis patient who lives in a society in which the word 'arthritis' covers a broader class of inflammations, including inflammations of the thigh of the sort Clara is now suffering. The twins differ not at all in their physical histories, nor even in their mental lives (provided we describe these 'nonintentionally', that is, describe them without reference to their intentional content, meaning, or significance should they have any).[6] Yet, Burge argues, we should say that, despite these important similarities, the twin has no beliefs at all about *arthritis*. Clara and her twin both use the word, of course, but they use it in such a way that it expresses different meanings. The beliefs we ascribe to the twins reflect this difference.

I have put this in terms of twins, though Burge's original example concerned an arthritis sufferer and *the very same sufferer* in a world in which linguistic institutions differed in the way I have described. We consider the original case and a *counterfactual* case that enables us to say what would be true of an agent's state of mind under different, counterfactual circumstances. Burge concludes that attention to such examples suggests that agents' states of mind depend on something more than the immediate, physical and men-

6 The twins, as we suppose, may have identical inner experiences and feelings, produce the same utterances, and the like. We leave open whether these experiences, feelings, and utterances are identical as well with respect to their intentional properties, their *meaning*. If Burge is right, they may well differ importantly in this regard.

tal condition of the agent, nonintentionally described. What makes it true that Clara's beliefs concern arthritis is not merely that she is in a certain physiological condition; two physiologically indiscernible agents might harbour thoughts with very different contents. The addition of *mental* components that are indiscernible in all nonintentional respects does not help.

Burge's suggestion is that what is required to put meanings into the picture (alternatively, what is required to account for the differences brought to light by the example) is the presence of a particular social environment. The original case and the counterfactual case differ in this respect. In the former, Clara inhabits a society in which norms governing the use of 'arthritis' restrict its application to certain inflammations of the joints; in the latter, the norms differ. The actual patient, Clara, and the counterfactual patient are thus 'responsible to' different sets of norms, and this is the crucial element in fixing the intentional content of their respective states of mind.[7]

While Burge emphasises the 'social environment', Putnam argues that terms designating natural kinds like 'water' depend for their meaning in part on the physical circumstances of agents who use them.[8] 'Water' means (something like) 'the stuff similar in chemical composition to the clear liquid stuff around here'. Because 'the stuff around here' differs on Twin Earth, the meaning of 'water' on Twin Earth differs from the meaning of 'water' on Earth.

It might be objected that this point concerns only an indexical dimension of the word 'water', not its meaning. When I use the

---

7 There is an important sense, then, in which individuals are not free to let words mean what they will. One may elect to use words – even 'arthritis' – idiosyncratically, but these words will possess an idiosyncratic *meaning* only so long as one is 'responsible' to other norms current in one's linguistic community. This, perhaps, is part of what is at issue in the 'private language' argument associated with Wittgenstein. See Burge (1979, p. 94); and Wittgenstein (1953/1968); see also Chapter 6 below.

8 This is somewhat misleading. Putnam, too, insists on the importance of the social dimension. He speaks, for instance, of a linguistic 'division of labour', arguing that we very often use terms without ourselves being in possession of reliable tests for their application. One may speak of gold, entertain thoughts of gold, etc., without necessarily being able to distinguish gold from various other yellowish metals. It does not follow, he contends, that the word means for us 'any one of many yellowish metals', or that our thoughts do not concern gold. We defer to others – 'experts' in a given domain – to make the relevant discriminations.

indexical expression 'here' in Poughkeepsie and you use the same expression in Schenectady, we refer to different places. It does not follow, however, that the *meaning* of 'here' is different for each of us. Although the reference of 'water' on Earth and Twin Earth is certainly different, this, Putnam argues, is due to differences in meaning. It is not that the liquid substance that counts as water varies from place of utterance to place of utterance – water is $H_2O$ on Earth, XYZ on Twin Earth – in the way the location that counts as *here* varies from place of utterance to place of utterance. There *is* no water on Twin Earth, no $H_2O$, only XYZ, twin water. If I visit Twin Earth and describe the liquid in lakes and rain puddles as water, I am in error – in a way that I am not in error in announcing 'I'm here!' after arriving in Schenectady.

Putnam and Burge, like Wittgenstein, distinguish sharply between the intrinsic qualities of agents' psychological states and the meanings of the terms they use. Wayne and his twin may both have the same mental imagery and 'verbalised thoughts', yet Wayne means *water* when he utters 'water', Dwayne does not. This suggests that the meaning of an utterance, or at least the meaning of some utterances, cannot be accounted for internalistically: Part of what fixes the meaning of 'water' or 'arthritis' includes states of affairs or goings-on external to individual speakers.

Suppose that this is right. It seems to follow that thoughts expressed by 'this is water' uttered by Wayne and Dwayne, respectively, are different: Wayne is thinking of water, Dwayne of twin water. Again, we can imagine Wayne and Dwayne being molecular duplicates, differing in none of their relevant intrinsic properties. In that case, however, the contents of the twins' thoughts must depend on something more than these intrinsic properties. This is the thesis of externalism.

Note that externalism does not require that the intentional content – the meaning or significance – of states of mind be determined *exclusively* by relations agents bear to external objects. Externalists hold only that the character of states of mind is determined *in part* by such relations. Imagine that Wayne and a twin who, at a particular time, $t$, bear relevantly similar relations to their surroundings, differ in certain of their intrinsic properties at $t$. Perhaps Wayne has an image of a glass of clear liquid and the 'verbalised thought', 'Oh, for a glass of water', whereas Dwayne has an image of a bowl of gnocchi, and the thought, 'Oh, for some pesto'. Other things equal, Wayne would, in that case, be thinking about water, Dwayne about pesto.[9]

Externalism can allow, as well, that some thoughts might depend *only* on intrinsic properties of thinkers. Thus, an agent altogether 'cut off' from the external world might nevertheless be in a position to entertain thoughts concerning mathematical propositions ('7 + 5 = 12'), or thoughts concerning his own states of mind ('I am thinking now', 'I feel warm'). What such an agent could not do, according to an externalist, is entertain thoughts concerning trees, gnocchi, or water.[10]

Does externalism imply that a thinker cut off from the external world be unable to entertain any thought at all about external objects? This seems unlikely. If having a thought that refers to an external object counts as having a thought *about* an external object, then an agent cut off from his surroundings – an isolated agent – in a world including just that agent and one other body might think about, hence refer to, that body by means of a predicate of the form, 'A thing noncontiguous to me'. An isolated agent in *this* world might succeed in referring to an object by entertaining a thought concerning 'An item existing at a distance from me equal to 100 times my girth', where, as it happens, something *does* exist there.[11]

Externalism, as I have depicted it, requires only that some of the thoughts we entertain possess their significance at least partly because of relations we bear to objects and states of affairs outside us. Different versions of externalism will insist on different relations and different *relata*. Since the focus here is on externalism, not on some particular externalist theory, I shall ignore differences of this sort. To simplify the exposition, however, we may envisage a

9 Of course an externalist will insist that Wayne's thoughts about water and his twin's thoughts about pesto bear the right sorts of relation to the world. But we can imagine that this is so, while imagining that the twins are, at the time their thoughts occur, similarly related to the environment but different internally – in the way that you and I might be as we stroll side by side while entertaining very different thoughts.

10 It might turn out that thoughts of this sort and of the sort mentioned below are possible only for beings for whom many other sorts of thought are possible, including thoughts the content of which is externally fixed; see Chapter 6. My point is just that, if this is *not* so, externalism is not thereby threatened.

11 I owe the example to C. B. Martin.

streamlined brand of externalism according to which thoughts acquire their significance in part from causal connections they bear to objects in the world. My thoughts about icebergs concern icebergs (and not, say, twin icebergs, XYZ-bergs) in part because those thoughts stand in a certain causal relation to icebergs (but not to twin icebergs).[12] The question is: What are the implications of such an externalist picture of mind for our commonsense conception of agency?

## 5. CAUSAL CAPACITIES: BROAD AND NARROW

Externalists argue that the contents of our states of mind, the 'about-ness' or 'of-ness' of our thoughts, hinge, not just on how we are, but on how things stand outside us, on our social, biological, and physical environment. Internalists imagine that thoughts take their significance from us alone, independently of our circumstances. Thoughts project outward from our minds in the way a searchlight beam projects outward, illuminating whatever it touches. There are times when a view of this sort seems inescapable. When I consider my own case, my perceptions, my thoughts about the world, it sometimes feels as though my thoughts 'reach out and touch reality' (as Wittgenstein puts it in the *Tractatus*), and that my perceptions illuminate a world that would otherwise remain in darkness.

Externalists believe that these feelings, and the metaphors that accommodate them, are deeply flawed. Even if we are sympathetic to their criticisms of internalism, however, we might wonder whether externalists are really in a better position than their internalist targets to explicate intentional phenomena. Thus, suppose we embrace the simplified version of externalism outlined at the end of § 4, and suppose we accept the notion that our intentional states of mind depend for their very identity in part on how things stand outside us. We are left, it would seem, with a pair of puzzles. First, if states of mind are somehow 'spread about', how can we account for the vast difference between our first-person and third-person access to those states of mind? How is it that *I* can know the

12 A causal theory of this sort, though crude, allows for the possibility of thoughts about nonexistent states of affairs. Suppose I entertain the thought that Wayne is the king of Idaho. My thought concerns a particular nonexistent state of affairs, Wayne's being the king of Idaho, partly because of causal relations that thought bears to Wayne, to Idaho, and to certain political institutions.

contents of my thoughts, within limits at least, immediately and with certainty, whereas you can know them only inferentially? If my thoughts depend for their content on things outside me, how can I know what I am thinking without first acquainting myself with those external things? I shall postpone these and related questions until Chapter 5.

A second puzzle concerns the causal role of intentional states of mind. Cartesian dualism trips over the problem of mental causation. If minds are substances entirely distinct from the physical substance of which bodies are modes, how can we suppose that bodies and minds interact causally? If we assume, as seems reasonable, that the physical domain is 'causally closed' – that is, the cause of every physical occurrence is itself a physical occurrence – we seem to guarantee the causal inefficacy of the mental in the physical world. It might appear that Descartes's problem could be addressed simply by abandoning dualism: Allow that mental events are themselves a species of physical event, and the Cartesian problem dissolves.

As we shall see in subsequent chapters, however, the abandonment of dualism merely shifts the Cartesian problem from one domain to another. The issues are complex, but there is one obvious difficulty for externalist accounts of intentional states of mind that can be previewed here. Suppose that I want to carve my initials in a certain tree and I believe that the tree in question is across the street. Assuming that I am free to do the deed, that my motivation is sufficiently strong, and that the world cooperates, I will proceed to the tree and begin carving. Here, my initial carving is *explained*, in part, by my mental condition, by my *desire* to carve my initials in the tree, and by my *belief* as to the tree's location. It is natural to suppose that the explanatory character of my mental condition is due to that condition's being causally connected to my subsequent behaviour. It is not merely that I *have* a certain desire and a certain belief, but that these together, and in concert perhaps with other states of mind, figure in the aetiology of my deed. Now, the intentional components of my mental condition, my aforementioned desire and belief, for instance, owe one essential aspect of *their* character to their intentional content. My belief about the tree is the belief it is largely because of its content, its being about a certain tree. Were it different in that regard, were it about spiders or muffins, it would not be the same belief. This, in turn, would be reflected in the role it plays in my psychological economy.

These observations are meant to be uncontroversial. They represent an important strand of our commonsense appreciation of agency, one that coalesces with our scientific dreams for psychology. How does this strand mesh with externalism? If the intentional content of my states of mind depends, even in part, on how things stand outside me, then it is not obvious how those states of mind could have a causal role in my behaviour. More precisely, if the intentional content of my states of mind depends on external factors, depends on my possession of certain *relational* characteristics, that content would seem to have no causal bearing whatever on what I do.

Imagine that we are explaining the behaviour of a collection of steel balls in the laboratory. Each ball has, let us suppose, the same volume but a different mass. We notice that, although balls differing in mass fall from an elevated platform into a box of sand at the same *rate*, the balls make impressions of different depths in the sand. Eventually we discover a simple linear relation between the mass of a given ball and the depth of the impression it makes. We conclude that the character of an impression made by each ball is caused, in part, by the ball's mass. We may think of mass, in this context anyway, as an intrinsic property possessed by individual balls. The causal capacities of each ball seem to be tied exclusively to its intrinsic properties.[13] What a given ball can *do* depends just on its here-and-now, nonrelational, intrinsic characteristics.

This may seem, at first, obviously wrong. Suppose ball *A* makes an impression in the sand one inch deep, and ball *B* makes a two-inch impression. Ball *B*, we might say, has the capacity to make a two-inch impression, and – holding constant the circumstances: the height of the platform, the relative location and consistency of the sand, gravitational forces, and the like – its possession of this capacity depends just on the intrinsic properties of ball *B*. Ball *B* seems, in addition, to have the capacity to make an impression that is *an inch deeper* than the impression made by ball *A*. Its having *this*

---

13 I shall not attempt an explicit definition of 'causal capacity'. The intended meaning will emerge in the course of the discussion to follow. In any case, I shall use the notion only in setting up a potential difficulty for externalism, not in its defense.

capacity depends not only on its intrinsic properties, however, but also on ball $A$ and *its* properties. Were we to change ball $A$ – by increasing its mass, for instance – then, even if we leave ball $B$ untouched, ball $B$ will lose the capacity to cause an impression an inch deeper than the impression caused by ball $A$. ·

I propose that we distinguish between an object's *broad* and *narrow* causal capacities.[14] A narrow causal capacity is one an object shares with every object similar to it with respect to its intrinsic properties. Although 'broad', 'narrow', and 'causal capacity' are terms of art, I shall use these expressions in a way intended to capture certain fundamental convictions most of us have concerning causal relations. Thus, two objects, $x$ and $y$, have the same narrow causal capacities, just in case they have the same intrinsic properties. (Alternatively, an object $x$ has the same narrow causal capacities in every world in which it has the same intrinsic properties.) A broad causal capacity, in contrast, is one that need not be shared by intrinsically similar objects. If $x$ and $y$ exist in different sorts of environments (or if an $x$ exists in a different environment in some other nomologically possible world), then $x$ and $y$ will differ in their broad causal capacities ($x$ will differ in its broad capacities across possible worlds).[15]

Once the distinction is made, we can see that every object possesses, in addition to whatever narrow causal capacities it possesses, endless broad capacities as well. Ball $B$ possesses the broad capacity to cause an impression one inch deeper than ball $A$, but it also possesses the broad capacity to cause an impression at noon today (were it dropped at noon), to cause an impression that is not as deep as the impression caused by ball $C$, to cause a lab assistant to smirk, and so on. If we drop ball $B$ at midnight, or change the respective masses of ball $A$ and ball $C$, or fire the lab assistant, we alter these broad capacities even though ball $B$, in one obvious sense, remains unchanged: Its capacities remain unaffected. Even the capacity to cause an impression two inches deep in the sand is, as it turns out, a broad capacity possessed by ball $B$. If we scatter the sand, or change its consistency, or if we imagine ball $B$ existing in a world with no

---

14 I owe the distinction to Alfred Mele (1992); see also Heil and Mele (1991).
15 It is time for the usual disclaimer concerning possible worlds. I shall employ talk of possible worlds simply to illuminate relevant modalities, and as a technique for the evaluation of certain counterfactuals and subjunctive conditionals.

sand, then ball $B$ may lack this capacity despite remaining un-changed intrinsically.

It may now seem that narrow causal capacities are mostly unin-teresting; what we care about – both in everyday life and in our scientific pursuits – are the capacities objects have to affect *other* objects, and these are invariably broad. What matters to me as I drive down the highway is that a Buick has the capacity to demolish my Yugo, but a raindrop does not. What matters to a chemist is that compound $C_1$ has the capacity to prevent rust, a capacity that $C_2$ lacks. Such capacities, however, are patently broad: Change the context in certain ways, and a Buick no longer crushes a Yugo, $C_1$ no longer prevents rust.

Despite appearances, however, narrow causal capacities are, in the end, fundamental. I know that a Buick has the capacity to crush my Yugo, but I know, as well, that anything at all relevantly similar to a Buick with respect to its intrinsic properties, has the very same capacity. I expect that an explanation of such objects' possession of this capacity will ultimately depend on their possession of certain shared intrinsic properties. I expect, as well, that objects possessing comparable intrinsic properties will behave in similar ways in simi-lar environments. In a world in which Yugos are made of armour-plate, a Buick may lack the capacity to crush my Yugo; but in that world objects comparable to a Buick with respect to mass (and acceleration) will also lack this capacity.

Even if this is so, it does not follow that our classification of causal capacities must be expressed in a vocabulary confined to narrow predicates, predicates ranging over just the intrinsic features of objects. I might elect to *identify* a narrow causal capacity by means of a description couched in terms of some broad capacity. Indeed, this may be typical. Thus, I might identify a certain narrow capacity possessed by Buicks via the phrase 'the capacity to demol-ish a Yugo'. In so doing, I might mean, roughly, the capacity, whatever it is, that, *in this world, under these circumstances*, leads to the demolishing of Yugos.[16]

16 The point is a general one. *How* we choose to identify features of the world depends, not only on the features we want to identify, but also on the context in which the identification is made and on innumerable pragmatic factors. I may identify a particular electromagnetic wavelength, for instance, by means of the description, 'my least favorite colour'. Here, as elsewhere, it is important to distinguish a mode of description from whatever is picked out by the descrip-tion.

I shall suppose, then, that it is both useful and important to distinguish between an object's narrow and broad causal capacities. Narrow capacities are tied to an object's intrinsic features, and shared by 'molecular duplicates'; broad capacities depend on narrow capacities and circumstances.

We may, similarly, distinguish an object's broad and narrow *conditions*. Narrow conditions are intrinsic conditions, conditions that comprise or that supervene on (or are otherwise determined by) an object's intrinsic properties. Broad conditions depend on relations the object bears to other objects, to a part of itself, or to itself at another time. My Yugo's being warm might be thought to be a narrow condition of my Yugo. Its being warm supervenes on motions of molecules making up its metallic surfaces. (That these molecules were set in motion by something external, sunlight, for instance, does not affect the narrowness of the condition of being warm.) Being old, in contrast, is a condition had by my Yugo broadly. My Yugo's being old entails that it has a longish history, hence that it has existed at some earlier time. If you took the trouble to construct a molecular duplicate of my Yugo in your basement workshop, that duplicate might be warm, but, lacking the appropriate causal history, it would not be old. Quantum oddities aside, every object and the condition of every object has *some* causal history or other. In speaking of an object's narrow condition, then, we abstract from its actual condition. It is this condition that accounts for the causal capacities of particular objects. An object's narrow causal capacities are traceable to its narrow condition; those capacities can be changed, but only by altering its narrow condition.

## 6. CAUSAL IRRELEVANCE

Given these observations on causal capacities, it is now possible to formulate more precisely a difficulty for externalism alluded to earlier. Recall that my carving my initials in a nearby tree was to be explained by reference to my mental condition, a condition that included a particular desire and belief: I wanted to carve my initials in a tree and believed that this tree was suitable. Let us suppose that the content of these attitudes is fixed in part by factors outside me. To make the case as simple as possible, we might pretend that my belief concerns a tree owing to its having been caused by a tree.

40

Notice that, if this is granted, my having this belief is partly a matter of my being in a certain broad condition. One – slightly artificial – way of looking at it is that, assuming externalism, my having this belief is determined by my being in a particular sort of narrow condition (perhaps a particular sort of neural condition) with a particular sort of causal history. A molecular twin might be in a comparable narrow condition yet, owing to differences in causal history, differ with respect to his broad condition and so, given our streamlined version of externalism, harbour some other belief.

Now, however, it is not easy to see how my belief could possibly be implicated causally in my behaviour. My belief depends on my broad condition, but what I *do*, how I move my body about, is a function just of my narrow condition. If my twin and I are intrinsically alike, then, whatever the character of our respective broad conditions, we will both move toward the tree and begin carving. My broad condition, and anything that depends essentially on its external components, seems *causally irrelevant* to my behaviour. Since my belief about the tree depends essentially on certain of those external components, that belief appears to be causally irrelevant to what I do. The point is perfectly general. It is not my Yugo's being old that causes it to rattle and vibrate, it is my Yugo's being in a certain narrow condition. A duplicate Yugo, assembled last night in your basement, possesses a similar narrow condition and, as a result, rattles and vibrates despite failing to be old.

In saying that whatever depends on the external components of an object's broad condition is causally irrelevant to the behaviour of that object, we need not imagine, either that (1) these external components are themselves causally inert, or (2) these external components play no causal role whatever in the object's behaviour. If the tree is an external component in my current broad condition, the tree itself is party to countless causal transactions: It is reflecting light, manufacturing chlorophyll, casting shadows. The tree's reflecting light that strikes my retina may be part of a complicated causal story as to why I am now moving my body as I am. In the latter case, the tree's reflecting light has a *distal* influence on my behaviour. That distal influence, however, is mediated by the state of my body at the time I act. Simply put, the tree influences my behaviour by causing me to be in a certain condition, the narrow aspects of which issue in my behaviour.[17]

The upshot appears to be that my mental condition is, to the extent that it depends on my broad condition, causally irrelevant to my behaviour. My narrow causal capacities include only those traceable to my narrow condition, but, as we have noted already, these seem, at bottom, to exhaust my causal capacities. If externalism is true, then, it looks as though one's mental condition, or an essential component of that condition, is beside the point behaviourally.

## 7. THE AUTONOMY PRINCIPLE

Thus far I have pitted externalism against internalism. Some externalists, however, have suggested ways out of this difficulty that depend on our embracing certain pared-down internalist notions. I shall, in this section and the next, discuss two such responses to the problem of causal relevance, then turn to a somewhat different response in Chapter 4.

In 'The Meaning of "Meaning"', Putnam offers the following description of internalist conceptions of mind:

When traditional philosophers talked about psychological states (or 'mental' states), they made an assumption which we may call the assumption of methodological solipsism. This assumption is the assumption that no psychological state, properly so called, presupposes the existence of any individual other than the subject to whom the state is ascribed. . . . Making this assumption is, of course, adopting a restrictive program – a program which deliberately limits the scope and nature of psychology to fit certain mentalistic preconceptions. . . . Just *how* restrictive the program is, however, often goes unnoticed. (Putnam 1975a/1975, p. 220)

Putnam offers the example of *being jealous*, a condition that might plausibly be thought to require the existence of some distinct *object* of jealousy. Such a condition would not be permitted by the assumption of methodological solipsism. Indeed, that assumption rules out all 'psychological states in the wide sense' and per-

---

17 Aficionados of Bell's theorem may smile at the crudeness of this picture. Perhaps reality is ultimately 'nonlocal', perhaps events can affect other events noncausally. This, I grant, may be so. But even if it is, what it bodes for ordinary causal transactions is unclear. I shall therefore bracket such considerations here.

mits only 'psychological states in the narrow sense' (1975a/1975b, p. 220).

The reconstruction required by methodological solipsism would be to reconstrue *jealousy* so that I can be jealous of my own hallucinations, or figments of my imagination, etc. Only if we assume that psychological states in the narrow sense have a significant degree of causal closure (so that restricting ourselves to psychological states in the narrow sense will facilitate the statement of psychological *laws*) is there any point in engaging in this reconstruction, or in making the assumption of methodological solipsism. (1975a/1975b, pp. 220–21)

Putnam concludes his discussion by observing that 'three centuries of failure of mentalistic psychology' provide 'tremendous evidence' against methodological solipsism (p. 221).

A pessimistic appraisal of this sort might be based either on doubts about the prospects for a *reduction* of ordinary 'wide' mental characteristics to 'narrow' counterparts, doubts that figure prominently in the externalist programme, or on doubts that a narrowing of focus in psychology would leave enough of the original subject matter to merit the designation. Others have been less timid about the assumption of methodological solipsism. Jerry Fodor, for instance, regards methodological solipsism as a more or less obvious *requirement* on psychological theorising and is led to defend the necessity of appeals to narrow psychological states in the explanation of behaviour. In a similar vein, Stephen Stich, no friend of intentionalistic psychology, holds that the explanation of behaviour is constrained by a 'principle of autonomy', according to which 'the states and processes that ought to be of concern to the psychologist are those that supervene on the current, internal, physical state of the organism.' Thus, 'any differences between organisms which do not manifest themselves as differences in their current, internal, physical states ought to be ignored by psychological theory' (Stich 1983, p. 164; see also Stich 1978). Stich's autonomy principle is related in obvious ways to the idea that explanations of the behaviour of anything at all ultimately rest on appeals to features of a thing's narrow condition. I shall discuss the principle here, then, in the section to follow, take up Fodor's arguments for narrow content and methodological solipsism.

Stich defends the autonomy principle by appealing to 'the replacement argument'. Imagine that, while you are asleep, you are kidnapped and replaced by an exact physical replica constructed on the spot.[18] If your kidnappers are clever, no one – excepting you and the kidnappers – would suspect that your replica was not you. Even the replica would suspect nothing. 'But . . . since psychology is the science which aspires to explain behavior, any states and processes which are not shared by [you and your] identically behaving replica must surely be irrelevant to psychology' (1983, pp. 165–66).

The replacement argument does not suppose that you and your replica are identical mentally, at least not to the extent that the character of agents' psychological states is determined by those agents' circumstances or history. Since you and your replica differ in countless ways historically, it seems likely, at least if externalism is correct, that you and your replica differ mentally in countless ways. What the argument is supposed to establish is that, despite these apparent differences, you and your replica *behave* identically. This, together with the plausible assumption that a central aim of psychology is the explanation of behaviour, suggests that psychology has no business appealing to states of mind in offering explanations of behaviour – or at least that psychology has no business appealing to states of mind the character of which is fixed externally.

Stich acknowledges that, if this argument is to succeed, it needs to be refined. As it stands, it is easy to doubt that your replica and you *do* behave identically. You, but not your replica, *remember* promising Wayne yesterday to help move a piano into his third-floor flat. The replica may *seem* to remember the promise, the replica may even, and with apparent sincerity, *say*, 'I promised yesterday to help Wayne move a piano into his flat'. The replica cannot *remember* the incident, however, because the replica did not exist at the time the incident occurred. Similarly, there is something you can now *do* that the replica cannot do, namely fulfil the promise to Wayne. The replica, not being on the scene, did not *make* the promise to Wayne, hence the replica cannot now fulfil the promise to Wayne. It is false, then, that you and your replica 'behave identically', and the replacement argument apparently fails.

One line of response to cases of this sort appeals to a distinction

18 Stich's argument, unlike those above, assumes the truth of a version of physicalism: Mental items depend exclusively on agents' physical conditions. Unless otherwise noted, I shall honour this assumption for the remainder of the chapter.

between broad and narrow *behaviour*. Narrow behaviour might be identified with the making of particular bodily motions. You and a replica, then, can be expected to engage in the same narrow behaviour. Broad behaviour consists of bodily motions, instances of narrow behaviour, with certain causal histories. When you and your replica utter the sentence 'I remember my promise to Wayne', you, but not your replica, might be said to express a memory. Part of the explanation of this difference is that the cause of your utterance, but not your replica's, includes a remembering. Similarly, your moving Wayne's piano constitutes promise keeping on your part but not on your replica's part because you, but not your replica, made a promise to Wayne, the satisfaction-conditions of which included your moving his piano.

Suppose you and your replica simultaneously shoot arrows toward identical targets under identical conditions. The arrows and shots are identical, yet you hit the bull's-eye, your replica does not. Could this happen? Certainly: An accomplice knocks down the replica's target after his arrow is in flight. In this case, you and your replica differ in respect to your broad behaviour. The difference, however, like the difference between your differing in respect to promise keeping is not a difference that we should want to require a plausible psychology to explain. Perhaps this is generally so: Psychology should concern itself exclusively with the explanation of narrow behaviour.[19] If it is fair to suppose that replicas, however they might differ in the intentional contents of their thoughts, however they might differ in their broad behaviour, will not differ in respect to their narrow behaviour, we can conclude that proper explanations in psychology must respect the autonomy principle. Agents intrinsically alike physically, whatever the character of their intentional states, must be treated alike by a proper science of behaviour.[20]

The same conclusion may be reached by a different route. I immerse a piece of litmus paper in a container of acid and the litmus paper turns red. This event, the litmus paper's turning red, delights

19 Or, as Stich might put it, psychology should rely on a narrow taxonomy of behaviours.
20 We are, recall, assuming with Stich that the mental depends on and is determined by the physical, that there are no mental differences without physical differences. It now seems to follow that there are no psychological differences without *narrow* physical differences.

Wayne who is standing nearby. The litmus paper's turning red *is* the event that delighted Wayne. We may say that there is one event here described in two different ways. Now, someone might insist that, although it is reasonable to expect a purely chemical explanation of the event 'under the first description', it is mad to expect a chemical explanation of it 'under the second description'. Although there is *something* right about this, it is misleadingly put. If we think of explanations as explaining events, particular, dated *occurrences*, then it scarcely makes sense to speak of explanations of 'events under descriptions'. If I explain the litmus paper's turning red via an appeal to physical chemistry, and if the event that delighted Wayne is the litmus paper's turning red, then I have *eo ipso* explained the event that delighted Wayne.[21]

What we *can* say, perhaps, is that an appeal to physical chemistry might reasonably be expected to explain the occurrence (or exemplification) of the *property* or *characteristic* identified by 'the litmus paper's turning red', but not the occurrence of the property or characteristic signified by 'the event that delighted Wayne'. Although these descriptions may pick out the selfsame event, an explanation of that event's satisfying each description will be very different. Why should we expect physical chemistry to explain why an event is one that delighted Wayne? Two events, identical with respect to their chemical attributes, might differ in all sorts of other ways (one delights Wayne, one does not). The difference, although perfectly genuine, is not a *chemical* difference; it is not, as it were, *chemically relevant*.

Applying this to the case at hand, we might say that broad differences between you and your replica are not *psychological* differences – at least they are not, given some suitably purified version of psychology. Psychology should be expected to explain why you are now moving your body in some particular way, but not why you are breaking your promise (even though in moving your body in that way you are breaking your promise). Similarly, if the cause of your moving your body as you are now moving it is a particular internal event, and if this internal event, owing to relations it bears to a particular external state of affairs, possesses a certain intentional

---

21 This seemingly innocuous point is easily missed. It will take on more significance in the discussion of mental causation in Chapter 4. In any case, the point is independent of one's views on 'event individuation', whether one thinks of events as fine-grained or coarse-grained.

content, the event's possessing that content is not behaviourally relevant. It is, in consequence, explanatorily epiphenomenal. One can, of course, allow that the event possesses the intentional property in question without thereby supposing that its occurrence is a matter of concern to a psychology that honours the principle of autonomy.

## 8. METHODOLOGICAL SOLIPSISM

It may seem outrageous to imagine that the intentional attitudes – desires, beliefs, intentions, emotions, and the like – are 'irrelevant to psychology'. The claim is something one is led naturally to so long as one is impressed by the autonomy principle, however. Or at least the claim seems natural so long as one is impressed simultaneously by externalist construals of intentional content and the autonomy principle. This dual commitment seemingly requires that we abandon traditional psychology and replace it with a science that explains behaviour exclusively by reference to agents' internal states and whatever supervenes on those states. And, again assuming externalism, it is not easy to see how such a science would differ from physiology or neurobiology.[22] Suppose, however, one keeps autonomy but tempers externalism. Thus, one might appeal to some notion of narrow psychological states, states characterisable by reference to their *narrow* representational content, a notion designed to satisfy the same intuitions that support the autonomy principle while preserving something resembling traditional intentional psychology. This is the tack taken by Jerry Fodor.

Putnam, as we have noted, criticises internalist semantic and psychological theories on the grounds that they result in methodological solipsism, a self-stultifying approach to psychological explanation. Fodor, in contrast, regards methodological solipsism as a promising – perhaps the only viable – 'research strategy' in psychology.[23] Fodor's argument is often complicated, but the overall conception is, in light of the foregoing, more or less straightforward.

22 Stich himself favours a 'syntactic theory of mind', a theory intermediate between neurobiology and traditional intentional psychology. I shall not discuss this option here.
23 See Fodor (1980/1981). I shall focus here on Fodor's more recent (1991) discussion of these issues.

Let us grant, as Fodor does, that Putnam and Burge are right in a general way about intentional content, and that internalists are wrong: The intentional content of states of mind is, on the whole, *broad*, determined by agents' circumstances. There are immediate and significant consequences of such a view for the philosophy of mind and for semantic theory. The consequences for psychology are less easy to gauge, however. Psychology, as we have already noted, might allow that replicas could differ mentally and behaviourally, but deny that they differ in a way that is *psychologically relevant*. Perhaps this need not result in a loss of theoretical independence for psychology; perhaps psychology need not be transformed into physiology or neurobiology. Psychologists might still invoke 'contentful' psychological states in explanations of behaviour, though the representational character of the states in question would be narrow, rather than broad. If a conception of narrow mental content could be made rich enough, perhaps it could serve as a basis for a psychology that honours both the convictions that underlie the autonomy principle and the commonsense view that psychology provides causal explanations of behaviour via appeals to states of mind distinguishable by reference to their content.

Suppose, as a first approximation, that causal capacities (Fodor calls these 'causal powers') are determined by the intrinsic features of objects. There are, on the face of it, obvious objections to the idea of a narrow psychology. As Fodor points out, however, some of these counterexamples violate a plausible contextual restriction on the comparison of objects with respect to their causal powers. The restriction is easily illustrated. Suppose you hold that requests for water and requests for twin water, despite their physical, nonintentional similarities, differ in their causal capacities: Requests for water typically bring it about that glasses of water are handed over, requests for twin water yield glasses of twin water. If the causal capacities of the requests are to be compared, however, they should be compared in similar contexts. When this is done, the apparent difference in causal capacities evaporates. On Earth, Wayne's requests for water yield water, and on Twin Earth Dwayne's physically indistinguishable requests result in twin water. If we transport Dwayne to Earth, however, his request for twin water ('May I have some water, please?') will likewise yield water. The situation is parallel if we imagine Wayne being transported to Twin Earth.

Even so, of course, Wayne and Dwayne, whatever their context, seem to be *doing* different things in uttering, 'May I have some water, please?' Wayne requests water; Dwayne requests twin water. If Wayne and Dwayne do different things, they *behave* differently, and it would seem that these behavioural differences should be psychologically relevant.

Fodor concedes that, in such cases, there is an obvious respect in which Wayne and Dwayne behave differently. The difference is one we might describe more generally: Two intrinsically similar events may be said to differ because their *causes* differ. Consider a pair of intrinsically similar events: two dippings of a slip of litmus paper into a beaker of acid. Now imagine that, in one case the litmus paper is placed in the acid by a lab technician with the flu, and in the other case the paper is handled by a healthy technician. Then, the events, the dippings, differ. One, we might say, is a 'healthy dipping', the other not. Similarly, Wayne's saying 'May I have some water, please' is a request for water, whereas Dwayne's identical utterance is not. This is because (to oversimplify) Wayne's utterance resulted from a state of mind the content of which includes 'water', though Dwayne's utterance has a different sort of causal history. (I shall, following Fodor, henceforth describe Wayne's mental condition as a 'water-thought' and Dwayne's condition as a 'twin water-thought'. Similarly, Wayne's behaviour – requesting water – will be described as 'water-behaviour', and Dwayne's behaviour as 'twin water-behaviour'.) Fodor's contention is that behavioural differences of the sort that distinguishes Wayne and his twin, although important in some domains, are not, or ought not be, of concern to the psychologist.

The idea is that, whereas the characteristic *being a water-thought* and the characteristic *being a twin water-thought* are distinct characteristics, they make no relevant difference to the causal capacities of agents' mental conditions. One might suppose that this is due to the *relational* character the two characteristics exhibit given externalism, but Fodor thinks that this is not so. The characteristics *being a planet* and *being a meteor* are relational characteristics possessed by 'chunks of rock' ('to be a planet is to be a rock . . . that is revolving around a star; to be a meteor is to be a rock . . . that is falling, or has fallen, into collision with another rock'; 1991, p. 12). Yet, according to Fodor, *being a planet* and *being a meteor* capture respectable causal capacities of objects satisfying them. What distinguishes *being a planet* from *being a water-thought* in this respect?

49

Fodor's answer comes down to the following. There is a 'conceptual connection' between a request's being a request for water and its being caused by a water-thought (similarly, there is a conceptual connection between a request's being a request for twin water and its being caused by a twin water-thought). Thus, it is a conceptual truth that an utterance of 'May I have some water, please' expresses a request for water if it is appropriately caused by a water-thought, and that a similar utterance appropriately caused by a twin water-thought expresses a request for twin water. Compare: It is a conceptual truth that $E$ is the effect of the cause of $E$. Just as, in this case, we do not suppose that something's having the characteristic of *being the cause of E* is a causal capacity had by that thing 'over and above' its other causal capacities, so we ought not to suppose that *being a water-thought* or *being a twin water-thought* are causal capacities something might have over and above whatever other capacities it possesses.

Something's *being a meteor*, however, is different:

Take a pair of rock twins such that one is a meteor and the other is not. Then (ceteris paribus) craters will be among the effects of the first but not among the effects of the second. And the relation between the difference between the rock-twins and the difference between their effects is nonconceptual. So it is all right for being a meteor (rather than a meteor twin) to be a causal power in virtue of the fact that meteors cause craters and meteor twins do not. (Fodor 1991, p. 20)

It is a contingent fact that meteors cause craters (they might, for instance, bounce harmlessly off bodies they strike) and that meteor twins do not (craters might be caused not by impacts but by rocks passing through a nearby region of space). Consider, however, the causing of water-requests by water-thoughts. Might water-requests have been differently produced? Might twin water-thoughts, for instance, produce water-requests? Might water-thoughts result in twin water-requests? The answer to such questions is, clearly, no, at least so long as we consider typical, nonwayward cases of mental causation.

Fodor takes considerations of this sort to show that, if characteristics of causes reflect differences in causal capacities, at least two conditions need to be satisfied.[24] First, the causes must exhibit

24 In speaking of causal capacities here – or, as Fodor does, of causal powers – the assumption is that *being a P* may fail to be a causal capacity vis à vis behaviour without failing to be a causal capacity *tout court*. A neural structure's being gray,

different effects in virtue of differences in these characteristics. Second, 'this difference in effects [must] be *nonconceptually* related to the difference between the causes' (1991, p. 24). It is this second condition that, Fodor believes, differences in externally fixed intentional content of agents' states of mind inevitably fail to satisfy. This is due, not to the relational character of the supervenience base – that is, the determinants – of mental characteristics, however. In principle, an agent's relational features (or features supervenient on an agent's relational characteristics) could be relevant to psychological accounts of the agent's behaviour. In this regard, Fodor's conception of psychological relevance appears weaker – that is, more liberal – than Stich's. Is this a virtue? That depends on whether Fodor's constraint lines up better than Stich's with distinctions fundamental in psychological explanation. In any case, Fodor's principle would be overturned if we could find a clear case in which an agent's 'broad' states of mind made a genuine, nonconceptual difference to that agent's behaviour. The point is one to which I shall return in Chapter 4. Meanwhile, two further matters must be addressed.

First, the reader may balk at my easy assumption (following Fodor) that the relation between mental states and behaviour is causal. After all, it was via considerations not altogether dissimilar to those addressed by Fodor, that a generation of English-speaking philosophers were led to doubt that this was so (see, for instance, Anscombe 1957; Dray 1957; Melden 1961; and Peters 1958). Perhaps in explaining behaviour by reference to agents' intentions, desires, beliefs, and the like, we are not offering a causal explanation. We are, rather, putting the behaviour into a context, or *illuminating* it, or making sense of it in the way we make sense of the activities of Wayne by coming to see those activities as chess playing.

I am inclined to think that such observations contain an important element of truth. That element of truth, however, is not that there is a sharp divide between causal explanation and psychologi-

___

for instance, may be causally irrelevant from the point of view of neurophysiology, though the structure's being gray means that it reflects light differently than it would were it blue or red. In denying that the difference between water-thoughts and twin water-thoughts signals a difference in causal capacities to be recognised by psychology, Fodor is not committed to the stronger claim that the difference has *no* causal significance.

cal explanation. I see no reason to deny that *one* relation mental states bear to behaviour is causal, and that this is important for the sorts of explanation we offer, both in psychology and in everyday life. Indeed, the causal character of the mental seems to me to be an integral part of our concept of agency (see Davidson 1963/1980; Goldman 1970).

Second, whatever our ultimate assessment of Fodor's argument, it would be wrong to imagine that he is making the mistake of supposing that conceptual relations *preclude* causal relations. Fodor is *not* arguing that, because there is a conceptual connection between water-thoughts and water-requests, that the former cannot be a cause of the latter. Although it is usual to speak of conceptual and contingent connections between characteristics, states, conditions, and events, strictly speaking such connections hold between *descriptions* of characteristics, states, conditions, and events. Reflect on a paradigmatic causal sequence: billiard ball *A*'s striking billiard ball *B* and ball *B*'s rebounding. Thus described, we can see that the relation between the two events is 'contingent': There is no 'conceptual necessity' in ball *B*'s behaving as it does when struck by ball *A*. Yet it is perfectly possible to redescribe the sequence in a way that makes this seem false. Thus, suppose we describe ball *A*'s striking ball *B* as 'the cause of ball *B*'s rebounding'. Now, although it is a 'conceptual truth' that the cause of ball *B*'s rebounding caused ball *B* to rebound, the relation picked out is both causal and contingent – that is, it is contingently true that the event described here as the cause of ball *B*'s rebounding had that result.

In the cases scrutinised by Fodor, however, the issue is not whether a causal transaction has occurred, or even whether a given mental event has caused a particular behavioural event. Fodor allows that Wayne's water-thoughts (and Dwayne's twin water-thoughts) inspire both Wayne and Dwayne to utter the sentence, 'May I have some water, please'. Fodor's question is whether differences in the intentional content of these thoughts (Wayne's thoughts concern water, Dwayne's are of twin water) result in behavioural differences that deserve to be reflected in a proper science of psychology. There is a causal connection and there are behavioural differences, Fodor concedes, but the differences do not reflect a difference in psychologically relevant causal capacities of Wayne's and Dwayne's respective states of mind. Rather, they are

52

like the difference between billiard ball $B$'s being struck by Wayne's favourite billiard ball and ball $B$'s twin being struck by Dwayne's favourite (where the effects on ball $B$ and twin $B$ are identical in 'all nonintentional respects'). Here we have two distinct sorts of effect: ball $B$'s being struck by Wayne's favourite and twin $B$'s being struck by Dwayne's favourite. These differences are explicable, however, not by reference to differences in the 'causal powers' of ball $B$ and its twin, but conceptually: A ball's being struck by another ball that happens to be Wayne's favourite *counts as* 'a striking by Wayne's favourite'. If we agree that the differences in these cases are not causal differences, then we may agree with Fodor's suggested criterion of causal capacityhood. [25]

There is undoubtedly much to be said for and against this way of identifying psychologically relevant causal capacities; however, I propose for now to let Fodor's reasoning stand. Later (Chapter 4) we shall see that a sensible conception of mental causation can accommodate that reasoning. Meanwhile, we are at last in a position to appreciate Fodor's conception of 'narrow content'.

Although Fodor may seem to be arguing against externalism, his aim is not to undermine the view that the intentional contents of a large number of states of mind are fixed by agents' circumstances, but to make clear the necessity for appeals to 'narrow content' in psychological explanation. In the case we have been discussing, Fodor would hold that Wayne and Dwayne, from the point of view of an appropriately scientific psychology, behave identically. The 'broad' differences in their thoughts are psychologically irrelevant; indeed, from the point of view of a scientific psychology, their thoughts are identical. Wayne and his twin, though different in a variety of important respects, are psychologically indiscernible. Our 'taxonomy' of psychological states, then, need not – indeed, had *better not* – coincide with taxonomies inspired by ordinary descriptions of those states or by consideration of the semantics of the twins' utterances. The appropriate research programme is 'methodologically solipsistic': The categories employed in psychological explanation must ignore differences among agents that fail

25 Fodor does not argue that it is *because* a conceptual connection holds in these cases that no causal power is revealed. It is rather that the criterion yields intuitively correct judgements in straightforward cases and plausible judgements in others.

to reflect behaviourally relevant causal capacities. In practice, though perhaps not in principle, this amounts to ignoring differences in states of mind that depend on agents' relational features.

Such a constraint on psychological theorising is not to be confused with a much weaker constraint. Suppose we explain Wayne's running by indicating that, when he rounded the bend he encountered a bear. An explanation of this sort takes hold only so long as we imagine that Wayne *noticed* the bear and, on that basis, fled. Had Wayne hallucinated a bear, or had he encountered a stuffed bear, he would have behaved exactly as he did. What matters is that Wayne came to *believe* that there is a bear in his path.

From the perspective of psychology, it may seem that what we do is a matter, not so much of how things stand in the world outside us, but of how we take the world to be, our beliefs about it. There is undoubtedly an interesting and important story to be told about our coming to have these beliefs. Psychology, however, may justifiably divide the labour here. Accounts of perceptual mechanisms are one thing, accounts of intelligent behaviour are something else again. A methodological stance of this sort, whatever its merits, certainly does not entail methodological solipsism. In explaining Wayne's running by appealing to his belief that there is a bear in his path, we appeal to a 'broad' state, a belief the intentional content of which seems to depend on Wayne's standing in certain causal relations to bears (as opposed, say, to twin bears). Fodor's suggestion is that the broad aspect of Wayne's thought does not affect that thought's causal capacities vis à vis Wayne's behaviour; hence it is irrelevant psychologically.

We are led thus to a conception of *narrow mental content*. It is not easy to say what such content is. Indeed, as Fodor points out, given that the meanings of terms in our language are largely externally fixed, those terms are particularly ill suited for descriptions of the content of narrow states of mind (see Fodor 1987, chap. 2).

One way to think about narrow content, though perhaps not Fodor's way, is to regard narrow content as mental content *shared* by molecular duplicates. Wayne has water-thoughts, Dwayne has twin water-thoughts. The narrow content of these thoughts is something they have in common. Perhaps this is a particular sort of 'phenomenal core', or perhaps it is something more abstract. If Fodor is right, we pick out narrow contents whenever we ascribe mental states in causal explanations of behaviour. Wayne fled, not because Wayne's thought literally concerned a bear, but because his thought had a certain, perhaps ineffable, narrow content, a content that would be shared by a replica of Wayne whose thoughts concerned twin bears.

Fodor's interest in narrow content stems from his conviction that psychological mechanisms operate exclusively on *formal* computational principles (see Fodor 1975, 1980/1981). We may think of formal operations as applying in symbolic domains. Symbols are entities possessing meaning. These entities are distinguished by their *shapes*.[26] Systems of symbols – natural languages, for instance – feature correlations between shapes and meanings. A capacity for thought, Fodor argues, depends on our possession of a 'language of thought', an internal system of symbols realised in the brain. It is our possession of a language of thought that enables us to see how thoughts can enter into causal relations, how thoughts can generate and be generated by other thoughts, and how thoughts can affect behaviour. The key, for Fodor, is to be found in the relation between the meanings of symbols, their semantic properties, and their formal – 'shape' – properties. Because these are correlated, an appropriately 'programmed' system that processes symbols by reference to their shapes will mirror a system that operated, as the mind appears to do, on purely semantic principles. Moreover, we can *understand* how a mechanism could 'process symbols' formally – computing machines are obvious examples of such mechanisms – though we have no idea at all how a device could operate just on semantic principles.[27]

Fodor's suggestion is that intelligent agents resemble computing machines in this respect at least: Their semantic operations are formally implemented. Wayne's water-thoughts have a formal realisation in Wayne's nervous system. This realisation incorporates whatever causal clout Wayne's thoughts may have. We might imagine

---

26 In reality, *shape* is not crucial. Symbols might be distinguished by size, by spatial location, by colour. An electrically realised symbol system might distinguish its elements along some electrical dimension. 'Shape', then, should be taken in an extended sense to include any sort of nonsemantic differentia of symbolic entities.

27 By 'semantic principles', I mean principles that range over meaningful or contentful items qua 'meaningful' or 'contentful'. It should be noted that Fodor's computationalism confronts head-on Descartes's contention that minds are incapable, in principle, of a physical realisation *because* minds operate on distinctively mentalistic principles that have no counterparts in the physical realm.

that Wayne's thoughts are realised by little sentence-like arrangements of neurons, by a biochemical 'code', or by patterns of electrical activity. Whatever the details, if neural levers are pulled, buttons
pushed, this pulling and pushing is accomplished by formal objects
solely in virtue of their formal properties. The system is semantically constrained only indirectly, only via its syntax.[28]

If this is the picture, then it is easy to see why Fodor needs a
notion of narrow content. Syntax mirrors semantics only to the
extent that we ignore broad semantic properties. Wayne and
Dwayne are syntactically – formally – identical, though they differ
semantically, they differ with respect to the broad intentional contents of their thoughts. If we could somehow *slice off* the broad
aspects of the content of these thoughts, then we could reasonably
expect a perfect correlation between syntax and semantics – between syntax and *narrow* semantics.

Fodor's view might be briefly summarised as follows. (1) Psychological explanation is prima facie a perfectly legitimate form of
causal explanation. (2) Psychological explanation is distinguished
from other forms of behavioural explanation – from neurobiological explanation, for instance – by its appeal to semantic properties
of agents, mental contents. (3) Semantic properties bear causally on
behaviour (or on anything at all, for that matter) only via their
formal realisations. (4) The semantic properties of states of mind
require a language of thought, a systematic formal implementation.
(5) Only those semantic properties that are appropriately mirrored
in the syntax of the language of thought are candidates for explanatory roles in a proper scientific psychology. (6) Broad semantic
properties are not mirrored in the syntax of the language of
thought. (7) Hence, broad semantic properties cannot figure in
psychological explanation. (8) Since psychological explanation is
manifestly legitimate, it must depend on appeals to narrow semantic properties, narrow mental content, content mirrored in the syntax of the language of thought.

If Fodor is right, we must either accept some notion of narrow

28 This is an oversimplification. What is important from Fodor's perspective is that
   neural operations implementing the language of thought conform to formal
   principles. The system must function *in accord with* syntactic rules, though the
   realising medium will certainly operate *on* very different principles. We build a
   syntactic engine by building a device the operation of which respects syntactic
   constraints.

content or abandon psychology. In opting for narrow content, we need not give up externalism or broad content, we need only realise that psychology per se has no use for broad content or for distinctions among states of mind tied exclusively to broad characteristics of agents.

Many philosophers are persuaded that something like this is plainly right. This may be due to their having been persuaded by Fodor and others that psychology must ultimately be computational, that psychological explanation must reduce to accounts of formal operations over symbols. Others may be sympathetic for reasons adduced by Stich. I have found that, in general, nonphilosophers seem to regard something like the autonomy principle or methodological solipsism, once it is explained to them, as *obviously* correct. Of course, most nonphilosophers do not see either autonomy or solipsism as a threat on ordinary 'broad' states of mind: Nonphilosophers tend to be all-out internalists when it comes to intentional content.

We are left, I think, with the following questions. Is there a viable conception of narrow content, one that avoids traditional internalist pitfalls (or is the appeal to narrow content merely an expression of closet internalism)? If we have doubts about narrow content, what are the prospects for psychology – and indeed for any theory, scientific or not, that appeals to intentional characteristics of agents in explanations of their actions? What are the prospects for a psychology founded on 'broad' intentional characteristics of agents? These are questions I shall address in the chapters that follow. In coming to grips with them we shall, perforce, come to grips with anti-Cartesian, externalist, conceptions of mind.

# 3

# *Supervenience*

## 1. THE SUPERVENIENCE HYPOTHESIS

It is time to explore in more detail the suggestion that mental characteristics of agents, more particularly agents' intentional attitudes, *supervene* on agents' physical conditions. I have designated this the *supervenience hypothesis*. In this chapter I propose to discuss the supervenience relation and explain why I am persuaded that the supervenience hypothesis is reasonable. I begin with a nontechnical characterisation of supervenience, move to a discussion of various philosophical refinements that have been suggested for this characterisation, and conclude with an overview of the metaphysical status of supervenience and the supervenience hypothesis. In Chapter 4, discussion will focus on some of the consequences of the supervenience hypothesis, especially its bearing on the causal standing of supervenient mental characteristics.

The supervenience hypothesis takes its inspiration from a much-quoted passage in Davidson's 'Mental Events':

Mental characteristics are in some sense dependent, or supervenient, on physical characteristics. Such supervenience might be taken to mean that there cannot be two events alike in all physical respects but differing in some mental respect, or that an object cannot alter in some mental respect without altering in some physical respect. (1970/1980, p. 214; see also 1973/1980, p. 253)

The supervenience relation holds, if and when it holds, between collections or 'families' of properties or characteristics.[1] If α-properties supervene on β-properties, then, following Davidson, α-prop-

---

1 A reminder: It is convenient to couch the discussion in terms of properties. I should, however, be happy to replace reference to properties with reference to predicates. I remain neutral on the question whether the relata in a supervenience relation must be genuine properties.

erties *depend on* and are *determined by* β-properties. More precisely, an object's *having* a given α-property depends on and is determined by its *having* a given β-property. I shall refer to cases of this sort as instances of α/β-*supervenience*. It is a *consequence* of α/β-supervenience that objects alike in all β-respects must be alike in their α-respects, though the converse need not hold: Objects may be alike in α-respects, while differing in various β-respects. If Wayne and Dwayne are physical duplicates, they must be mental duplicates as well, but Wayne and Clara may share the same thoughts without sharing physiques. Further, again following Davidson, when α/β-supervenience holds, an object cannot change in some α-respect without changing in some β-respect. If, at *t*, Wayne acquires the intention to order a Whopper, Wayne must, at *t*, undergo some physical change or other.

Supervenience relations are by no means confined to the mental domain. Liquidity, for instance, might be thought to supervene on molecular structure.[2] That is, something's being liquid apparently *depends on* and *is determined by* its possessing a certain sort of molecular structure.[3] Let us pretend that this is so. It follows that substances possessing identical molecular structures will be identical with respect to liquidity. It follows as well that, should a substance change its state, cease to be liquid, and become solid, for instance, its 'underlying' molecular structure must change as well. Indeed, we should say that its change in state is *due to* some change at the molecular level.

We require a conception of supervenience insofar as we regard our world as *layered* or *sedimented*, as consisting of *hierarchies* of characteristics in which the upper tiers of the hierarchy are fixed by those in the lower tiers. There are, admittedly, alternatives to this layered picture of the world. We might, for instance, regard every characteristic as standing on its own. Something's being liquid, then, might be a characteristic it possessed *along side* the characteristic of possessing a certain molecular structure; and its possessing that molecular structure would be a feature it possessed *along side* the characteristic of possessing certain atomic features. Alter-

2 I do not contend that being a liquid *does in fact* supervene on molecular structure, though I suppose there is reason to think that it does.

3 Although it is controversial, this amounts, I think, to its possessing the characteristic of liquidity *in virtue of* its possession of this molecular structure; it is liquid *because* it possesses this molecular structure; see below.

natively, we might imagine that liquidity is *nothing but* molecular structure; what appear to us to be distinct characteristics are in fact one and the same. Nonhierarchical conceptions, of which these are but two examples, encourage us to abandon efforts to explain or understand higher-level characteristics in terms of those at a lower level. Atomic characteristics certainly *seem* to be distinct from, yet responsible for, hence explanatory of, molecular characteristics, and these, in turn, *seem* to be distinct from, yet responsible for, hence explanatory of, the possession of observable characteristics like liquidity. Moreover, such relations of dependence and determination, and explanations framed in light of these, exhibit a definite *directionality* and *transitivity*. Features of molecules depend on, are determined by, and so are explained by, features of atoms, not vice versa, and the observable characteristics of a substance depend on, are determined by, and so are explained by, but do not themselves explain, its molecular characteristics.

This conception of the world as comprising layers of subvenient and supervenient characteristics, then, stands in contrast to non-layered, nonhierarchical, *flat* images of the world. But the conception is also to be contrasted with hierarchical conceptions that allow for *downward influence*. We suppose that a substance's having a certain sort of molecular structure determines, hence accounts for, and so partly explains, certain observable features of that substance, including its being liquid. If the relation is one of supervenience, then we suppose that the determination goes in one direction: from molecular characteristics to observable features. It is possible, however, to hold onto the hierarchical picture while denying or modifying this directionality. Thus one might be attracted to the view that certain lower-level features are *themselves* influenced by various higher-level features, the higher-level features exert a measure of downward influence on the lower-level. I shall call a picture of this sort *emergentist*.

I believe that it is largely an empirical question whether the world is layered, whether it exhibits a hierarchical or a nonhierarchical structure. Our science and our everyday experience, however, strongly suggest that the question is to be answered in the affirmative. I shall, then, accept that this is so while granting that, if it is so, its being so is not a conceptual truth. It is also an empirical question whether particular characteristics, like liquidity, or families of characteristics, are supervenient or emergent. I shall say more about emergence in Chapter 4. For the present I shall simply assert without argument that, although there may be nothing conceptually incoherent (or empirically unthinkable) about the emergentist picture, there are no very good empirical reasons to think that there are cases of downward influence.[4] We are left, then, with supervenience as a pervasive feature of our world, a feature underlying the layered structure that manifests itself wherever we turn.

Even if this is so, of course, it remains to be seen what supervenience relations actually obtain. And that, I have contended, is largely a matter for empirical inquiry. Does this mean that I am in possession of telling empirical evidence for the supervenience hypothesis, that I am prepared to set out an empirical demonstration of mental/physical supervenience? No, I merely offer the hypothesis as one with at least this much to be said for it: The supervenience hypothesis provides a powerful and natural way of fitting together elements of our overall picture of intelligent agency. Consider, for instance, our toleration of both psychological and non-psychological (physiological or neurobiological) explanations of behaviour. We appeal to states of mind to explain intelligent behaviour, while recognising that physiology and neurobiology stand ready to explain in very different ways what is, in one obvious sense, the same behaviour. If we suppose that an agent's states of mind depend on and are determined by that agent's biological condition, that states of mind are possessed in virtue of agents' possession of certain biological characteristics, then we are in a position to understand this otherwise puzzling relationship. Explanations framed in terms of an object's supervenient characteristics and explanations appealing to the subvenient basis in that object of the those characteristics, though importantly different in many respects, are bound to be synchronised. To be sure, synchronicity does not, by itself, yield the sort of directionality required by supervenience. That directionality, in the mental/physical case, is inspired by empirical work on brains and mental functioning.

I should emphasise that I am not contending that experimental work on the brain provides anything so grand as *direct* evidence for

4 Quantum mechanics might be offered as a counterexample to this claim. If certain attributes of an electron depend on its being measured, then it would seem that downward influence is ubiquitous. Given the murky character of issues surrounding the interpretation of quantum physics, however, I doubt that quantum measurement should be offered as a *clear* case of downward influence.

the supervenience hypothesis. It is, however, uniformly consistent with that hypothesis. Indeed, it may nowadays be close to unthinkable that neurobiology and psychology might begin to diverge.[5] Still, it is important to bear in mind that, although it may be an empirical question whether states of mind supervene on agents' physical characteristics, the supervenience relation itself is metaphysically saturated. In this respect, supervenience resembles causality. Although it is an empirical question whether one event causes another, the causal relation itself is metaphysically, not empirically, specifiable. Thus, whatever empirical evidence we may have that inclines us to the belief that some $C$ caused some $E$, that evidence is consistent with the noncausal co-occurrence of $C$'s and $E$'s.

In the case of causality, of course, we advance causal *laws* that we regard as both explanatory of, and confirmed by, their instances. Are there comparable nomological generalisations covering supervenience relations? Talk of nomological generalisations incites long-standing fears of 'reductionism'. Davidson's appeal to supervenience occurs in the course of a defense of 'anomalous monism', a doctrine according to which (1) mental events are (that is, are identical with) physical events, events falling under strict laws, though (2) there are no strict laws relating sorts of mental event and sorts of physical event. Against this background, it is scarcely surprising that supervenience is usually billed as a 'nonreductive' relation. I propose, however, to leave open whether supervenience is nonreductive, and thus whether, if $\alpha$'s supervene on $\beta$'s, there are strict laws relating instances of $\alpha$–characteristics to instances of $\beta$–characteristics.[6] Even so, evidence for the supervenience of $\alpha$'s on $\beta$'s typically includes evidence for the presence of nonaccidental, principled relations between $\alpha$'s and $\beta$'s. These relations appear to exhibit the sort of directionality associated with supervenience: We regard the occurrence of a $\beta$ as underlying, hence explaining, an $\alpha$–occurrence, but not vice versa. In this way we may come to

---

5 Unthinkable, except by eliminativists, science-fiction writers, and those members of philosophy faculties adept at thinking the unthinkable.
6 By 'strict law' here, and elsewhere, I am following Davidson's usage. A strict law is an exceptionless law, one that belongs to a closed and comprehensive system of laws (of the sort we presumably strive for in ground-floor physics). Strict laws are to be distinguished from ordinary lawlike generalisations, 'hedged' laws, ceteris paribus laws, and the like. I take anomalous monism to ban only *strict* psychophysical laws (see Davidson 1992).

regard neural conditions of certain sorts as explaining certain mental capacities or deficits, but not the latter as explaining the former.

I do not pretend that these remarks provide anything close to an air-tight case for the supervenience hypothesis. This is perfectly in keeping with my claim that supervenience relations are to be empirically supported, however. In fact, given my philosophical purposes, I need only show that the supervenience hypothesis has some reasonable chance of success. It would, of course, be desirable for that hypothesis to possess a large measure of empirical plausibility. My suggestion is that it does, though, as a philosopher (a *mere* philosopher), I can only direct the reader to the immense body of empirical literature that endeavours to connect mental and neurobiological characteristics.[7]

A sceptic might retort that this literature better supports some version of the identity theory according to which mental properties (or types) are taken to be identical with certain physical properties (types), or that it supports the out-and-out *elimination* of mental properties. I shall not argue against eliminativism here (see Chapter 1, § 3). I shall, however, say a word about property or type identities.

The supervenience hypothesis as I have explicated it thus far is compatible with the 'token identity' of mental and physical particulars. By this I mean that the supervenience of mental characteristics on physical characteristics is consistent with, though does not imply, the notion that every mental particular is a physical particular.[8] Given that $\alpha$'s supervene on $\beta$'s, what supervenience rules out is just that $\alpha$ and $\beta$ are the very same *property*. Supervenience is, in this respect, a weaker relation than a relation of property identity. Still, we might think that empirical evidence for the supervenience of $\alpha$'s on $\beta$'s must also be evidence that $\alpha$ and $\beta$ are one and the same. If that is so, what reason, other than a reluctance to endorse a

---

7 Classics in this domain include Gazzaniga (1970); Lashley (1950); Linneberg (1967); Luria (1973); Penfield (1967); and Sperry (1952). More recent sources: Cotman and McGaugh (1980); Hubel and Wiesel (1979); Kertesz (1983); Oakley (1985).

8 If we employ a fine-grained individuation of events in the style of Kim and Goldman (according to which an event is the exemplification of an event property at a time), then token identity is ruled out immediately for mental and physical events. Thus, $\alpha$'s being mental event $M$ at $t$ and $\alpha$'s being neural event $N$ at $t$ are distinct events – unless $M$ and $N$ are identical. See Goldman (1970); Kim (1973).

stronger thesis when a weaker alternative is available, is there to prefer supervenience?

There is little agreement among philosophers as to the criteria of property or type identity. Nevertheless, there are various prima facie grounds for favouring supervenience over identity in the mental/physical case. One reason is the apparent 'multiple realisability' of mental characteristics. Most mental characteristics seem capable of being instantiated in a wide range of physical media. Can a computing machine think? One may doubt that this is so, but few nowadays would base their doubts solely on the notion that computing machines are made of the wrong 'stuff'. Moreover, it seems entirely within the realm of physical possibility that there are creatures elsewhere in the universe that share various mental characteristics with us but whose 'biology' is vastly different from ours. We need not appeal to science-fiction cases, however, to make the same point. We unhesitatingly ascribe mental states across species, despite large differences in underlying physiology. Even within our own species, it seems unlikely that particular mental characteristics are invariably realised in identical neural structures.

Multiple realisability, however, need not deter a determined identity theorist. It is open to such a theorist, for instance, to argue that the relevant subvenient characteristic is, in fact, disjunctive in character. That is, it might be that, in you, mental feature $M$ is realised in neural structure $N$, whereas in an octopus, $M$ is realised in a different sort of neural structure, $N'$. Would this undermine type identity? It would not, unless we assume that $M$ might not be identical with the *disjunctive* characteristic $<N$ or $N'>$. It could happen that the characteristic in question is a disjunction of *dozens* of characteristics, even, in principle, an infinite number of characteristics.[9]

The most prominent motivation for doubting property identity is, I suspect, the brute conviction that the property *being a thought of Vienna* is just obviously a different property from the physical property *being neural process $N$* (or *being neural process $N$ in context $C$,* or even *being neural process $N$ or $N'$ or $N''$ . . . in context $C$ or $C'$ or $C''$ . . .* ). What accounts for this conviction? Perhaps, as identity theorists have long warned, it is a mere prejudice to be overcome

---

9 Further reservations concerning the bearing of multiple realisability on property identity surface in Chapter 4, § 5.

by further empirical investigation (see, e.g., Smart 1959). Lacking a theory of type identity, I shall fall back on a point made at the outset: A commitment to supervenience is weaker than a commitment to type identity. In the absence of some further reason to prefer identity, therefore, I shall throw in my lot with supervenience.[10]

Before pushing ahead, I might say a word concerning the utility of the concept of supervenience. Thus far I have touted the metaphysical and empirical plausibility of the supervenience hypothesis, the hypothesis that states of mind depend on and are determined by agents' physical conditions, that we enjoy a mental life in virtue of our possession of a certain sort of complex physical constitution. I have described supervenience as a relation holding between properties or characteristics according to which (1) the instantiation of some property or family of properties (or characteristics), $\alpha$, *depends upon* the instantiation of some other property or family of properties (or characteristics), $\beta$, and (2) $\beta$ *determines* $\alpha$. The relations of dependence and determination, as I shall deploy them here, are *directional* and *transitive*: If $\alpha$'s depend upon $\beta$'s, then $\beta$'s do not depend upon $\alpha$'s; and if $\beta$'s determine $\alpha$'s, then $\alpha$'s do not determine $\beta$'s. Further, if $\alpha$'s depend upon and are determined by $\beta$'s, and $\beta$'s depend upon and are determined by $\gamma$'s, then $\alpha$'s depend upon and are determined by $\gamma$'s.

I do not offer supervenience as a one-step solution to the mind–body problem. I do not offer it as a *solution* to anything. I accept Simon Blackburn's observation that, in many ways, 'supervenience is usually quite uninteresting by itself. What is interesting is the reason why it holds' (Blackburn 1984, p. 186). My suggestion has been that mind–body supervenience is simply one manifestation of a pervasive metaphysical feature of our world: Properties are distributed hierarchically, those in lower tiers of the hierarchy determining the distribution in higher tiers, those at higher levels depending on distributions at lower levels. Intentional states of mind arise in this way from the natural order. This is sometimes put by saying that once God has fixed the basic physical facts, all the other

10 An identity theorist might point out that *parsimony* is on his side, and so it is not obvious that the supervenience hypothesis really is weaker than an identity hypothesis. In response, one might appeal to the apparent fact that scientific and everyday explanatory practices treat the types in question as distinct. Supervenience, then conserves – but does not add to – our list of admissible types.

facts are thereby fixed. The image is misleading, however, unless we think that 'all the other facts' are purely logical consequences of the basic facts. The conception I am advocating is more modest. In addition to fixing the basic physical facts, God must establish the relevant dependence/determination relations among properties. These could vary across logically possible worlds.

The picture is a stirring one, but it lacks precision. In the sections to follow, I shall survey some recent attempts to tame the notion of supervenience, to say more definitely what supervenience encompasses and what it implies. It should be born in mind, however, that philosophical accounts of supervenience may well fall short of their quarry. Indeed, if history is our guide, this seems inevitable. The fault, if it is a fault, reflects, perhaps, less on the concept of supervenience than on the character of philosophical inquiry.

A final thought before moving on. I shall, in discussing various supervenience theses, avail myself of talk about possible worlds. I do so for two reasons. First, certain of the issues to be discussed involve modal claims that are often formulated by reference to possible worlds. It is, I think, simpler to stick to this way of talking than to translate it into a blander idiom. Second, in many cases, appeal to possible worlds streamlines the discussion. We may use talk about possible worlds to illuminate modal relations without thereby committing ourselves to the out-and-out existence of any world other than the actual world. One might, of course, doubt that talk about worlds other than the actual world *is* illuminating. The doubt is one with which I have considerable sympathy. My hope, however, is that I have employed reference to possible worlds in a way that does not skew the central themes of this chapter.

## 2. 'WEAK' AND 'STRONG' SUPERVENIENCE

In drawing a bead on the notion of supervenience, ordinary language provides little in the way of guidance. Although 'supervene', 'supervenience', and 'supervenient' are entirely respectable English words, their use by philosophers differs from that endorsed by lexicographers. The entry for 'supervene' in my *Shorter Oxford English Dictionary*, for instance, explains that, for one thing to supervene on another, is for it 'to come or occur as something additional or extraneous; . . . to follow closely upon some other occurrence or condition'. A headache might, in this sense, supervene on my discovering that my chequing account is overdrawn. This usage echoes Aristotle, who, in the *Nicomachean Ethics* (1174b31–33), characterises pleasure as 'coming upon' or supervening on pleasurable activities: 'Pleasure completes the activity not as the corresponding permanent state does, by its immanence, but as an end that supervenes (ἐπιγινόμενόν) as the bloom of youth does on those in the flower of their age'.

Contemporary discussion of supervenience begins, perhaps, with R. M. Hare's contention that evaluative judgements about agents or actions are supervenient on purely descriptive nonevaluative judgements about those agents or actions.[11] Hare's idea is straightforward. If I judge that St. Francis is good on the grounds that he sets out saucers of milk for homeless cats, I seem bound, other things equal, to judge the same of anyone who behaves similarly. My failing to do so would signal a puzzling inconsistency on my part. Hare's avowed aim is to elucidate the requirement of consistency in the application of evaluative judgements without resorting either to the notion that normative predicates are definable in terms of some finite set of purely 'descriptive' features of evaluated items, or the view that such predicates denote characteristics possessed by things independently of our nonnormative assessments of them. The correctness of my judgement that St. Francis is good is grounded in or *depends*, perhaps, on St. Francis's possession of a host of natural qualities: He feeds homeless cats, cares for sick birds, saves scraps for dogs. According to Hare, however, it does not follow that goodness is definable in terms of, and is thereby reducible to, the possession of these qualities. Moral characteristics are supervenient on nonmoral characteristics just in the sense that moral discourse obliges us to treat like cases alike. Paraphrasing Davidson: There could not be two acts alike in all nonmoral respects but differing in some moral respect, nor could an agent alter in some moral respect

---

11 See Hare (1952, 1984). G. E. Moore had, some years earlier, advanced an account of the relation of moral to 'natural' properties that is sometimes cited as the inaugural philosophical use of the notion of supervenience (Moore 1903/1968). Moore, however, did not use the word. 'Supervenience' surfaces as a synonym for 'emergence' in discussions of 'emergentism' (see, e.g., Morgan 1923; Pepper 1926; Meehl and Sellars 1956). A useful account of the history and philosophical metamorphosis of the term may be found in Kim (1990).

without altering in some nonmoral respect. This, according to Hare, is at least a part of what moral theorists have in mind in insisting on the *universalisability* of moral judgement.

Hare's conception of supervenience differs in at least one crucial respect from the conception I have invoked in advancing the supervenience hypothesis. Whereas I have taken supervenience to characterise a dependence/determination relation between families of properties or characteristics, Hare applies supervenience to *judgements* or property *ascriptions*.[12] The conceptions need not be thought to be utterly unrelated, of course. One who held a metaphysical doctrine of supervenience for a certain domain might well appeal to that doctrine by way of an explanation of the sorts of judgement warranted in that domain. In any case, the focus here will be on explicitly metaphysical accounts of supervenience.

Much of the present-day discussion of supervenience takes as its starting point the work of Jaegwon Kim.[13] Kim has identified two distinct conceptions of supervenience, *weak supervenience* (*WS*), and *strong supervenience* (*SS*).[14]

$WS_{pw}$  If $\alpha$'s weakly supervene on $\beta$'s, then no possible world contains objects that are identical in all $\beta$-respects, but different in some $\alpha$-respect.

$SS_{pw}$  If $\alpha$'s strongly supervene on $\beta$'s, then, for any two possible worlds, $w_i$ and $w_j$, and any two objects, $x$ and $y$, if $x$ in $w_i$, is identical in all $\beta$-respects with $y$ in $w_j$, then $x$ in $w_i$ and $y$ in $w_j$ are identical in every $\alpha$-respect.

$SS_{pw}$ differs from $WS_{pw}$ in comparing objects *across* worlds. It is consistent with $WS_{pw}$, but not with $SS_{pw}$, that objects in different worlds agree in all $\beta$-respects, yet differ in some $\alpha$-respect. What $WS_{pw}$ prohibits is the existence, in a given world, of objects that are $\beta$-indiscernible but $\alpha$-discernible.

---

12 Blackburn (1984, chap. 6) sides with Hare in the case of evaluative predicates, while leaving open the character of supervenience in other domains. On the distinction between supervenience as applied to judgements and as a metaphysical thesis, see Klagge (1988).

13 See Kim (1978, 1979, 1982, 1984a, 1990). My discussion is centered on Kim (1990).

14 The formulations here are borrowed from Kim (1990). I shall employ subscripts to distinguish different expressions of *WS* and *SS*. Thus, $WS_{pw}$ is weak supervenience formulated by reference to possible worlds, while $WS_{mo}$ is a formulation of weak supervenience by means of modal operators to be discussed below. In contexts in which differences in formulation are irrelevant, subscripts are omitted.

In remaining silent about across-world comparisons, $WS_{pw}$ affords limited help in the evaluation of counterfactual and subjunctive conditionals (but see § 3 below). Imagine that we take liquidity to supervene weakly on the possession of a certain sort of molecular structure. We can be sure, then, that, if a particular substance is liquid, any substances we happen upon that are indiscernible from that substance with respect to their molecular structure will be liquid as well. But suppose we wonder whether a given nonliquid substance, a piece of granite, for instance, *were counterfactually to take on* this same molecular structure, it would be liquid. $WS_{pw}$ provides no guidance. It is apparently perfectly compatible with the weak supervenience of liquidity on molecular structure, that, in the nearest worlds in which the piece of granite possesses the molecular structure possessed by a liquid in this world, it is not liquid. In fact, it is consistent with the weak supervenience of liquidity on molecular structure that there are worlds indiscernible from our world with respect to molecular structure, yet, in some of those worlds, nothing is liquid, and in others, everything is.

The character of $WS_{pw}$ may be illustrated in a slightly different way. Suppose we believe that liquidity weakly supervenes on molecular structure, and that, in the actual world, molecular structure $M$ is a 'supervenience base' for liquidity. It follows from this that all (that is, all *actual*) substances possessing $M$ were, are, and will be liquid. What does not follow is that there is some *necessity* that this is so, that, in some sense, whatever is $M$ *must* be liquid. Our attitude toward the connection between a substance's possessing $M$ and its being liquid would resemble our attitude toward the connection between something's being a person and its being less than twelve feet tall. In such cases our stance differs dramatically from the stance we take toward the connection between something's being triangular and its being three-sided, or the connection between something's being acid and its having a certain atomic character. In these cases, we regard the connection as one that *must* hold, as a matter of logic or as a matter of natural law.

We might, then, reformulate $WS_{pw}$ – and, while we are at it, $SS_{pw}$ – so as to highlight these modal characteristics. So doing obliges us to distinguish explicitly between properties and the 'families' to which they belong. Thus, suppose that α-properties supervene on β-properties. We might imagine, as well, that the α-properties include $A$ and $A'$, and that the β-properties include $B$

69

and $B'$. We can then distinguish weak from strong supervenience as follows. (Again, I shall employ formulations suggested by Kim 1990. For those comfortable with formal representations, these are included as well.)

$WS_{mo}$  Necessarily, if anything has property $A$ in $\alpha$, then there is a property $B$ in $\beta$, such that the thing has $B$, and anything that has $B$ has $A$.
$\Box\forall A\forall x[Ax \rightarrow \exists B(Bx \wedge \forall y(By \rightarrow Ay))]$

$SS_{mo}$  Necessarily, if anything has property $A$ in $\alpha$, then there is a property $B$ in $\beta$, such that the thing has $B$, and, *necessarily*, anything that has $B$ has $A$. $\Box\forall A\forall x[Ax \rightarrow \exists B(Bx \wedge \Box\forall y(By \rightarrow Ay))]$

In these formulations, the difference between weak and strong supervenience is easy to spot. $SS_{mo}$ differs from $WS_{mo}$ in containing a second occurrence of 'necessarily', a second necessity operator, $\Box$. This reflects the fact that $SS_{mo}$ brings with it the notion that, if structure $M$, for instance, suffices for liquidity in one world, it does so in other worlds as well: $M$'s sufficing for liquidity is a matter of necessity. It is the lack of this embedded necessity in the formulation of $WS_{mo}$ that distinguishes it from $SS_{mo}$.

The formulations of $WS$ and $SS$ we have been scrutinising leave open the precise nature of the modalities involved. When $WS$ and $SS$ tell us, for instance, that certain relations between properties hold across possible worlds, are we to understand this as referring to all logically possible worlds? Or are the characterisations meant to apply across some more restricted set of worlds – those that are metaphysically possible, perhaps, or those that are physically or nomologically possible? Kim has suggested that we can allow each of these options to specify a distinct concept of supervenience (see, e.g., Kim 1984a). It is then up to a proponent of a particular supervenience claim to indicate the claim's intended modal force. In the case of mental/physical supervenience, no one other than a logical behaviourist is likely to claim that the supervenience of states of mind on the physical conditions of agents is logically necessary. It is far more plausible to suppose that the necessity is physical, nomological, or metaphysical (leaving open that these might turn out to be equivalent). A proponent of $SS_{mo}$ is, moreover, free to interpret each instance of the necessity operator differently. Thus, if there are three distinct shades of necessity, there are, at least in principle, eight distinct concepts of strong supervenience.

A Kim-style analysis of supervenience, then, yields a number of different supervenience concepts. We have seen that Kim formu-

70

lates both *WS* and *SS* in terms of possible worlds and by means of modal operators. Are there, then, bracketing questions about grades of necessity, two distinct conceptions of both *WS* and *SS*, or is it the case that, holding the necessities involved fixed, $WS_{pw}$ and $SS_{pw}$ are logically equivalent to $WS_{mo}$ and $SS_{mo}$, respectively? Kim defends the latter possibility; that is, he holds that the possible world renditions of *WS* and *SS* respectively imply their modal operator counterparts and vice versa.[15] The claim is more difficult to evaluate than one might expect. Although we may readily grant that modal operator formulations of *WS* and *SS* imply the corresponding possible world formulations, it is less obvious that the latter imply the former.

Consider the case of *WS*. $WS_{mo}$ tells us that it is a necessary truth that, if $\alpha$'s supervene on $\beta$'s, for any object, $x$, that possesses a certain $\alpha$-property, $A$, there is some $\beta$-property, $B$, possessed by x, and every object that has B has $A$. If this is so, there is no possible world in which two objects are indiscernible with respect to their $\beta$-properties – both have exactly one $\beta$-property, $B$, for instance – but discernible with respect to their $\alpha$-properties – one has and the other lacks A. $WS_{mo}$, then, evidently implies $WS_{pw}$. What is less clear, however, is that 'no possible world contains objects that are identical in all $\alpha$-respects, but different in some $\beta$-respect' implies that 'if anything has $A$, then there is some $\beta$-property, $B$, such that everything that has $B$ has $A$'.

Kim's proof that $WS_{pw}$ implies $WS_{mo}$ makes use of the assumption that the supervenient and subvenient families of properties, $\alpha$ and $\beta$, are 'closed under the usual Boolean property-forming operations, complementation, conjunction, and disjunction' (1984a, p. 158). Such an assumption is, however, less than perfectly obvious. How plausible is it to think that very long, possibly infinite, disjunctions of properties are themselves properties? If, as Kim himself points out (1990, p. 21), *being red* and *being round* are properties, must we suppose that *being red or round* is a property?

It is unlikely that such things are decidable purely a priori. *Being red or round* could easily turn out to have a significance that would incline us to count it as a perfectly respectable property. Imagine

---

15  See Kim (1984a). Van Cleve (1990b) and Post (1991, chap. 5) dispute the equivalence.

that mating behaviour in a certain species of fish is triggered by the approach of a fish of the same species but of the opposite sex with a marking that is either red or round. We might then be perfectly happy to postulate 'red or round detectors' in the species, detectors that respond to a feature of our world that we should most naturally pick out by means of a disjunctive predicate. I doubt, then, that there is any deep objection to disjunctive property construction.[16]

Matters are quite otherwise when we consider the complements of properties. John Post, for one, has argued that Kim's requirement that families of properties party to supervenience relations be closed under Boolean operations, including complementation, yields the surprising result that the property of *lacking mass* is a physical property (Post 1987, 1991; see also Van Cleve 1990b). If that were so, then disembodied spirits, abstract entities, and nonexistent objects would all possess innumerable physical properties. Worse, a world containing a disembodied spirit that possessed the complements of every physical property would apparently be consistent with even the strong supervenience of the mental on the physical.

The worry is that, if we allow the complements of physical properties to count as physical properties, supervenience theses will be reduced to triviality. To block this result, James Van Cleve has advanced a restricted closure principle:

CP 'If the thesis under discussion is that α-properties supervene on β-properties, then let the base set be closed under a given operation if and only if β-hood is preserved by that operation' (1990b, p. 228).

On this principle, the family of physical properties would be 'closed under complementation' just in case the complements of physical properties are themselves physical properties. Since this condition seems not to be satisfied – the complements of some physical properties are not themselves physical properties – we should be wary of Kim's assumption that, in general, families of properties party to supervenience relations are closed under complementation, conjunction, and disjunction.

Where does this leave the question whether $WS_{pw}$ implies $WS_{mo}$?

16 This is not to say that the measure of whether a given characteristic is to count as a genuine property is whether a detector can be built to detect its instances. The example is meant only to suggest that characteristics that may, at first, strike us as artificial or gerrymandered, might turn out to have a perfectly natural basis. See Fodor (1991, pp. 13–14).

Kim's strategy for demonstrating this hinges on the constructability of a class of 'β-maximal' properties for the subvenient family. The class of β-maximal properties consists of 'the strongest consistent properties constructable in β' (1984a, p. 158). Suppose, for instance, that β contains just $B$, $B'$, and that β is closed under complementation, conjunction, and disjunction. Then the β-maximal properties are $<B$ and $B'>$, $<\bar{B}$ and $B'>$, $<B$ and $\bar{B}'>$, $<\bar{B}$ and $\bar{B}'>$, $<B$ or $B'>$, $<\bar{B}$ or $B'>$, $<B$ or $\bar{B}>$, and $<\bar{B}$ or $\bar{B}'>$. Since the properties in this set are mutually exclusive, every object must have exactly one of them. Objects indiscernible with respect to their β-properties, then, possess the same β-maximal property, and $WS_{pw}$ implies that two objects with the same β-maximal property must have the same α-property. But under the assumption that β-maximal properties are β-properties, this is equivalent to $WS_{mo}$; hence $WS_{pw}$ implies $WS_{mo}$. The trouble is, the proof relies on such questionable 'β-properties' as $<\bar{B}$ and $\bar{B}'>$.

We can disallow such properties by disallowing closure under complementation and opting for $CP$. In so doing, however, we undercut the proof. Consider, for instance, the hypothesis that there is at least one disembodied spirit. This hypothesis is *consistent* with mental/physical supervenience interpreted as $WS_{pw}$ or $SS_{pw}$, with or without closure under complementation, but consistent with $WS_{mo}$ and $SS_{mo}$ only assuming closure under complementation. To see why, suppose, first, that we exclude closure under complementation. Recall what is required by $WS$. $WS_{pw}$ says that no world contains objects physically alike, but mentally different. This is consistent with there being in some world, $w$, an object, $S$, that possesses mental properties but only the complements of physical properties. $WS_{mo}$, however, is falsified if $S$ has mental properties but lacks a physical property since, in excluding closure under complementation, $S$'s possession of the complement of every physical property need not count as the possession of a physical property. Next, suppose we allow closure under complementation for the family of physical properties, then $S$ will possess a physical property, namely, the complement of every physical property.[17] In this

---

17 Notice that, assuming closure under complementation and Leibniz's law, no world could contain more than one such disembodied spirit. If $S$ and $S'$ both possess the complement of every physical property, then $S$ and $S'$ are physically indiscernible. If supervenience holds, then they are mentally indiscernible, as well, and unless they are otherwise discernible, $S = S'$.

case, $S$ is consistent both with $WS_{pw}$ and with $WS_{mo}$. Parallel reasoning can be used to show that Kim requires closure under complementation to demonstrate the equivalence of $SS_{pw}$ and $SS_{mo}$.

We must conclude, I think, that the possible worlds formulations of $WS$ and $SS$ are not equivalent to their modal operator counterparts; the former are, in an obvious sense, weaker than the latter. Is there any reason to prefer one to the other? One might opt for the stronger modal operator formulations on the grounds that, in allowing cases of the sort illustrated by the existence of a disembodied spirit – that is, instances of $\alpha$ without corresponding instances of $\beta$ – $WS_{pw}$ and $SS_{pw}$ are too weak to capture plausible, preanalytical conceptions of mental/physical – $\alpha/\beta$ – supervenience. Let us suppose that this is so: Let us suppose that a notion of weak supervenience is best captured by $WS_{mo}$, and a notion of strong supervenience is most sensibly expressed by $SS_{mo}$. Van Cleve (1990b) argues if we grant this, and if we allow closure under disjunction – but not closure under complementation – Kim is right in supposing that if $\alpha$'s supervene on $\beta$'s, then $\alpha$'s and $\beta$'s turn out to be *coextensive*, and, given strong supervenience, if $\alpha$'s supervene on $\beta$'s, then $\alpha$'s and $\beta$'s are *necessarily* coextensive.

If correct, this is an interesting result. It is common to tie property *reduction* to property coextension: If $\alpha$'s are reducible to $\beta$'s, then every $\alpha$-property is necessarily coextensive with some $\beta$-property. If Kim and Van Cleve are right, strong supervenience yields an important component of property reduction. Van Cleve's argument is straightforward. Assume $SS_{mo}$, and for each $\alpha$-property, $A$, locate a $\beta$-property, $B^*$, where $B^*$ is a (possibly infinite) disjunction of $\beta$-properties, each disjunct of which suffices, in some world, for an object's possessing $A$. $B^*$, then, entails $A$, and, given strong supervenience, $A$ entails $B^*$. $A$ and $B^*$, thus, are necessarily coextensive.

The procedure can be illustrated in the moral case. Think of every instance of goodness and the property or properties in which the instance of goodness is grounded. Now imagine a property, $D^*$, consisting of the disjunction of each of these grounding properties. It will be true that, whenever something has $D^*$, it is good, and whenever something is good, it has $D^*$. If goodness is strongly supervenient, then goodness and $D^*$ are, not merely coextensive, but *necessarily* coextensive.

One might balk at the notion that β-properties might be constructed from infinite disjunctions of β-properties. I have suggested already that there is nothing objectionable per se in the notion of a disjunctive property. Is there then some special difficulty in the notion of a property comprising an infinite (or even a very large) number of disjuncts? One might worry, for instance, that the possession of such a property would not be explanatory. What is important in the present context, however, is that the properties we are imagining satisfy the closure principle, *CP*. If we are considering a property formed from the disjunction of an infinite number of physical properties, for instance, that property must itself be a physical property. Why should anyone *doubt* that such a property is a physical property? And, if it is a physical property, why should it not be potentially explanatory?

Of course, even if one accepts the idea that infinite disjunctions of β-properties could themselves be β-properties, one might balk at the character of $B^*$. In constructing $B^*$, we left the possibility open that $B^*$'s disjuncts will include the *complements* of various β-properties. This would be so if, for instance, some β-properties sufficed for the instantiation of some particular α-property only in the *absence* of certain other β-properties. Is this cause for worry?

There is nothing, I think, especially odd in the notion that complex properties might include property complements as subcomponents. Recall St. Francis. St. Francis's being good might depend both on his doing certain good deeds and on his refraining from other good deeds. In order to cure a sick bird, for instance, St. Francis can administer potion $P$ or administer potion $Q$, either of which will effect the cure, though, taken together, $P$ and $Q$ are fatal. St. Francis's administering potion $P$ is good-making only in the absence of his administering $Q$, although his administering $Q$ would, in itself, be a good thing.[18] Are we then once more in the position of having to regard every complement of a β-property as itself a β-property? Not at all. The property complements at issue here are not introduced via an abstract property-generating procedure. They are, rather, independently motivated constituents of complex properties whose β-hood is unquestioned. In the present

---

18 These cases resemble those in which an agent's warrant for the belief that $p$ is defeated by his acquiring an additional warranted belief that $q$.

case, it is not the failure to administer $Q$ that is good-making, but the administering of $P$ *together with* the withholding of $Q$, $P$ coupled with the absence of a certain defeater.

I conclude that there is no special reason to doubt Kim's contention that $WS$ implies property coextension, and that $SS$ implies necessary coextension. Does this push us uncomfortably close to the possibility of reduction? Again, it seems to me a mistake to put excessive weight on the prospects of reduction in evaluating a supervenience hypothesis. Who knows; we might find that the hypothesis in question is independently plausible and so concede reduction. More to the point, it needs to be shown why reduction of the sort envisaged here should be regarded as objectionable. I shall remain steadfastly agnostic on the matter.

One loose end requires tying up. If Kim and Van Cleve are right, then necessary coextension follows from $SS$. Is there any reason to prefer $SS$ to $WS$, however? Before we can answer this question, we must be clear on the relation between $WS$ and $SS$. Kim argues that $SS$ implies $WS$, but that $WS$ does not imply $SS$. This seems clearly correct. Consider that, while $WS$ is silent about relations across worlds, it is at least consistent with those relations being in accord with $SS$. Thus, if $SS$ holds, $WS$ holds, though, as we have seen already, $WS$ may hold without $SS$ holding. The question we must eventually face is, which (if either) of the two, $WS$ or $SS$, best captures the preanalytical conception of supervenience with which we began our discussion?

## 3. HARE, DAVIDSON, AND SUPERVENIENCE

In order to answer this question, we might first compare what Hare and Davidson say about supervenience with Kim's taxonomy of supervenience concepts.

Hare is on record as suggesting that what *he* has 'always had in mind is not what Kim now calls "strong" supervenience. It is nearer to his "weak" supervenience'.[19] Hare regards supervenience as being 'a feature, not just of evaluative words, properties, or judge-

19 Hare (1984); see also Blackburn (1984, chap. 6). Although I shall not address the matter explicitly, the discussion here bears in obvious ways on Blackburn's contention that the weak supervenience of moral properties on nonmoral properties, together with their alleged failure to supervene strongly, provides support for projectivist antirealist accounts of moral properties.

ments, but of the wider class of judgements which have to have . . . reasons, or grounds, or explanations' (1984, p. 1). We have seen that Hare's conception of supervenience is, by his own accounting, best understood as a consequence of the requirement of 'universalisability': If we judge St. Francis to be good *because* he feeds birds, nurses sick cats, and speaks kindly to everyone, then we seem obliged, other things equal, to judge similarly of anyone who does the same. Moreover, according to Hare, 'as the link with universalisability shows, supervenience brings with it the claim *that there is* some "law" which binds what supervenes to what it supervenes upon' (1984, p. 3). The notion that there is a 'law' connecting subvenient to supervenient properties, however, strongly suggests that what Hare has 'always had in mind' is in fact something more nearly resembling Kim's *strong* supervenience. The latter, though not weak supervenience, implies that, when α's supervene on β's, modal generalisations of the form, 'necessarily, for all $x$, if $x$ has $B$, then $x$ has $A$' hold. And such generalisations are at least law*like*.

Other remarks of Hare's, admittedly, might be read as suggesting that moral/nonmoral supervenience requires only a much weaker, nonmodal generalisation: 'For all $x$, if $x$ has $B$, then $x$ has $A$':

If I call one room of that kind nice, there must be some universal, though perhaps highly specific and by me unspecifiable, aesthetic attitude that I have; in other words I have to be subscribing to some universal premiss from which, in conjunction with facts about the room, it follows that the room is nice. But my tastes might have been different. (1984, p. 5)

To this we might add that if the tastes – or moral views – of others disagree with ours, we may suppose them wrong without thereby supposing that they are confused, as we should were we to imagine that there is a necessary – conceptual – connection between particular nonaesthetic qualities possessed by rooms and those rooms' being nice (see Blackburn 1984, p. 184).

Let me expand on this last, somewhat cryptic point. Hare assumes that, for the domains that concern him, it is conceptually necessary that normative judgements are constrained by nonnormative judgements. It is a conceptual truth that if something is judged to be good, for instance, there is some nonmoral characteristic possessed by the thing and anything possessing that characteristic must also (and other things equal) be judged good. But this differs from the much stronger claim that it is a conceptual truth that (again, other things equal) anything possessing the property in question is good (or must be judged to be good by any rational agent). Suppose I judge that St. Francis's caring for injured birds is good. I am, according to Hare, thereby committed to judging that *your* caring for injured birds – other things equal – is good. But I need not suppose that it is a conceptual truth that caring for sick birds is good. I might, then, regard those who do not share my judgement as morally in error, but not as being conceptually out of bounds. And this, Hare supposes, rules out strong moral/nonmoral supervenience. The latter would license inferences of the form, 'necessarily, if anything has nonmoral feature $B$, then it has moral feature $A$'.

Despite his protestations, the conception of supervenience Hare invokes seems clearly to be more robust than $WS$. As evidence, I offer the parallel drawn by Hare between causal judgements and moral judgements. Just as moral judgements imply suitable generalisations, so causal judgements imply causal *laws*. In both cases, the relevant generalisations support 'hypothetical' claims, that is, subjunctive conditionals and counterfactuals, and in both cases, they undergird the notion that something holds 'because of' or 'in virtue of' the holding of something else (see Hare 1984, p. 10). Hare concedes that generalisations with this character afford 'a sense of "necessity"', though not, certainly, conceptual necessity. Hume taught us that there is no conceptual necessity in $C$'s causing $E$'s. It seems clear, as well, that, for many $\alpha$'s and $\beta$'s, there is no conceptual necessity in the supervenience of $\alpha$'s on $\beta$'s. Hare suggests that, in the moral case, the pertinent necessity might be 'physical' (1984, p. 11). But if that is so, then Hare might, after all, be committed to something resembling $SS_{mo}$, a version of $SS_{mo}$, perhaps, for which the necessity operators are interpreted differently in each of their occurrences. Thus, it might be a 'conceptual' truth that if anything is good it possesses some nonmoral feature, while it is merely 'physically necessary' that anything possessing this nonmoral feature is good.

It may seem odd to speak of 'physical necessity' in this context, but I am merely taking Hare at his word. The point is just that $SS_{mo}$ is open to weaker interpretations of the second modal operator than Hare acknowledges. And Hare's insistence that moral principles support counterfactuals ('Had Nixon been honest, he would have been a good man') and 'in virtue of' claims ('It is in virtue of St.

Frances's attitudes and behaviour toward animals that he is a good man') apparently commits him to *some* modal interpretation of the generalisations implied by his view. This modal interpretation is yielded by *SS*, but apparently not by *WS*.

Like Hare, Davidson has contended that his notion of supervenience is 'very close to' Kim's notion of weak supervenience.[20] The contention appears in the context of a discussion of 'anomalous monism', a doctrine that, it will be recalled, rules out strict psychophysical laws and strong reductive mental-physical generalisations. It might seem that *SS*, in sanctioning modal generalisations of the form, 'necessarily, if something is *B*, then it is *A*', threatens the anomalous character of the mental. Perhaps, as Hare suggests,

At the very least, if mental events are supervenient . . . on physical events, there are going to be some true universal propositions, although we may not be able to say what they are, which link the two. It is not enough that there should be merely physical laws that enable us to predict the mental events which, on this view, are token-identical with physical events. The laws will have actually to mention mental events, and indeed, since they are universal propositions, not individual mental events but kinds of mental event. (Hare 1984, p. 15)

Davidson insists, however, that anomalous monism is consistent with there being laws connecting the mental and the physical. Anomalous monism merely denies that these laws could be refined into or derived from the sorts of *strict* law thought to be characteristic of basic physics. Thus, although *SS* underwrites modal, lawlike psychophysical generalisations, these need pose no threat in principle to anomalous monism. A proponent of anomalous monism is free to interpret the embedded modality in such a way that it represents 'nonstrict' nomological necessity. Is there any reason, then, for Davidson to prefer *SS* to *WS*?

It is certainly arguable that *SS* better fits Davidson's original

---

20 See Davidson (1992). Unfortunately, in the same context Davidson cites as equivalent an apparently much weaker conception he had advanced earlier: 'A predicate *p* is supervenient on a set of predicates *S* if for every pair of objects such that *p* is true of one and not of the other there is a predicate of *S* that is true of one and not of the other' (1985, p. 242). This conception would seem to allow, e.g., *being a Nobel Prize winner* to supervene on *having an odd number of freckles*, providing it happens to be true that only Nobel laureates have an odd number of freckles. It is likely, however, that in describing this characterisation of supervenience as one 'intended' to be equivalent to his considered view, a view 'close to' *WS*, he has in mind the stronger conception. My suggestion here is that Davidson, like Hare, needs something stronger still. See § 5 below.

sketch of mental/physical supervenience than does *WS*: 'Supervenience might be taken to mean that there *cannot* be two events alike in all physical respects but differing in some mental respect, or that an object *cannot* alter in some mental respect without altering in some physical respect' (1970/1980, p. 214; emphasis added). Occurrences of 'cannot' here, suggest that the supervenience relation envisaged by Davidson is meant to be strong enough to support counterfactual and subjunctive conditionals: 'If Wayne and Dwayne were physically indiscernible, they would be mentally indiscernible as well'. Moreover, references to 'dependence or supervenience' suggest that the relation Davidson has in mind is stronger than that sustained by *WS*. *WS* implies only contingent generalisations. And these fall well short of providing a basis for a dependence relation.

Perhaps I am wrong about this, however. William Seager (1988) has argued that *WS* does in fact afford support for counterfactual and subjunctive conditionals of the sort apparently endorsed by Davidson. In evaluating these counterfactuals, we hold constant contingent features of the world consistent with the truth of the antecedent. According to Seager, supervenience relations are themselves among those contingent features to be held constant. If this is done, however, counterfactuals supported by *WS* might seem to come out just as we should expect them to do.

By way of illustration, suppose that liquidity and solidity only weakly supervene on microstructural properties of substances, and that, in the actual world, the substance in Wayne's glass is liquid. In the actual world, then, any substance microphysically indiscernible from the substance in Wayne's glass will be liquid as well. In other worlds, however, the substance in Wayne's glass, while microphysically indistinguishable from the substance in Wayne's glass in the actual world, is altogether different with respect to its macroproperties. In those worlds the substance in Wayne's glass is solid, perhaps, or gaseous. Now suppose we think, of the substance in Wayne's glass in the actual world, that had it been solid, its molecular structure would have been different. In evaluating this counterfactual judgement, we inspect nearby worlds in which its antecedent is true, that is, worlds in which the substance in Wayne's glass is solid, and determine whether, in those worlds, the consequent is true, whether the molecular structure of the substance in Wayne's glass is different from what it is in the actual world.

*WS* allows for worlds in which the antecedent of this counterfactual is true and its consequent false, worlds, for instance, in which Wayne's glass contains a gaseous cloud the molecular structure of which is no different from the molecular structure of the liquid in Wayne's glass in the actual world. Perhaps these worlds are remote from the actual world, however. This is precisely Seager's contention: 'Counterfactuals are evaluated in worlds which are most similar to the actual world. Would it not be natural to say that one measure of similarity is the extent and kinds of supervenience relations holding at the worlds in question?' (Seager, p. 706).

This is oddly put, however. *WS* itself places no constraints of the pertinent sort across worlds. *WS* provides no particular reason to expect objects in nearby worlds similar in all subvenient respects to objects in this world to resemble objects in this world with respect to their supervenient characteristics. Suppose we imagine worlds arranged in a similarity continuum based exclusively on *WS* considerations, as Seager suggests. Worlds in which the generalisations expressing *WS* relations more nearly match those true in the actual world will be closer to the actual world; worlds in which *WS* generalisations true in the actual world are false will be more remote.

Less abstractly, suppose that, in the actual world, substances with molecular structure $M$, $M$-substances, are liquid whereas, in some other world, $M$-substances determine some radically different macro-characteristic, solidity, for instance. Then worlds in which $M$-substances, or substances with structures similar to $M$, are liquid, will be closer along this continuum than worlds in which $M$-substances are solid. Call a continuum of worlds constructed on this principle the *WS-continuum*, and call the continuum of worlds based on overall, all-things-considered similarity the *ATC-continuum*. Is there any reason to think that the *WS*-continuum would correspond to the *ATC*-continuum, that *WS*-remote worlds would not be nearby, all things considered? Again, *WS* alone provides no evidence that nearby *ATC*-worlds preserve *WS*-generalisations. True, nearby *ATC*-worlds will resemble the actual world with respect to all sorts of contingent facts. The behaviour of *WS*-generalisations across worlds is difficult to assess a priori, however. Weak $\alpha/\beta$-supervenience, *by itself*, gives us no reason to regard worlds in which $\alpha/\beta$-generalisations resemble those holding in our world as closer to our world than worlds in which these generalisations differ. This is simply one remarkable aspect of *WS*, an aspect that illustrates just how weak *WS* is. It is doubtful, then, that Seager could be right in supposing that *WS* provides adequate support for the evaluation of the sorts of counterfactual claims that proponents of supervenience relations like Davidson find congenial.

Imagine, however, that Seager were not wrong. After all, the ranking of worlds on a similarity continuum is a vexed issue. The question remains whether *WS* yields an adequate sense of dependence or determination. Seager imagines that, in the case of mental/physical supervenience, although it is a necessary truth that every mental state depends on some physical condition or other, there is no necessity whatever in the relation between sorts of mental state and the physical conditions on which those states depend in our world. The notion that states of mind are in this respect 'accidentally dependent' on agents' physical conditions appears, on the face of it, unduly mysterious. We should wonder: What could possibly account for the differences between worlds in which headaches were associated with certain neurological occurrences, and physically indiscernible worlds in which they were associated with something altogether different? Further, if such worlds are nomologically or metaphysically possible, what accounts for what Blackburn (1984, p. 184) calls the 'ban on mixed worlds', that is, the absence of worlds in which neurological occurrences of certain sorts sometimes do and sometimes do not result in headaches?

On the basis of such considerations, I conclude that *WS* fails to capture the intent of perhaps the two most prominent supervenience theses. These, it appears, require something stronger, something on the order of *SS*, perhaps. Before considering *SS* further, however, a reminder is in order concerning the relation of supervenience and reduction.

Owing largely to Davidson's introduction of supervenience in the course of defending anomalous monism, supervenience is most often characterised as a nonreductive relation: The supervenience of $\alpha$'s on $\beta$'s does not imply that $\alpha$'s are *reducible* to $\beta$'s. Some philosophers have gone to great lengths to promote supervenience as the principal hope for theorists with materialist leanings who imagine that the prospects for reduction of nonmaterial properties or entities to material properties or entities are dim (see, e.g., Post 1987, 1991). And such theorists, as we have noted already, might worry that *SS* smooths the way for reduction.

It would be useful to introduce a clear characterisation of reduction and a list of reasons so many philosophers find the prospect of reduction repellant. The exercise would be unnecessary, tedious, and almost certainly inconclusive.[21] I have already expressed my intention to remain neutral on the question whether the supervenience hypothesis does or does not suffice for the reduction of the mental to the physical. My reasons are unexciting. First, I find the supervenience hypothesis an independently attractive one for reasons mentioned already. If supervenience provides a vehicle for an interesting sort of reduction, then I should be surprised, perhaps, but not thereby put off. Second, it is quite unclear why reduction per se should be regarded as a threat. The reduction of $\alpha$'s to $\beta$'s, just in itself, implies neither the *elimination* of $\alpha$'s, nor the notion that $\alpha$'s are 'nothing but' $\beta$'s. Nor does reduction imply the definability of $\alpha$'s in terms of $\beta$'s. My strategy, then, will be to defend the plausibility of the supervenience hypothesis and, as concerning reduction, let the chips fall where they may.

## 4. 'GLOBAL' SUPERVENIENCE

The prospects of combining the supervenience hypothesis with a reductionist programme turn on the character of the supervenience relation. *WS*, perhaps, provides no special encouragement to reductionists. As we have seen, however, it is not easy to appreciate why anyone attracted to the supervenience hypothesis would not be better served by *SS*. Still, *SS* may, justifiably or not, simultaneously raise the expectations of eliminativist-minded reductionists and lead proponents of the intentional attitudes to despair. There is, as it happens, an alternative conception of supervenience, one designed by its advocates to promote an explicitly nonreductive physicalism. It will be useful to examine this conception and discover how it compares with weak and strong supervenience, and whether it meshes with the informal characterisation of supervenience that underlies the supervenience hypothesis advanced in § 1.

The conception of supervenience in question is what has come to

---

21 The classical account of reduction can be found in Nagel (1961, chap. 11). For discussions bearing on the present context, see Churchland (1985); Hellman and Thompson (1975); and Kim (1989b).

be called *global supervenience* (GS).[22] Whereas it is convenient to think of *WS* and *SS* as applying to properties or characteristics of individuals, in its simplest form, *GS* applies to properties or characteristics of *whole worlds*. Suppose that α's globally supervene on β's. Then worlds indiscernible with respect to the distribution of β-properties are indiscernible with respect to α-properties:

GS For any worlds $w_i$ and $w_j$, if $w_i$ and $w_j$ are β-indiscernible, then $w_i$ and $w_j$ are α-indiscernible.

Applying *GS* to the supervenience hypothesis: If mental properties globally supervene on physical properties, then physically indiscernible worlds are mentally indiscernible.

As noted already, *GS* is usually touted as patently nonreductive. Moreover, *GS* provides a way around what might be thought to be a fatal defect with *SS*. I have made much of externalism, the doctrine that the intentional content of states of mind is fixed, in part, by factors extrinsic to agents. Put now in terms of supervenience, we might say that externalism requires that the supervenience base of agents' intentional states includes, not only the intrinsic features of those agents, but features of their circumstances as well. *GS* seems eminently suited to doctrines of this sort. Both *WS* and *SS* are characterised in terms of properties or characteristics of individuals. States of mind may not supervene on features of individuals, however, but on more complex wholes of which the individuals to whom the states of mind are ascribed are merely components. These more complex wholes might include contexts, restricted world regions, or even complete worlds.

This line of reasoning masks a confusion. Although *WS* and *SS* define supervenience over features of individuals, this is perfectly consistent with the supervenience base of some characteristics possessed by individuals, encompassing *relations* those individuals bear to other individuals or to states of affairs. If we allow relational properties in the supervenience base, however, it is hard to see how *GS* could be thought to provide an advantage over *WS* or *SS* in coming to terms with externalism.

Kim has, in fact, argued that *SS* and *GS* are equivalent – *SS* implies *GS* and *GS* implies *SS* (Kim 1984a). The former implication seems obvious. If α's strongly supervene on β's, then there can be no

22 Versions of *GS* are articulated and defended in Haugeland (1982); Hellman and Thompson (1975); Horgan (1982); Lewis (1983a); and Post (1987, 1991).

worlds indiscernible with respect to β's that differ in some α-respect. It is less clear, however, that $GS$ implies $SS$. An argument to the conclusion that $SS$ does not imply $GS$ has been advanced by Bradford Petrie (1987). The argument is worth examining because of the light it sheds on the concept of global supervenience and its bearing on the question of reduction.

Petrie provides a schematic representation of two worlds that appear to be inconsistent with $SS$ but not inconsistent with $GS$. If Petrie were right, were it possible for a pair of worlds to satisfy $GS$ while failing to satisfying $SS$, then $GS$ does not imply $SS$, and $GS$ and $SS$ are not equivalent. Before turning to Petrie's schemata, we should note that the construction of an example that 'falsifies' – that is, an example inconsistent with – either $WS$ or $SS$, requires the consideration of only a single world. The formulation of $WS$ and $SS$ refers to *all* worlds, to all possibilities. The production of a single world in which there is, for instance, an α-difference without a corresponding β-difference, is inconsistent with the weak supervenience of α's on β's. Since $WS$ is implied by $SS$, that possibility defeats $SS$ as well. The falsification of α/β global supervenience, in contrast, requires a *pair* of worlds that are (1) indiscernible with respect to the distribution of β's, while (2) differing with respect to the distribution of α's.

Petrie's strategy reflects this requirement. He asks us to imagine a pair of worlds, $w_1$ and $w_2$, each containing two objects, $x$ and $y$, one β-property, $B$, and one α-property, $A$. In $w_1$, both $x$ and $y$ possess $B$, and $x$, but not $y$ has $A$. In $w_2$, $x$ but not $y$ possesses $B$, and neither possesses $A$. The idea can be made more concrete by means of the chart in Figure 3.1. Petrie argues that the two worlds, $w_1$ and $w_2$, though inconsistent with the strong supervenience of α's on β's, are not inconsistent with α's globally supervening on β's. $GS$, in that case, would be shown not to imply $SS$. If Petrie's argument is correct, notice, then $GS$ does not even imply $WS$, since in $w_1$, $x$ and $y$ are β-indiscernible, but α-discernible. This suggests that $GS$ may be weaker even than $WS$, a conclusion that might be regarded as severely dampening the prospects of α/β-reduction.

What are we to make of Petrie's argument? It is tempting to describe the Petrie example as one in which we exhibit a pair of worlds, $w_1$ and $w_2$, that are *consistent* with the global supervenience of α's on β's, though inconsistent with strong (or weak) α/β-super-

| $w_1$ | | $w_2$ | |
|---|---|---|---|
| $x$ | $y$ | $x$ | $y$ |
| $B$ | $B$ | $B$ | $\overline{B}$ |
| $A$ | $\overline{A}$ | $\overline{A}$ | $\overline{A}$ |

Figure 3.1

venience. This is unobjectionable so long as our concern is with the class of logically possible worlds. Petrie's $w_1$ and $w_2$ do indeed seem logically possible. Since $w_1$ is logically consistent with $GS$ but not with $WS$ or $SS$, it follows that $GS$ does not logically imply either $WS$ or $SS$. What are we to conclude from this? We can say, perhaps, that the *concept* of global supervenience differs from the concepts of weak and strong supervenience. This is an interesting result. We might continue to wonder, however, about the broadly metaphysical character of $WS$, $SS$, and $GS$. Might Petrie's argument be extended to show, for instance, that $GS$ does not *metaphysically* (or nomologically) imply $WS$ or $SS$? Is it metaphysically (or nomologically) possible for $GS$ to hold when $WS$ and $SS$ fail to hold? Are Petrie's $w_1$ and $w_2$ metaphysically (or nomologically) consistent with $GS$? These are difficult questions. Petrie 'worlds' are world *schemata*, not worlds. Whether worlds satisfying these schemata are metaphysically or nomologically possible worlds, given global $\alpha/\beta$-supervenience, is by no means clear.

There is perhaps some reason to doubt that $w_1$ and $w_2$ are metaphysically consistent with $GS$. If $w_1$ and $w_2$ are metaphysically possible, it seems natural to suppose that there is a world, $w_3$, that resembles $w_1$ with respect to $\beta$, and $w_2$ with respect to $\alpha$.[23] Thus, in $w_3$, neither $x$ nor $y$ has $B$, and neither has $A$. Figure 3.2 represents worlds $w_1$, $w_2$, and $w_3$ schematically. However, $w_1$ and $w_3$, taken together, falsify $GS$, they are $\beta$-indiscernible, but $\alpha$-discernible.

One might wonder whether this is a fluke, or whether it is invariably possible, in cases of this sort, cases in which a pair of metaphysically possible worlds appears consistent with $GS$ and

23 I owe this example to Brian McLaughlin.

| $w_1$ | | $w_2$ | | $w_3$ | |
|---|---|---|---|---|---|
| $x$ | $y$ | $x$ | $y$ | $x$ | $y$ |
| $B$ | $B$ | $B$ | $\bar{B}$ | $B$ | $B$ |
| $A$ | $\bar{A}$ | $\bar{A}$ | $\bar{A}$ | $\bar{A}$ | $\bar{A}$ |

Figure 3.2

inconsistent with *SS*, to find a third metaphysically possible world that cancels *GS*. In one respect, it would be surprising if this were not so. Petrie's invented properties are queer ducks. They must be such that worlds $w_1$ and $w_2$ are logically possible worlds, but $w_3$ is not – since otherwise *GS* would be falsified, and the counterexample would be undermined. It is not easy to imagine metaphysically or nomologically possible properties that would satisfy this requirement.

Let us suppose, however, that Petrie is right, that *GS* is distinctive: It logically implies neither *SS* nor *WS*. Let us suppose, further, that *GS* does not *metaphysically* imply *SS*: *GS* is consistent with there being metaphysically possible worlds that falsify *SS*. We need now to ask whether a relation of this sort could capture an interesting notion of dependence and determination. One immediate worry is that *GS*, like *WS*, seems not to require the sorts of *systematic* constraint we should expect in instances of genuine dependence and determination. As Kim points out, in the context of a discussion of mental/physical supervenience,

Before we accept global psychophysical supervenience as a significant form of materialism we should consider this: It is consistent with this version of materialism for there to be a world which differs physically from this world in some most trifling respect (say, Saturn's rings in that world contain one more ammonia molecule) but which is entirely devoid of consciousness, or has a radically different, perhaps totally irregular, distribution of mental characteristics over its inhabitants (say, creatures with brains have no mentality while rocks are conscious). As long as that world differs from this one in some physical respect, however minuscule or seemingly irrelevant, it could be as different as you please in any psychological respect you choose. (1987, p. 321)

Although Kim's point is important, it would be a mistake, I think, to focus exclusively on the 'trifling' nature of differences in such cases. Where dependencies are concerned, the magnitude of a difference is not something easily assessable a priori. As studies in weather prediction have made clear, a seemingly insignificant change in base conditions may yield a large difference in outcome – recall the straw that broke the camel's back and the missing nail that resulted in a kingdom's loss. Consider a simple example. Suppose that all the electrical power for Manhattan is supplied by a ridiculously long extension cord plugged into an outlet in Atlantic City. Imagine, now, that Wayne trips over the cord, pulling the plug from the outlet. This apparently insignificant event might have momentous consequences indeed. Turning to Kim's example, it could happen that all the consciousness in the universe is 'plugged into' a receptacle orbiting in the rings of Saturn, and that the absence of a single molecule would be just enough to sever the connection.

Turning the argument around, it should be noted that strong mental/physical supervenience requires that there are no mental differences – among persons, for instance – without corresponding physical differences. This is consistent, however, with there being two agents who are altogether different mentally, but who differ physically only with respect to a single, 'trifling' molecule.[24] To paraphrase Kim, as long as one agent differs from the other in some physical respect, however minuscule or seemingly irrelevant, they could be as different as you please in any psychological respect at all.

If relational properties are allowed in the physical supervenience base, then the cases Kim finds troublesome for GS appear no less troublesome for SS. Imagine a world identical to our world in every physical respect except that, in that world, a single molecule is missing from Saturn's rings. Call our world $W_a$, the less-populated world, $W_b$. Every individual in $W_a$ differs physically from every individual in $W_b$ in at least this respect: Every individual in $W_a$ bears some spatial-temporal relation to a molecule in Saturn's rings, but no individual in $W_b$ bears any physical relation at all to that molecule – since it is absent from $W_b$. But if every individual in $W_a$ is physically discernible from every individual in $W_b$, then it is

24 The example is Brian McLaughlin's.

consistent with strong mental/physical supervenience – just as it was with $GS$ – that every individual in $W_a$ differs from every individual in $W_b$ with respect to that individual's mental characteristics.

In coming to terms with supervenience, we must focus, not on what may or may not be trifling differences, but on the systematic character of differences and their outcomes. A plausible case for the supervenience hypothesis rests on the discovery of evidence that agents' mental lives vary nonaccidentally and systematically with their physical conditions and circumstances. What variations might or might not be relevant is not something likely to be revealed at a glance. A single, well-placed molecule could have a crucial role in the function of a complex biological system. (Imagine the effect on a delicate biological system of a missing $DNA$ molecule.) If I am right in regarding supervenience as a pervasive metaphysical characteristic of our world, then the supervenience hypothesis has a certain initial, pretheoretical plausibility. A wealth of empirical evidence of systematic mental–physical relationships and an emerging picture of intentional states as depending on agents' biological characteristics and their circumstances provide the supervenience hypothesis with additional empirical and conceptual credence. The interesting question, perhaps, is whether there is any good reason to doubt that hypothesis, to doubt that states of mind depend on and are determined by agents' nonmental, physical conditions.

## 5. IS THE SUPERVENIENCE HYPOTHESIS TRIVIAL?

The foregoing section may kindle worries that the supervenience relation is uninteresting, that the supervenience hypothesis, even interpreted as expressing $SS$, strong supervenience, is trivially satisfied. Suppose that proponents of $GS$ are right, and $GS$ is weaker even than $WS$. It might seem unlikely that a relation this weak could capture what we have in mind in regarding mental characteristics of agents to depend on and to be determined by the physical characteristics of those agents. Reasoning thus, we may be led to embrace $SS$. As we have just seen, a plausible construal of strong mental/physical supervenience may require the inclusion of relational characteristics in the physical supervenience base. Once we allow relational characteristics in, however, we seem obliged to admit that any two individuals, however much they seem to be alike, are nevertheless different when they are embedded in worlds that differ in any physical respect at all, however insignificant seeming. In this sense, *SS* threatens to dissolve into *GS*, and in a way unlikely to please advocates of *SS*.

A criticism of this form has been advanced by Richard Miller (1990). Miller believes it 'trivially' true that 'the nonphysical supervenes on the physical'. Worse,

> it is equally true that the physical supervenes on the moral, the mental, and the aesthetic. 'No difference without a physical difference' is an excellent slogan. The gist of this paper can also be summarized with slogans. 'No difference without a moral difference', 'no difference without a mental difference', and 'no difference without an aesthetic difference', are as (trivially) true as the physicalist slogan. (1990, p. 695)

According to Miller, (1) the supervenience of the nonphysical on the physical is 'trivial'; and (2) the supervenience relation is invariably *symmetrical*: When α's supervene on β's, the supervenience of β's on α's is 'all but guaranteed'. Together, these claims yield 'the metaphysical insignificance of the supervenience relation'(1990, p. 696). Miller, I think, is wrong on both counts. The charge of triviality hinges on an implausibly weak notion of supervenience, and once this notion is replaced by something more apt, the symmetry Miller finds in every supervenience relation evaporates.

Miller characterises supervenience as follows:

$S*$  For a class of properties [α] to supervene on a class of properties [β] is for it to be true that for any two things to differ in their [α] properties is for them to differ in their [β] properties. (1990, p. 696)

Miller's first claim, that everything 'trivially' supervenes on the physical, is a consequence of $S*$ together with what I shall call the *discernibility thesis*: Every object differs from every other in some physical detail. If every object differs from every other with respect to its β-properties, then, 'trivially', there are no α-differences without β-differences. The supervenience of every property on physical properties is assured.

Why should we grant that every object differs from every other in some physical respect? Miller holds that 'physical language' incorporates the resources to distinguish any two physical objects however similar they seem. Objects so distinguishable, are physically distinguishable, hence physically discernible. A proponent of the supervenience hypothesis, he supposes, must include relational and historical characteristics in the physical supervenience base, along with dispositional and 'undetectable' characteristics. Consider, for instance, the physical supervenience base for moral characteristics. As we have noted already, it is plausible to suppose that this base will be 'broad', that it would include relational and dispositional features of agents. If St. Francis is a good man in part because of deeds done and temptations overcome, a molecular replica of St. Francis constructed last night in a Tijuana laboratory, lacking many of St. Francis's historical features, would, in consequence, lack many of St. Francis's moral characteristics. Externalist considerations lead to a parallel conclusion in the case of mental characteristics. 'The base properties upon which moral [and mental] properties supervene include relations, noncontemporaneous properties, and dispositional properties, none of which need be detectable. Moreover, these properties are mathematicized to allow an infinity of distinctions to be drawn' (1990, pp. 397–98).[25]

It is, Miller contends, an immediate consequence of our including relational, dispositional, and undetectable characteristics in the physical base together with the 'mathematization' of physical language, that the supervenience of every characteristic on physical characteristics is 'trivialised'. Since it will always be possible to draw *some* physical distinction between any two physical objects (this one's origin differs from that one's, this one occupies a different spatial-temporal region than that one, this one is composed of fewer molecules than that one, and so on), it follows that every physical object differs physically from every other. Since no two things are physically indiscernible, the discernibility thesis is satisfied – there are no differences without physical differences – and, given S*, 'everything' supervenes on the physical.[26]

When we consider the complexity of the actual world, plus the fact that the supervenience relation is supported by undetectable differences, relational

---

25 Miller slides back and forth between talk of properties and talk of linguistic 'distinctions'. His characterisation of supervenience makes reference to properties, but his worries about the 'metaphysically trivial' character of supervenience are couched in terms of distinctions afforded by actual and ideal 'languages'. Were there a simple, one-to-one correspondence between properties and 'distinctions', this vacillation might be dismissed as mere stylistic quirk. Without assuming the correspondence, I shall grant it here for the sake of argument.

26 In fact, the supervenience of all properties on physical properties does not follow from this result, not if there are nonphysical particulars – Cartesian souls, for instance, or abstract particulars – that altogether lack physical properties.

properties, and dispositional properties, the mathematization of physics ensures supervenience. . . . It is the expressive power of physical language which allows us to assume physical differences where none are detectable. (1990, p. 698)

This brings us to Miller's second contention: Supervenience is invariably symmetrical, a 'two-way street'. If moral characteristics, for instance, and aesthetic characteristics, supervene on physical characteristics, it is no less true that physical characteristics supervene on moral and aesthetic characteristics. The idea is straightforward. Suppose we regard α-characteristics as supervenient on β-characteristics, and take this to be a 'trivial' consequence of the β-discernibility of every object. If it turns out that every object differs from every other in some α-respect as well, then, on $S^*$, every characteristic, including the β-characteristics, supervenes on α-characteristics. In the moral case,

the apparent asymmetry of the supervenience relation . . . is an artifact of certain contingent features of our actual physical and moral languages. Actual physical language is far subtler and closer to an ideal physical language than actual moral language is to an ideal moral language. Actual physical language has incorporated mathematics, while actual moral language, despite the efforts of Jeremy Bentham, has not. (1990, p. 696)

As a result, there is a 'vast preponderance in the number of physical distinctions we can make in the actual physical language compared to the actual moral language' (1990, p. 696). Comparable 'expressive power' should be made available to the moralist, however.

Just as it is unfair to allow one team to use a different set of rules from another team, it is inappropriate to compare actual moral language to idealized physical language. The illicit comparison of an anaemic qualitative moral vocabulary with a robust quantitative physical vocabulary creates the illusion of a metaphysical primacy for the physical. (1990, p. 699)

If we allow both teams to 'play by the same rules', however, 'the result is a draw' (p. 699). That is, if we permit moralists to 'mathematize' familiar moral distinctions, and if we suppose that the family of moral properties might include 'undetectable differences, relational properties, and dispositional properties', it looks as though every object could be said to differ from every other in some moral respect. Why should we imagine that the pencil on my desk or a bit of rock orbiting a distant star possess distinctive moral characteristics? Perhaps both have 'some slight disposition to affect human flourishing' (1990, p. 700). We can, in this way, concoct a unique assignment of moral characteristics to every object just as we did in the case of physical characteristics. But if we can do that, then, since no two things are morally indistinguishable, there are no physical differences without moral differences, and every characteristic (including every physical characteristic) turns out to supervene on the family of moral characteristics. Moreover, 'A similar case can be made for the supervenience of the physical on suitable strengthened aesthetic or psychological languages. Give these languages the same resources for generating distinctions as the physical now has, and both will constitute a set of base properties upon which everything may supervene' (1990, pp. 700–701).

Consider just the supervenience of the physical on the mental ('no physical difference without a mental difference'). If we include undetectable relational, dispositional, and 'mathematized' characteristics in the mental supervenience base, then it is plausible to imagine that every object differs in some mental respect or other. The tree in the quad differs from a similar tree in the forest, for instance, in having once been observed by George. For its part, the tree in the forest occupies a unique region, $R$, of space-time relative to the observed tree in virtue of which it possesses a certain exotic feature: It is $n$ feet to the northeast of a tree observed by George. If this mental characteristic seems contrived, it is only because we usually rest content with coarse-grained mental distinctions. An 'idealised' psychological language, however, would incorporate resources for the construction of endless mental distinctions. And if this is so, it would seem to follow that every object whatever differs in some mental respect from every other.[27] The supervenience of the mental on the physical and the physical on the mental is thus 'all but guaranteed'. More generally, it is in the nature of things that whenever $\alpha$'s supervene on $\beta$'s, $\beta$'s will supervene on $\alpha$'s. And this, as Miller rightly points out, is not what advocates of the supervenience hypothesis have in mind in appealing to $S^*$. $S^*$ licenses 'two-way' supervenience relations, but these seem incompatible with the kind of dependence and determination relation hankered after by proponents of supervenience.

This, if it shows anything, may show only that $S^*$ is defective. It

27 Or, at any rate, every object in a world in which some object has some mental property. The caveat is important; see below.

is certainly an open question whether $S^*$ captures the notion of dependence and determination that inspires proponents of supervenience hypotheses. Miller grants as much: 'It is impossible to give a definition of supervenience that will satisfy all participants in the discussion' (1990, p. 696n.). Still, Miller's choice of $S^*$ is puzzling. $S^*$ is distinctively *nonmodal*. Advocates of the supervenience hypothesis, however, seem on the whole to favour one or another *modal* conception of the notion.[28] Thus, as we have noted already, supervenience is typically regarded as a relation holding with necessity, holding *across* some range of possible worlds.

Perhaps this does not matter, however. Recall the initial characterisation of strong $\alpha/\beta$-supervenience:

$SS_{pw}$  If $\alpha$'s strongly supervene on $\beta$'s, then, for any two possible worlds, $w_i$ and $w_j$, and any two objects, $x$ and $y$, if $x$ in $w_i$, is identical in all $\beta$-respects to $y$ in $w_j$, then $x$ in $w_i$ and $y$ in $w_j$ are identical in every $\alpha$-respect.

If $\alpha$'s strongly supervene on $\beta$'s, can we invoke Miller's strategy so as to yield the strong supervenience of $\beta$'s on $\alpha$'s? Note that, given Miller's insistence that relational and quantitative characteristics be included in the supervenience base, $x$ in $w_i$ and $y$ in $w_j$ will be $\beta$-indiscernible just in case $x = y$ and $w_i = w_j$. To see why this is so, consider again a world exactly like the actual world in every physical respect save for the lack of a particular molecule orbiting in the rings of Saturn. Every object in that world will differ physically from every object in our world. The Washington Monument in our world stands at a certain distance from a collection of $n$ molecules orbiting in Saturn's rings; in that world, the Washington Monument has a different relational physical feature: It stands at that distance from an orbiting collection of molecules having $n - 1$ members. Since no two physically distinct worlds can contain physically indiscernible objects, then, if every world contains some physical object, every characteristic strongly supervenes on physical characteristics.

What of the strong supervenience of physical characteristics on moral or mental characteristics? Here Miller's thesis runs into a snag. It is consistent with strong moral/physical supervenience that there are worlds in which no moral properties are instantiated. Worlds in which sentient life is nomologically excluded might be of

28  Or, at any rate, most do; see note 20 above.

this sort (see Hellman 1992). But if there are such worlds, then the physical does not strongly supervene on the moral: There are possible objects that differ physically, but not morally.[29] In general, if it is consistent with the strong supervenience of α's on β's (strong α/β-supervenience) that there are worlds with β-characteristics but devoid of α-characteristics, then Miller's strategy will not generate the symmetrical result he claims for it.

Parallel reasoning applies for other conceptions of supervenience. The weak supervenience of α's on β's, for instance, is consistent with the existence of worlds instantiating β-characteristics, but nomologically excluding α-characteristics. Such worlds – those, for instance, composed entirely of matter in the form taken by matter in our world at the time of the Big Bang – falsify strong β/α-supervenience, but they falsify, as well, *weak* and *global* β/α-supervenience. In such worlds, objects differing in respect to their β-characteristics do not differ in respect to their α-characteristics. But then there are worlds that are β-discernible, and not α-discernible. Miller's suggestion that the supervenience relation is a de facto symmetrical relation, then, holds, if at all, only for a nonmodal conception of supervenience like $S^*$. Since most advocates of supervenience embrace, not $S^*$, but $SS$, $WS$, or $GS$, Miller's conclusion loses interest.[30]

Let us return now to Miller's first point, the contention that the supervenience of the moral, the mental, and the aesthetic on the physical is simply a 'trivial' consequence of the fact that every physical object is discernible from every other. If we grant the discernibility thesis and accept one of the formulations, $S^*$, $SS$, $WS$, $GS$, as definitive of supervenience, it follows that every characteristic supervenes on physical characteristics only if it is also true that every possible object has some physical characteristic (or, in the case of $GS$, only if every world instantiates some physical

---

29 It might be argued that, (1) the complements of moral properties, for instance, are instantiated in such worlds, and (2) the complement of a moral property is itself a moral property, so (3) such worlds do contain moral properties after all. Ignoring the question of whether (2) is plausible, the problem is that in these worlds every object is morally indiscernible, though not physically indiscernible, so physical/moral supervenience fails.

30 It is true, nevertheless, that supervenience, as characterised in $SS$, $WS$, and $GS$, is a nonsymmetrical relation. It is *consistent* with supervenience characterised in any of these ways that β's supervene on α's when α's supervene on β's. See Kim (1990); Grimes (1988).

property). Let us concede the point for the sake of argument. Does this concession 'trivialise' supervenience? I doubt it.

Suppose we restrict in some way subvenient relational characteristics to those that are *relevant*. Then, although individuals and worlds might invariably differ physically, they need not diverge in physically relevant respects. Wayne, who exists in the actual world, and his counterpart, who exists in a world identical to the actual world save for a single missing molecule, are physically different, though perhaps not in a way that bears on their possession of particular mental, or moral, or aesthetic characteristics.

The suggestion has merit, but it faces an immediate difficulty. How, without begging the question, might we specify what is to count as a *relevant* physical characteristic? We have seen already that we are unlikely to discover a priori what is or is not relevant in a given dependence-determination relation. Perhaps we could take a relevant physical characteristic to be one that figures in the determination of some $\alpha$-characteristic. But this suggestion requires that we have some notion of determination (or dependence) specifiable without reference to a favoured conception of supervenience. The point of introducing the notion of supervenience, however, was to articulate this very relation.

Worries of this sort, however, ignore the empirical aspect of a supervenience hypothesis. An advocate of mental/physical supervenience, for instance, need not imagine that individuals' physical characteristics are, one and all, relevant to the possession, by those individuals, of particular mental characteristics. The point is likely to be forgotten so long as we consider only Kim-style $\beta$-maximal properties. In advancing a concrete supervenience claim, however, one is compelled to identify particular subvenient characteristics as those responsible for particular supervenient characteristics. Individuals indiscernible with respect to *these* features must be indiscernible with respect to the supervenient feature in question. A narrowed supervenience claim of this sort would be shown false if it could be shown that there are two individuals, occupants of metaphysically or nomologically possible worlds, who shared these subvenient characteristics but who differed with respect to the supervenient characteristic − their differing in other physical respects would be beside the point. We attempt to discover whether there are such individuals or possible individuals by conducting empirical tests.

We must distinguish, then, generic supervenience hypotheses – the mental supervenes on the physical, for instance – from particular empirically constrained hypotheses. We can do so without rejecting the formulations of supervenience already in play if we limit the domains of $\alpha$ and $\beta$ to some subclass of available subvenient and supervenient characteristics. Thoughts and conscious states might be taken to supervene on agents' neurological characteristics, for instance, or, as is more likely, on some restricted subclass of these. Differences between agents' hair colour, or weight, or cardiovascular functioning would then be treated as irrelevant. We should suppose that agents indiscernible with respect to these neurological characteristics would be indiscernible with respect to their thoughts. Restrictions of this sort could be motivated by what we know about physiology, and psychology, and by some preferred theory of intentionality. An externalist, then, might allow $\beta$ to range over some, though certainly not all, of an individual's physical relational features. An internalist, in contrast, would restrict $\beta$'s domain to some subclass of an individual's intrinsic physical features.

It should be noted that this strategy is open to proponents of GS, as well as to those favouring SS. That is, for any particular supervenient characteristic, we can restrict world comparisons to subsets of worlds' physical characteristics and so avoid trivialising a supervenience claim. Once advocates of GS move in this direction, however, it becomes difficult to distinguish them from proponents of SS.[31] The original attraction of moving from talk of individuals to talk of worlds vanishes when we narrow down characteristics of worlds to characteristics, including pertinent relational characteristics, of individuals in those worlds. It seems likely that the initial appeal of GS stems from a desire to reconcile externalism with the notion that mental characteristics depend on and are determined by physical characteristics. Once we allow individuals' relational characteristics to count, however, it appears that externalism is entirely compatible with SS. Indeed, SS seems preferable to GS in one regard at least. SS ties mental characteristics of agents to the physical conditions of those very agents. The picture we have from GS is of mental characteristics 'spread out' into the world. This, in my judgement, is a picture we ought to resist.

31 For a sustained attempt to uphold the distinction, see Post (1991, chap. 5).

## 6. SUPERVENIENCE AND DETERMINATION

I have argued that both weak supervenience and a weakened conception of global supervenience (the conception identified by Petrie, for instance) fail to capture the concept of supervenience that informs the supervenience hypothesis with which this chapter opened. That concept includes a notion of the dependence of a thing's possession of certain sorts of characteristic on its possession of other sorts of characteristic, and the determination of the former by the latter. Whatever the precise nature of dependence and determination, it is clear that these involve more than mere intraworld correlations of the kind envisaged by *WS*. They involve, as well, a measure of systematicity that may be absent from *GS*. Perhaps, then, *SS*, Kim's concept of strong supervenience captures what we are after.

This suggestion is advanced by Van Cleve (1990a). Earlier, we characterised strong α/β-supervenience as follows:

$SS_{mo}$    Necessarily, if anything has property $A$ in α, then there is a property $B$ in β, such that the thing has $B$, and, necessarily, anything that has $B$ has $A$. $\Box\forall A\forall x[Ax \rightarrow \exists B(Bx \wedge \Box\forall y(By \rightarrow Ay))]$

Van Cleve suggests that α/β-dependence is just the requirement that, as a matter of necessity, nothing can have α-characteristics unless it has β-characteristics: $\Box\forall A\forall x[Ax \rightarrow \exists B(Bx)]$.[32] Similarly, α/β-*determination* might boil down to the requirement that nothing can be indiscernible with respect to its β-characteristics without being α-indiscernible as well: $\Box\forall y(By \rightarrow Ay)$. As Van Cleve puts it, 'the two components can be neatly expressed in the pair of slogans "every α-property, some β-property" and "same β-properties, same α-properties"' (1990a, p. 221).

These slogans, however, bring to the fore an apparent difficulty for anyone who takes *SS* to capture a supervenience relation that includes dependence and determination. For consider: Both slogans would hold if α's and β's were appropriately *correlated*, perhaps by virtue of each depending on some third, unmentioned, family of properties, γ. The point is not confined to the supervenience relation, but applies, as well, to any dependence relation: Dependencies

---

32 In what follows I shall assume the domains of α and β to be restricted as suggested in § 5.

imply correlations, but are not themselves constituted exclusively by correlations – even nonaccidental, lawlike correlations. Changes in the colours of leaves might be correlated with falling temperatures without thereby depending on falling temperatures. This would be so if both falling temperatures and changes in colouration were due to some third factor, diminishing hours of daylight, for instance. In that case, the slogan, 'no change in colour without a change in temperature', would hold, and hold nonaccidentally, although not because of a dependence relation between temperature changes and changes in colour.

Worse, at least from our perspective, $SS$ leaves open the possibility that, while $\alpha$'s strongly supervene on $\beta$'s, $\beta$'s strongly supervene on $\alpha$'s.[33] Consider the relation between the area of a square and the length of its sides. Area strongly supervenes on side-length (squares identical with respect to the length of their sides must be identical with respect to their area), but the reverse holds as well: Side-length strongly supervenes on area (squares identical with respect to area will be identical with respect to the length of their sides). However, the relation between the area of a square and the length of its sides seems not to be one of dependence or determination (except perhaps in a purely mathematical sense in which values are functions of – depend on, are determined by – other values). Part of the problem stems from the explicitly *non*symmetrical character of Kim's $SS$. The relation we have in mind in supposing states of mind to supervene on physical characteristics of agents is resoundingly asymmetrical. An agent's states of mind are dependent on and determined by certain of his physical characteristics, but his physical characteristics are not dependent on or determined by his states of mind. The same asymmetry is present in the idea that moral characteristics (or perhaps judgements) supervene on nonmoral characteristics (judgements) or that liquidity supervenes on molecular structure. The question is whether $SS$ might be supplemented to accommodate this element of directionality.

One possible strategy is to stick with $SS$, but to require that, when $SS$ holds in the $\alpha/\beta$-direction (when $\alpha$'s strongly supervene

33 Ted Honderich (1988) characterises a 'Correlation Hypothesis' according to which mental and neural events stand in definite nomic relations, but lack the directionality implicit in the notion of supervenience. It may be that $SS$ comes close to modelling the relation Honderich has in mind. See Honderich (1988, pp. 107–9).

99

on β's), $SS$ does not hold in the β/α-direction. The additional requirement is satisfied by many, maybe all, apparent cases of supervenient dependence and determination. Perhaps, then, it constitutes at least a plausible necessary condition for a suitably asymmetrical supervenience relation.

It is doubtful, however, that a requirement of this sort is sufficient, that it captures all there is to dependence and determination. Again, it seems easy to imagine cases in which $SS$ is satisfied in the α/β-direction, excluded in the β/α-direction, but in which α's nevertheless intuitively fail either to depend on or to be determined by β's. This could happen when α's and β's are correlated in a certain way in virtue of their both depending on some third kind of thing, γ, as in the case discussed above. Suppose that both the colour and texture of objects depend on the molecular configuration of the surfaces of those objects. And suppose, as well, that the relation of colours to textures is one–many: Surfaces alike in texture will exhibit the same colours, but two objects can be similarly coloured, yet differ in texture. Colours might then, in the sense of $SS$, strongly supervene on textures while textures fail in this sense to supervene strongly on colours. Yet the grounds for the correlation between colour and texture would lie, not in a relation of dependence or determination between colours and textures, but in a dependence relation both colour and texture bear to a third thing, molecular structure.

## 7. CONCLUDING REMARKS

It would be premature to conclude from such considerations that supervenience is a 'myth' or that the notion of supervenience has no useful theoretical or explanatory application.[34] Attempts to analyse causality, too, have proved notoriously fragile, but it would be naïve to conclude that this shows that there are no causal relations, that causality is a 'myth'. Granted, what I have been calling supervenience might be regarded as far less clear cut, far less central to our perspective on the world than the notion of causality. I concede that 'supervenience' is a philosophical term of art. Yet the idea it is intended to encompass is, I have insisted, utterly fundamental to our outlook. We find, or seem to find, the world to be layered; and

34 This point is made by Kim (1990); cf. Grimes (1988).

we find, or seem to find, characteristics associated with one layer to depend on, to be determined by, and to be explicable by reference to those associated with other, 'more basic' layers. Objects possess some characteristics in virtue of their possession of other characteristics. The asymmetry built into this relation accounts for a prominent explanatory asymmetry: The possession of 'higher-level' characteristics is explicable by reference to 'lower-level' characteristics, but not vice versa. The root idea probably goes back to the dawn of reflection – recall Democritus's contention that observable qualitative features of objects 'arise from' purely quantitative spatial features of their constituent atoms. The idea is shared historically by reductionist-minded philosophers and their anti-reductionist opponents; and the idea is implicit in our scientific practice: We seek, and expect to find, the explanation of phenomena by appeals to entities and processes we take to 'underlie' those phenomena.

To be sure, one might accept this layered picture of the world and the conception of supervenience that is partly constitutive of it, but then doubt that it illuminates the relation of the mental and the physical. Again, although the denial of mental/physical supervenience is perfectly coherent, it is importantly at odds with another idea that has proved remarkably resilient: At the most fundamental level, our world consists of physical items distributed in space and time; the tangible inhabitants of the world and their properties are determined exclusively by these. It is important to distinguish this idea from two stronger theses. First, that *all there is* are the atoms and the void. Second, that everything is, conceptually or logically, reducible to the atoms and the void. Neither of these theses is implied by the idea of supervenience to which I have appealed here. Of course, if dependence and determination imply reduction in some weaker sense, then reduction in that weaker sense follows. But if that is so, then it is far from clear why reduction should be regarded as a threatening prospect.

My aim in this chapter has been to make the supervenience hypothesis plausible. I began with a nontechnical characterisation of the notion of supervenience inspired by Davidson, then discussed some attempts at analysing and refining the notion. Those attempts turned out ultimately to leave us some distance from our goal. I have insisted that it would be unwise to conclude, as do some recent critics, that the supervenience relation itself, as opposed to one or

101

another philosophical analysis of supervenience, is lacking in application or importance. Are we left then, where we began, with a notion for which we have a definite intuitive feel, but for which we have no precise characterisation?

I believe, on the contrary, we have made considerable progress. We have discovered that the notion of supervenience is not easy to capture by means of a purely modal analysis. Although modal notions constitute an important ingredient of the concept of supervenience, they do not exhaust that concept. Supposing, then, that *SS* illuminates at most one aspect of our notion of supervenience, we might inquire as to the remaining aspects. These include, first, a notion of dependence, according to which a property or characteristic in the supervenient family requires for its instantiation the instantiation of a property or characteristic in the subvenient family; and, second, a notion of determination, according to which supervenient properties or characteristics are instantiated *in virtue of* or *because of* the instantiation of some subvenient property or characteristic. These elements bring with them the requisite metaphysical and explanatory asymmetry lacking in *SS* (or anything resembling *SS*) taken straight.

Offered as an analysis of supervenience, these remarks would be excessively thin. We should want to know what dependence and determination amounted to, and how they bear on explanation. We can spell out the modal aspects of these notions, indeed these aspects are included, as we have seen, in *SS* itself. The difficulty is to say what *more* they include. This difficulty is, I have suggested, parallel to that faced by those offering explications of the concept of causality. And it is one about which I have nothing exciting or original to suggest. Even so, I shall, in the chapters that follow, avail myself of the supervenience hypothesis with a clear conscience. There is, I believe, ample reason to think that supervenience relations are ubiquitous, and good reason to take states of mind to stand in some such relation to agents' physical constitutions. The question we must face now is, '*So what?*'

# 4

## *Mental causation*

### 1. AGENCY AND CAUSALITY

In Chapter 1, I stuck out my neck and sided with Aristotle, cognitive psychology, and common sense in according an important causal role to the intentional attitudes. What we *do* depends in part on what we *think*, and the dependence in question is straightforwardly causal. Now I shall try to make clear what is and what is not involved in a commitment to this causal perspective. The *what is not* is as important as the *what is*. There is a tendency, in thinking about mental causation, to set inappropriate standards for causality, then to conclude on the basis of appeals to these standards either that mental causation is impossible, or that the causation in question is attenuated or in some other respect second-class. Part of what I hope to do here is to provide a credible picture of one important facet of causal explanation and to show that mental causation accords with this picture.

I begin with a pair of caveats. First, a reminder: I shall not offer an argument against *eliminativism* (see Chapter 1, § 3). In part this is because it is not altogether clear what I should be arguing against. Eliminativists sometimes seem to endorse strong claims: Current work in the neurosciences shows, or at least gives us ample reason to suppose, that there are no intentional states of mind. The thesis is exciting, but patently false. Sometimes, however, eliminativists express their views more cautiously: It is possible, or likely, or reasonable to expect that the neurosciences will one day replace intentional psychology. This thesis, while not obviously wrong, is not nearly so exciting either. In any case, its truth hinges on empirical developments that no one, least of all a philosopher, is in any position to forecast. I readily concede that it is possible that eliminativists of this stripe are right, that we shall one day cease to

103

appeal to intentional attitudes in scientific (or even ordinary) explanations of behaviour. I see no compelling reason now to believe this is inevitable, however, or even that it is very likely.

Second, I am not interested in defending common sense and cognitive psychology – especially the latter – down to the last detail. For all I or anyone else knows, the intentional concepts we now find congenial may be replaced by finer-grained intentional concepts, or intentional concepts of a very different sort from those now in use; their use may even fizzle out altogether, as eliminativists hope. My aim, rather, is to show that there is a good deal of room for a sensible notion of mental causation, and that there is every reason to think that common sense and cognitive psychology are sometimes successful in explaining the behaviour of intelligent agents by citing mental causes of that behaviour.

Before turning to a positive account of mental causation, I shall first discuss the sorts of consideration that have led some philosophers to abandon hope of finding a place for mental causation, and discuss one sort of response to these considerations. This will provide a background against which the position on mental causation I shall defend can be more easily appreciated.

## 2. CAUSAL RELEVANCE

It might appear at first that the supervenience hypothesis automatically underwrites the possibility of mental causation. Thus, if we suppose that the mental supervenes on the physical, and that mental causes supervene on physical causes, then, given that *physical* causation is unproblematic, mental causation might seem to be assured. Although this line of reasoning has a certain initial plausibility, it is, as it stands, inadequate. I shall try to make that inadequacy vivid by means of simple examples. In discussing those examples, I shall adopt a coarse-grained perspective on events (see Chapter 1, § 5). This is a matter of convenience, not a reflection of principle. What I have to say could be reformulated in terms of the fine-grained conception. Where this is not obvious, I shall comment explicitly. Otherwise, I shall leave it to readers so inclined to supply an appropriate translation.

Consider an event pair, $<c, e>$, in which $c$ is Wayne's dialing, and $e$ is the ringing of Clara's telephone. Wayne's dialing, $c$, causes

$e$, the telephone's ringing. Let us suppose, further, that $c$ has the feature of being a left-handed dialing. In this case, $c$ causes $e$, and $c$ possesses a certain characteristic, that of being a left-handed dialing, although that characteristic appears to have no 'causal relevance' for the occurrence of $e$: Wayne's dialing his telephone with his left hand – rather than with his right hand or his nose – has no causal bearing on the ringing of Clara's telephone.[1]

Strictly speaking, this latter claim is false. Were $c$ to lack the characteristic in question, then $e$ would lack a corresponding feature, namely, that of being a ringing caused by a left-handed dialing, an '$L$-ringing'. So perhaps $c$'s possession of this feature *is* relevant to the occurrence of $e$, at least in the sense that $e$ would have been different had $c$ lacked the feature. From this perspective, *every* characteristic of a cause is relevant to *some* feature of its effect. Yet there remains an obvious sense in which $c$'s possession of the characteristic of being a left-handed dialing plays no causal role in the telephone's *ringing*, that is, it has no bearing on $e$'s possessing the characteristic of being a ringing.

More generally, the possession, by a cause, of a certain feature, $F$, need not figure causally in the possession, by an effect, of a feature, $G$.[2] Neither Wayne's telephone's being white nor its being manufactured in Kannapolis has any obvious bearing on $e$'s being a ringing, although it is not literally true that his telephone's being white or its being manufactured in Kannapolis lack causal relevance *tout court*: A ringing produced by Wayne's dialing a white telephone, or by his dialing a telephone manufactured in Kannapolis, differs in various ways from a ringing produced by Wayne's dialing a black telephone, or a ringing produced by his dialing a telephone manufactured in Cornelius.[3] It is natural, though entirely interest

---

1 On a fine-grained construal of events, Wayne's dialing left-handed and Wayne's dialing are distinct events, though the former includes the latter as a part. The case nicely illustrates a fine-grained conceptualisation of the causal relevance problem. The cause of the ringing of Clara's telephone is Wayne's dialing left-handed, though only a part of this event, namely Wayne's dialing, does any 'causal work' in the production of the ringing.

2 In a fine-grained idiom: An $F$-event need not be the cause of a $G$-event even though these events include events that are causally related.

3 How? White objects and black objects scatter photons differently. A ringing produced by Wayne's dialing a white telephone, then, differs from one produced by his dialing a black telephone in this respect: The former ringing has the charac-

relative, to regard particular features of a given event as causally inert. We focus on certain aspects of the telephone's ringing, and these seem unaffected by the colour of Wayne's telephone or its place of manufacture. What matters – what matters *to us* – is that Wayne's dialing produces an electrical pulse that travels over a wire and in virtue of which a contact inside Clara's telephone closes and her telephone rings.

An event, $c$, may possess a property, $P$, and $c$ may cause $e$, without our being inclined to suppose that $c$'s possession of $P$ had any bearing at all on $c$'s causing $e$: $c$ might have caused $e$, even in the absence of $P$, for instance. The point is difficult to put precisely, however, for reasons that have emerged already. If we imagine $c$ to lack $P$, then we must imagine $e$ to differ as well (if nothing else, $e$ will lack the property of having been caused by an event possessing $P$). This points, I think, to an irreducibly *pragmatic* element at the centre of our notion of causal relevance. We regard $P$ as causally irrelevant when its absence from $c$ would make no difference *we care about* to $e$.

Returning, then, to mental events, we might ask whether an event's being mental could be causally relevant to its production of an effect, *behaviour*, with certain features. Recall the discussion in Chapter 2, § 8. There it was noted that some characteristics of an effect may be *causally necessitated*, others *conceptually necessitated*. Wayne dials his telephone and, a moment later, Clara's telephone rings. The ringing of Clara's telephone is causally, but not conceptually, necessitated by Wayne's dialing. There are conceptually possible worlds in which Wayne dials his telephone but Clara's telephone fails to ring. In all nearby nomologically possible worlds, however – in all nomologically possible worlds in which characteristics of the two telephones, the telephone lines, and background factors are held constant – Wayne's dialing his telephone results in the ringing of Clara's telephone. Compare $e$'s possession of the characteristic of being an 'L-ringing', that is, a ringing caused by a left-handed dialing. This characteristic is conceptually necessitated: In every conceptually possible world in which $c$, the cause of $e$, is a

teristic of being a ringing produced by an event involving an object that scatters photons in pattern $P$; the latter ringing lacks this characteristic. Similarly, dialing a telephone manufactured in Kannapolis produces a pattern of electrons, $E$, that differs from the pattern, $F$, produced by telephones manufactured in Cornelius. Although both patterns produce ringings, they do so in different ways.

left-handed dialing, $e$ possesses the characteristic of being an '$L$-ringing'.

A sensible notion of mental causation requires that mental characteristics of causes be related to their effects – behaviour, for instance – in the way Wayne's dialing is related to the ringing of Clara's telephone, and not in the way Wayne's dialing left-handed is related to the occurrence of an '$L$-ringing'. It is not that left-handed dialings fail to cause '$L$-ringings', but that the characteristic of being an '$L$-ringing' is one possessed by an event solely in virtue of a conceptual connection it bears to a particular feature of a distinct event, its cause.

Imagine now that, at $t_1$, Clara acquires the intention to wave at Wayne at $t_2$, and as a result, at $t_2$, moves her arm in a way characteristic of waving. Let us suppose that intentions supervene on agents' neurological conditions, and that it is in virtue of coming to be in neurological condition $N$ that Clara comes to have the intention to wave at Wayne. To complete the picture, let us pretend that Clara's coming to be in condition $N$ causes, $B$, her arm-waving behaviour. Since Clara's coming to be in neurological condition $N$ causes $B$, and since intentions supervene on neurological conditions, Clara's coming to be in $N$ might possess the (supervenient) characteristic, *being the acquisition of an intention to wave*. On this basis, then, $B$ could be seen to possess a feature, namely, that of being an intentional waving, a feature $B$ would not have possessed had it not been caused by an event with a corresponding mental characteristic.[4] Yet it seems right to say that $B$'s possession of this characteristic is at best a *conceptual*, as distinct from a *causal*, consequence of Clara's acquiring the intention to wave.

As I have formulated it, the question of mental causation is the question whether mental features of agents are ever *causally* relevant to their behaviour. Although causal relevance may not be ruled out by the sort of conceptual relation illustrated above, it is not implied by it either. If we are to establish that an event, $c$'s, possession of a mental characteristic, $\psi$, for instance, is straightforwardly causally relevant to the possession, by an effect, $e$, of some characteristic, $\varphi$, we need something more than a conceptual link between $c$'s pos-

4 Strictly, an intentional $A$-ing need not be caused by an intention to $A$. Nevertheless, as a first approximation, an $A$-ing is intentional only if it is caused by some intention or other. See Mele (1992, chap. 8).

sessing ψ and $e$'s possessing φ. Less abstractly, we must show that an event's being, say, the acquiring of an intention to wave might bear causally on Clara's arm's moving as it does.

One possibility is that causal relevance turns on the existence of a causal *law* connecting ψ's and φ's: $ψ → φ$. Thus, if $c$'s possession of some mental characteristic, ψ, is linked *nomologically* to $e$'s possession of φ – to Clara's arm's moving being an arm moving (or a waving), for instance, as opposed merely to her arm's moving being an intentional arm moving – we are entitled to suppose that $c$'s possessing ψ is causally relevant to $e$'s possessing φ.[5] The law in question, it might be thought, need not be 'strict', that is, it need not be exceptionless and context-independent. Indeed, there is ample reason to suppose that 'strict' laws are to be found, if at all, only at the level of our most basic physics. Nevertheless, 'nonstrict' laws – 'hedged laws', 'ceteris paribus laws' – might suffice for the causal relevance of characteristics not associated with basic physics. Thus a sequence, $<c, e>$, might be accounted a causal sequence in virtue of instantiating a nonstrict law.[6]

Although a view of this sort has a certain allure, I am sceptical that it can be put to work in the present case. It is, I think, at least *unlikely* that there are genuine psychological or psychophysical laws, laws relating mental properties to other mental characteristics or to physical characteristics. True, we can say things of the following sort with confidence:

L If $x$ intends to $A$, then $x$ will $A$, ceteris paribus.

It is unclear, however, that L expresses a law. One difficulty surfaces when we attempt to fill in the ceteris paribus condition, when we set out to specify when 'other things' *are* equal, in such a way as to preserve the distinctively psychological character of the resulting conditional.[7]

---

5 Reverting to a fine-grained characterisation: To establish that an exemplifying of ψ is causally related to an exemplifying of φ, we must do more than establish that the object exemplifying ψ is a constituent of a causal transaction of which the object exemplifying φ is also a constituent.
6 If Davidson (1970/1980) is right, then $<c, e>$ is a causal sequence in virtue of instantiating a strict law. This is consistent, however, with $<c, e>$'s (1) instantiating a less-than-strict law, and (2) counting as a causal sequence in virtue of (1). Compare: My being mortal in virtue of being a sentient creature does not rule out my being mortal in virtue of being a human being. See McLaughlin (1989).
7 The argument sketched here is spelled out in Schiffer (1991, pp. 2–10).

Suppose we take $L$ to be a law, and ask what is involved in discharging the ceteris paribus condition.[8] Such conditions might be interpreted in either of two very different ways. First, they might be thought to have a completion in the vocabulary of the science to which $L$ belongs. We might suppose that, among other things, if $x$ intends to $A$, then $x$ will $A$ only if $x$ does not abandon this intention, and only if $x$'s desires and beliefs remain mostly unchanged. Second, ceteris paribus conditions might be discharged by means of truths couched in the vocabulary of some 'lower-level' science, neurophysiology or basic physics, perhaps. There is reason to favour the second of these two possibilities. In considering $L$, for instance, it seems clear that, having acquired the intention to $A$, $x$ will $A$, only if $x$'s nervous system is functioning normally. When we attempt to spell out what might count as a normally functioning nervous system, however, we must appeal, not to $x$'s intending, or to some other aspect of $x$'s intentional condition, but to some 'lower-level' specification of the physical basis of that intending. In elaborating $L$, then, we eventually revert to generalisations that range exclusively over 'lower-level' physical items. When this happens, the psychological expressions with which we began drop out of the picture, and we are left with something resembling a strict law couched in a purely physical vocabulary. Such a law is not a *psychological* law.

One ready response to this line of argument involves appealing to the track records of the special sciences: biology, chemistry, astronomy, geology, meteorology, and the like. These, it is claimed, are *in fact* successful at explaining events that fall within their respective domains by means of appropriate less-than-strict, ceteris paribus causal laws. Suppose it turned out that psychological explanation invokes generalisations that resemble such laws. This would mean that psychology is at least no worse off with respect to causal explanation than any of the special sciences. If we reject the possibility of causal explanation in psychology on the grounds that

8 One might balk at the notion that ceteris paribus conditions *can* be discharged. Certainly, on some conceptions of ceteris paribus laws, such conditions are in-eliminable. However, as Fodor (1987, pp. 4–6) points out, ineliminable ceteris paribus conditions threaten vacuity. The White Knight's song brings tears to the eyes of those who hear it, ceteris paribus – 'unless it doesn't'. According to Fodor, a ceteris paribus law is not one that lacks a completion, but one that lacks a completion in the vocabulary of the special science to which it belongs.

putative causal transactions involving mental events are inadequately grounded, then we shall be obliged to reject causal explanations offered in these other sciences. Since few philosophers are willing to do that – it is permissible to evince scepticism about psychology, but not about the special *sciences* – we are invited to conclude that appeals to ceteris paribus laws in psychology are sufficient to ground mental causal relations.

A response of this sort carries conviction, however, only if we agree in advance *both* that characteristics mentioned in explanations offered in the special sciences have an uncontroversial sort of causal relevance *and* that their having causal relevance hinges on their figuring in ceteris paribus laws. The first conjunct is closely related to the question at issue, and the second conjunct seems doubtful. I do not deny that psychology and the special sciences offer informative true generalisations, even that these are lawlike in character. It is not obvious, however, that such generalisations either constitute or imply genuine laws. This is a large issue, however, and I shall not pursue it here. Rather I shall approach the matter from an altogether different direction. Later, I shall return to the matter of psychological laws.

## 3. CAUSAL PREEMPTION

A wonderfully vivid statement of the hurdles to be faced by anyone offering an account of mental causation may be found in Norman Malcolm's 'The Conceivability of Mechanism' (1968).[9] Malcolm begins with a characterisation of a doctrine he labels 'mechanism':

By 'mechanism' I am going to understand a special application of physical determinism – namely, to all organisms with neurological systems, including human beings. The version of mechanism I wish to study assumes a neurophysiological theory which is adequate to explain and predict all movements of human bodies except those caused by outside forces. The human body is assumed to be as complete a causal system as is a gasoline engine. Neurological states and processes are conceived to be correlated by general laws with the mechanisms that produce movements. Chemical and electrical changes in the nervous tissue of the body are assumed to cause muscle contractions, which in turn cause movements such as blinking, breathing, and puckering of the lips, as well as movements of fingers, limbs, and head. Such movements are sometimes produced by forces

9 My way of setting up the problem of causal preemption owes much to Kim (1989a, 1989b).

(pushes and pulls) applied externally to the body. If someone forced my arm up over my head, the theory could not explain that movement of my arm. But it could explain any movement not due to an external push or pull. It could explain, and predict, the movements that occur when a person signals a taxi, plays chess, writes an essay, or walks to the store. (1968, p. 45)

In endorsing the supervenience hypothesis, I have come close to endorsing mechanism. I have supposed that agents' mental characteristics are entirely dependent on their physical characteristics. If we couple this assumption with the notion that the physical world is 'causally closed', we obtain a version of mechanism approaching what Malcolm seems to envisage.[10]

There is, I believe, something deeply compelling about the notion that the physical domain is autonomous.[11] It is difficult not to imagine that causal relations at the 'most basic level' depend on fundamental physical characteristics of the world, and on these alone. Supervenient – 'higher-level' – characteristics are then determined by basic characteristics. To give up autonomy is to suppose that some basic physical occurrences call for 'higher-level' explanations. This prospect, though conceivable, does not sit well with our layered picture of the world, a picture that, if I am right, we must respect.

We explain the operation of a clock by reference to clockwork principles, principles governing the behaviour of gears, springs, and levers. In so doing, we 'factor out' effects on the clock of 'outside influences'. If we placed the clock in a strong magnetic field, for instance, or if we smashed it with a hammer, we should need to look beyond clockwork principles to explain its behaviour. This is one reason there are no strict exceptionless clockwork laws, laws governing the behaviour of clocks qua clocks. When we consider the fundamental physical entities and processes, however, there is nothing left over to count as an outside influence.

'Emergentists', in the nineteenth and early twentieth centuries, held that certain features of complex physical systems – conscious-

10 How close that version is to Malcolm's depends partly on what Malcolm has in mind in describing mechanism as 'a special application of physical determinism'. Whether, and to what extent, the physical domain is deterministic is, I take it, an empirical question.
11 The autonomy enjoyed by the physical realm is absolute and to be distinguished from the notion that psychological explanation is autonomous. See, Chapter 2, § 7.

ness, for instance – exerted a kind of *downward* causal influence on systems in which they emerged.[12] According to emergentists, fundamental physical occurrences are sometimes affected by emergent (or supervenient – the terms were used interchangeably) characteristics of the systems to which they belong. On such a view, the behaviour of basic entities might turn out not to be explicable solely by reference to elementary laws governing those entities. Explanations of their behaviour might then require reference to emergent laws as well.

There is reason to think that emergentism, while not conceptually incoherent, is empirically false (see McLaughlin 1992). Emergentism is, in addition, at odds with the 'layered' metaphysical picture endorsed in Chapter 3. That picture accommodates the emergence of 'new' properties given new combinations of 'old' properties. This is just the supervenience hypothesis broadly construed. What emergentism challenges is the notion that the basic physical system is self-contained, or as I have put it, autonomous. Admittedly, the notion of causal autonomy would be difficult to spell out. The leading idea is straightforward, however. What happens at the 'basic level' determines what happens at 'higher levels'. The relation between the basic stuff and what depends on the basic stuff is asymmetrical. Causal relations are initiated and guided by fundamental entities and processes; 'higher-level' characteristics supervene on characteristics of these fundamental items. Although observable objects and events exhibit supervenient characteristics, characteristics not possessed by the fundamental entities considered individually, these 'higher level' characteristics 'make no difference' at all to the basic entities. Vertical determination goes in one direction only: upward.

Applying this picture to the behaviour of intelligent creatures, we obtain mechanism. What we do depends, at bottom, on the character and disposition of our physical constituents. A complete neurophysiological theory, while not providing us with the sort of account of intelligent behaviour we might expect from basic physics, would at least move us in the direction of such an account. Further, as Malcolm puts it,

---

12 Consciousness was by no means special in this regard. Emergentists regarded consciousness as but one among many *physical* characteristics capable of 'downward' causal influence.

The neurophysiological theory we are envisaging would . . . be rich enough to provide systematic causal explanations of all bodily movements not due to external causes. These explanations would be understood as stating *sufficient* conditions of movement and not merely necessary conditions. They would employ laws that connect neurophysiological states or processes with movements. (1968, pp. 45–46)

In short, the envisaged theory would explain behaviour, not by reference to intentional characteristics of agents, but by reference to the neurophysiological supervenience base of those characteristics.

It should be emphasized that this theory makes no provision for desires, aims, goals, purposes, motives, or intentions. In explaining such an occurrence as a man's walking across a room, it will be a matter of indifference to the theory whether the man's purpose, intention, or desire was to open a window, or even whether his walking across the room was intentional. This aspect of the theory can be indicated by saying that it is a 'nonpurposive' system of explanation. (1968, p. 46)

We are now led to ask how neurophysiological explanations of behaviour are related to 'purposive' explanations, those framed in terms of beliefs, desires, intentions – the intentional attitudes.

Some students of behavior have believed that purposive explanations of behavior will be found to be less basic than the explanations that will arise from a future neurological theory. They think that the principles of purposive explanation will turn out to be dependent on the neurophysiological laws. On this view, our ordinary explanations of behavior will often be true: but the neural explanations will also be true – and they will be *more fundamental*. Thus we could, theoretically, *by-pass* explanations of behavior in terms of purpose, and the day might come when they simply fall into disuse. (1968, p. 50)

Students of behaviour who embrace a view of this kind are convinced that mechanistic explanations do not *compete* with ordinary purposive explanations of behaviour. Rather, purposive explanations are *underwritten* by their 'more fundamental' mechanistic counterparts. If I explain Clara's waving by citing her reasons, the truth of my explanation rests on there being a corresponding 'lower-level' neurophysiological explanation of this same behaviour.

Other philosophers have supposed that purposive and mechanistic explanations are not in competition because they 'explain different things'. 'Purposive explanations explain actions. Neurophysiological explanations explain movements. Both explain behavior:

113

but we can say this only because we use the latter word ambiguously to cover both actions and movements' (1968, pp. 51–52).

According to Malcolm, however, such sanguine views of the status of purposive explanations are unacceptable. Consider a man climbing a ladder to retrieve his hat, which has blown onto a roof. We say that he is climbing the ladder *because* he wants to retrieve his hat and believes that he can do so by climbing the ladder. 'A neurophysiological explanation of his climbing would say nothing about his intention but would connect his movements on the ladder with chemical changes in body tissue or with the firing of neurons' (1968, p. 52). How are these accounts related? Do they complement one another, or are they in conflict?

I believe there *would* be a collision between the two accounts if they were offered as explanations of one and the same occurrence of a man's climbing a ladder. We will recall that the envisaged neurophysiological theory was supposed to provide *sufficient* causal explanations of behavior. Thus the movements of the man on the ladder would be *completely* accounted for in terms of electrical, chemical, and mechanical processes in his body. This would surely imply that his desire or intention to retrieve his hat had nothing to do with his movement up the ladder. It would imply that on this same occasion he would have moved up the ladder in exactly this way even if he had no intention to retrieve his hat, or even no intention to climb the ladder. Given the antecedent neurological states of his bodily system together with general laws correlating these states with the contractions of muscles and the movements of limbs, he would have moved as he did regardless of his desire or intention. If every movement of his was completely accounted for by his antecedent neurological states (his 'programming'), then it was not true that those movements occurred *because* he wanted or intended to get his hat. (1968, pp. 52–53)

Mechanistic explanation, then, might be thought to *preempt* explanations framed in terms of desires, intentions, beliefs. If the man climbs a ladder because certain things happen in his nervous system, then it is false that he climbs the ladder for a reason, false that he climbs it because he wants his hat and believes that climbing the ladder will enable him to satisfy this want – even if he in some sense possesses this belief and this want.

If a comprehensive neurophysiological theory is true, then people's intentions never are causal factors in behavior. . . . [I]n no cases would desires, intentions, purposes be necessary conditions of any human movements. It would never be true that a man would *not* have moved as he did if he had *not* had such and such an intention. Nor would it ever be true that a certain movement of his was due to, or brought about by, or caused by his having

114

a certain intention or purpose. Purposive explanations of human bodily movements would *never* be true. (1968, p. 63)

It should be noted that this argument takes for granted that both purposive explanations of behaviour and their mechanistic counterparts are causal. In explaining a man's climbing a ladder by citing his reasons, we allude to putative causes of his climbing. If we suspect, however, that there is a complete neurophysiological explanation of the very same behaviour and at the same time allow that an explanation of this sort is in some sense more fundamental than one couched in terms of purposes, we seem driven to Malcolm's conclusion. The point is echoed by Kim. 'The problem . . . seems to arise from the fact that a cause, or causal explanation, of an event, when it is regarded as a full, sufficient cause or explanation, appears to *exclude* other . . . purported causes or causal explanations of it' (1989b, p. 44; see also Kim 1989a). One might try to circumvent this conclusion by denying that purposive, reason-giving explanations explain behaviour by adverting to causes of that behaviour. Perhaps in ascribing reasons to Clara we merely 'illuminate' her behaviour or render it 'intelligible' in the way we render speech intelligible, not by specifying its causes, but by interpreting it. Were that so, mechanistic and purposive explanations need not be considered rivals, and there need be no question that the former might preempt the latter.

The notion that explanations of intelligent behaviour framed in terms of reasons are noncausal has been considered already (Chapter 2, § 8), and rejected. The *because* in 'He climbed the ladder because he wanted to retrieve his hat and believed he could retrieve it by climbing' looks for all the world like the *because* in 'His arms moved because his muscles contracted'. In ascribing reasons to Clara, we may illuminate or make sense of her behaviour, but only insofar as we take Clara's reasons to be causally implicated in her behaviour. We distinguish, for instance, reasons Clara *has* for a given action from the reason, or reasons, *for which* she acts. Clara may *have* a reason to wave, and wave for a reason, without waving for *that* reason. A reason for which Clara acts is one that leads her so to act. It would seem, then, that if reasons explain behaviour, they do so at least partly in virtue of figuring causally in the production of behaviour. The problem is to reconcile the causal role of reasons with the supervenience hypothesis and with the notion that the physical system is autonomous, causally closed.

115

In accepting the supervenience hypothesis, we are supposing that the mental supervenes on the physical. This leaves open the possibility that, while the physical realm is autonomous, mental items could acquire causal significance somehow via their supervenience bases. In evaluating this possibility, it is simplest, I think, to begin with a concrete case. Suppose Wayne acquires the intention to climb a ladder and, apparently on this basis, climbs a nearby ladder. Let us suppose, as well, that intentions of the sort in question supervene on neurological conditions of certain sorts. Call Wayne's acquiring the intention to climb a ladder, $\psi_1$, and call Wayne's coming to be in the neurological condition that 'realises' this intention, $\varphi_1$. (I shall discuss the realising relation presently. For the moment, let us suppose that Wayne's neurological condition realises certain mental characteristics in virtue of these mental characteristics' supervening on neurological conditions of the pertinent sort.) Finally, let us designate Wayne's climbing the ladder – that is, Wayne's limbs moving in a certain way – $\varphi_2$. Wayne's acquiring the intention to climb a ladder, then, might be thought to 'work through' its neurological realisation, and in this way produce the appropriate behaviour. The arrangement is represented in Figure 4.1.[13] The horizontal arrow, $\rightarrow$, signals a causal relation, and the vertical arrow, $\Uparrow$, indicates the holding of an appropriate supervenience relation. Figure 4.1, then, depicts a case in which $\varphi_1$ causes $\varphi_2$, and $\psi_1$ acquires causal standing indirectly, by way of $\varphi_1$.

Why should we credit $\psi_1$ with a causal role in the production of the bodily movement, $\varphi_2$, however? If being an intention to climb a ladder were just a particular sort of neurological condition, we could replace the vertical arrow with an identity sign, and the problem might vanish. Supervenience, however, implies, not property or type identity, but dependence. A characteristic cannot supervene on itself – at least it cannot given the account of supervenience offered in Chapter 3. If liquidity supervenes on molecular structure, a substance has the property or characteristic of being liquid in virtue of its possession of a certain (distinct) molecular property or characteristic. If $\psi_1$ and $\varphi_1$ are in some sense distinct, however, how does $\psi_1$ figure in the causal picture? More particularly, how does $\psi_1$ figure in the causing of $\varphi_2$?

13 I owe the inspiration for this figure, the figures that follow, and the line of
   reasoning they support to Jaegwon Kim.

Figure 4.1

In Figure 4.1, $\psi_1$ *dangles* in a way that suggests causal impotence.[14] This impression is reinforced by the apparent fact that an event neurologically resembling $\varphi_1$ might have occurred and caused an event resembling $\varphi_2$, even in the absence of $\psi_1$. As Malcolm puts it in discussing the ladder climber, 'given the antecedent neurological states of his bodily system together with general laws correlating these states with the contractions of muscles and the movements of limbs, he would have moved as he did regardless of his desire or intention' (1968, p. 53). To appreciate the point, we need only imagine a molecular twin of the climber who, owing to differences in his circumstances, lacks a counterpart of $\psi_1$. Given that the physical realm is causally closed, assuming sameness of physical laws and background conditions, and putting to one side instances of causal overdetermination, the twins' bodily motions will be indistinguishable. Malcolm's point, then, might be expressed as follows: (1) $\varphi_1$ is causally sufficient for the occurrence of $\varphi_2$; (2) $\psi_1$ is not necessary for the occurrence of $\varphi_2$; and this suggests that (3) $\psi_1$ is causally irrelevant to the occurrence of $\varphi_2$.

Perhaps – reverting to a suggestion of Malcolm's – we have erred in taking states of mind and the neurological conditions on which these might supervene to have common effects. Perhaps reasons cause and thereby explain *behaviour* or *action*, whereas neurological states and processes cause merely *bodily motions*. Behaviour (or action) might be bodily motion produced by a certain sort of cause, for instance. Behaviour would then supervene on bodily motions only when these possessed the right kinds of causal history. Were that so, we might allow that an ideal neurophysiological theory could completely account for the occurrence of bodily motions, without imagining that this preempts causal explanations of behaviour that advert to reasons. Letting $\psi_2$ represent a piece of be-

14 The claim is not one a reader should attempt to deconstruct.

haviour – Wayne's climbing intentionally, perhaps – we might be attracted to the arrangement represented in Figure 4.2.

What are we to make of the causal arrow connecting $\psi_1$ and $\psi_2$ in Figure 4.2? That arrow indicates that $\psi_1$ causally suffices for $\psi_2$. Given the (noncausal) dependence of $\psi_2$ on $\varphi_2$, it looks as though an occurrence of $\psi_1$ could induce $\psi_2$, only *obliquely*, only by inducing an occurrence of whatever it is that realises $\psi_2$, namely, $\varphi_2$. This would yield an arrangement of the sort depicted in Figure 4.3. Now, however, $\varphi_2$ is apparently causally overdetermined: $\varphi_1$ is *already* causally sufficient for $\varphi_2$. What, then is the causal contribution of $\psi_1$? Recall that $\psi_1$ is metaphysically dependent on $\varphi_1$, so the occurrence of $\varphi_1$ suffices for *both* $\psi_1$ and $\varphi_2$. Under the circumstances, it might seem preferable to revert to an arrangement of the sort depicted in Figure 4.4 and regard $\psi_1$ and $\psi_2$ as riding 'piggyback' on $\varphi_1$ and $\varphi_2$, respectively (see LePore and Loewer 1989). The worry is that in so doing, we render $\psi_1$ and $\psi_2$ *epiphenomenal*, we concede, in effect, that $\psi_1$ and $\psi_2$, at bottom, contribute nothing to causal transactions in which they (or their realising bases) figure, and we are again confronted with Malcolm's problem.

Two possible responses suggest themselves. First, it might be thought that, despite appearances, $\varphi_1$ does not causally suffice for $\varphi_2$. Perhaps $\varphi_2$ requires *both* $\varphi_1$ and $\psi_1$. The occurrence of $\varphi_1$, then, though causally *necessary*, is not after all causally *sufficient* for $\varphi_2$; it is only in conjunction with $\psi_1$ that $\varphi_1$ brings about $\varphi_2$ – and thereby brings about $\psi_2$. Were that so, there would be an obvious respect in which $\psi_1$ would be causally relevant to the production of *both* $\varphi_2$ and $\psi_2$, and we are back with the arrangement illustrated by Figure 4.3. Alternatively, one might reason as follows. Since $\varphi_1$ suffices for $\psi_1$, events of the latter sort are bound to accompany occurrences of the former sort. Any reason we might have for thinking that $\varphi_1$ is causally responsible for $\varphi_2$, then, would equally be evidence that $\varphi_1$-plus-$\psi_1$ caused $\varphi_2$.[15]

A second possibility is that $\varphi_1$ and $\psi_1$ are independently causally sufficient for $\varphi_2$: $\varphi_2$, like Caesar's death, is causally overdetermined. True, $\varphi_1$ realises $\psi_1$. This leaves open the possibility that a counterpart of $\psi_1$ might have a very different sort of realisation. Perhaps,

15 Notice that this possibility fails to square with an externalist theory according to which, given differences in circumstances, an event of the sort of which $\varphi_1$ is an instance might occur in the absence of anything resembling $\psi_1$. Indeed, this is precisely what Twin Earth cases are supposed to show.

Figure 4.2

Figure 4.3

Figure 4.4

then, the occurrence of such a counterpart would give rise to an occurrence of something very like $\varphi_2$, independently of an occurrence of anything resembling $\varphi_1$. Less abstractly, Wayne's acquiring the intention to climb, though realised by a different sort of neural occurrence, might have resulted in his body's moving just as it does now.

Both suggestions compete with the notion that the physical domain is, in the end, causally closed: Every physical occurrence is entirely explicable by reference to comparable physical occurrences. It is this ban on 'downward' causal influences that, in concert with the causal requirement – mental states and events explain behaviour only to the extent that they have a causal part in its production – that gives rise to Malcolm's problem. On the one hand, we offer psychological explanations of intelligent behaviour by reference to apparent intentional mental causes. On the other hand, we recognise that behaviour can be explained by reference to nonintentional physical states and processes in a way that apparently preempts psychological, reason–giving explanations. We recognise, as well, that the physical realm is both causally closed and in

119

some sense causally 'more fundamental' than the psychological domain. The *real* work is done at the 'physical level', ultimately at the level of the basic entities and processes. We are in this way pushed back in the direction of the arrangement depicted in Figure 4.4.

## 4. EPIPHENOMENALISM

We have seen that an arrangement of the sort represented in Figure 4.4 obliges us to face the possibility that mental characteristics – indeed, supervenient characteristics generally – are causally inert, *epiphenomenal*. There, $\psi$-characteristics appear to *dangle* (see Smart 1959). They accompany occurrences of $\varphi$-characteristics on which they depend, but they themselves seem to possess no causal authority.

Traditionally, *epiphenomenalists* have focused on putative relations holding between mental and physical *events*. Thus, according to C. D. Broad, 'epiphenomenalism is just one-sided action of body on mind': '(1) Certain bodily events cause certain mental events. (2) No mental event plays any part in the causation of any bodily event. (3) No mental event plays any part in the causation of any other mental event. Consequently (4) all mental events are caused by bodily events and by them only' (Broad 1925/1960, p. 118).

Epiphenomenalism, thus characterised, entails *event dualism*: If epiphenomenalism is true then, (a) there are mental events, and (b) mental events are caused by, though distinct from, physical events. The relation between mental and physical events would be something like that represented in Figure 4.4, with one crucial difference: The vertical arrows indicating a supervenience or realising relation would be replaced by arrows indicating a causal relation (Figure 4.5).

The difference is significant. Many philosophers would reject (b), reject the notion that mental events are caused by, but distinct from, physical events. Davidson, for instance, regards mental and physical events as events satisfying, respectively, mental and physical descriptions. Since, according to Davidson, every event satisfies *some* physical description, every event, including every mental event, is a physical event. Suppose we refer to some mental event by means of an intentional attitude ascription: Clara's acquiring the intention to wave. On a view of this sort, if our ascription is correct, we have picked out a particular physical event, that is, an event

120

$$\begin{array}{ccc} \psi_1 & & \psi_2 \\ \uparrow & & \uparrow \\ \phi_1 & \rightarrow & \phi_2 \end{array}$$

Figure 4.5

satisfying some physical description or other – an occurrence in Clara's brain, perhaps. This event possesses both mental and physical characteristics in virtue of which it answers to both mental and physical descriptions. Thus epiphenomenalism of the kind spelled out in the quoted passage is blocked.[16]

Does this mean that the threat of epiphenomenalism is overrated? If we take epiphenomenalism in its traditional guise, then perhaps it is. Still, one may suspect that a response of this sort does not touch the fundamental issue. Our original worries over the causal significance of the mental stemmed, not from doubts about one-way causal relations between physical events and nonphysical, mental events, but from the appearance of causal irrelevance in the case of mental properties or characteristics. Expressed in terms of a coarse-grained view of events (and subject to qualifications discussed in § 2, above): An event's possession of a given mental characteristic seems to make no contribution to the causal capacities of that event. The core epiphenomenalist idea apparently survives: The exemplifying of a mental characteristic 'makes no causal difference' to subsequent physical or mental states or events. Broad, as it happens, was well aware of this possibility:

Epiphenomenalism may be taken to assert . . . that certain events which have physiological characteristics have *also* mental characteristics, and that no events which lack physiological characteristics have mental characteristics. That many events which have physiological characteristics are not known to have mental characteristics. And that *an event which has mental characteristics never causes another event in virtue of its mental characteristics, but only in virtue of its physiological characteristics.* (Broad 1925/1960, p. 472)[17]

---

16 On a fine-grained account of events, physical events and mental events must be distinct so long as we take physical and mental properties or characteristics to be distinct. A fine-grained theorist, then, could accept (a), (b), and Broad's (1). Such a theorist need not accept (2) or (3), however.

17 Emphasis added in the final sentence. Cf. Huxley (1917, chap. 5). According to Huxley, 'our mental conditions are simply the symbols in consciousness of the

An epiphenomenalism of this sort, what Brian McLaughlin (1989) has labelled *type* epiphenomenalism, *begins* with the notion, endorsed by Davidson, that every mental event is a physical event. A type epiphenomenalist denies that any event causes another 'in virtue of' its mental characteristics (or in virtue of satisfying a mental description).[18]

One sort of response to type epiphenomenalism appeals, first, to the idea (discussed briefly in § 2) that sequences are *causal* sequences in virtue of instantiating causal laws, and, second, to the presence in the special sciences and psychology of causal laws relating mental and physical types. Thus, imagine that an event, *c*, causes an event, *e*, only if this sequence instantiates a causal law. Since laws range over *types* of event, we could carve out a place for mental causation by allowing for laws relating mental and physical types or characteristics. The laws in question would undoubtedly fail to be strict laws, though this in itself need not prevent them from grounding causal transactions.[19]

I have expressed reservations about such strategies already. On the one hand, the envisaged grounding laws may well be unavailable. On the other hand, if we allow for the possibility of such laws, and allow as well that they signal the presence of genuine causal relations, we seem driven back to the arrangement depicted in Figure 4.3. That arrangement, however, has little to recommend it – or so I claim.

Once more we seem to be compelled to choose between a commitment to the autonomy of the physical domain and the conviction that mental characteristics must 'make a difference' causally. Regarded in this light, however, the problem seems not to be confined to the mental realm. Precisely analogous difficulties can be raised for supervenient characteristics generally. What difference, if

---

changes which take place automatically in the *organism*; . . . to take an extreme illustration, the feeling we call volition is not the cause of the voluntary act, but the symbol of that state of the brain which is the immediate cause of that act' (p. 244). I am not sure what Huxley means here by 'symbol'.

18 McLaughlin defines type epiphenomenalism as follows: '(a) Events can be causes in virtue of falling under physical types, but (b) events cannot be causes in virtue of falling under mental types' (1989, p. 109).

19 If we suppose that events are related causally only if they instantiate a *strict* law, then a less-than-strict , i.e., ceteris paribus, law can ground a causal claim only if ceteris paribus laws themselves are grounded by strict laws. On one construal of 'ceteris paribus law', this is precisely what we should expect. See above, § 2.

any, might we reasonably expect such characteristics to make to the causal structure of the world?

As a preliminary to answering this question, let us turn again to the property of being liquid. Pretend that this property supervenes on a certain sort of dynamic molecular structure, $S$, and that some substances are liquid in virtue of their possessing $S$. In light of this presumption, consider the operation of the hydraulic braking system in my Yugo. That system consists of an arrangement of tubes filled with braking fluid, a cylinder that compresses this fluid when the brake pedal is depressed, and another cylinder that responds by forcing a brake shoe against the rim of a wheel. For the braking system to function, the fluid must be kept in a liquid state. If the fluid turned granular, for instance, or if we lowered the temperature so that it became solid, the system would bog down. Imagine now that we wonder whether the braking system's operation depends on the fluid's possessing structure $S$ or whether it depends *rather*, or *in addition*, on the fluid's being liquid. *Whatever* one is inclined to say here, it is *not*, I think, that the braking fluid's being liquid contributes a causal capacity 'over and above' whatever might be contributed by $S$.

We can, to be sure, bring it about that the braking system ceases to function by bringing it about that the substance it contains is no longer liquid. We do so, however, only obliquely, only by bringing it about that this substance ceases to possess structure $S$. This is not to suggest, incidentally, that we could not appeal to the fluid's being liquid in an ordinary causal explanation of the operation of the braking system. Yet this might be so even though the 'real' causal work is accomplished by those basic physical characteristics in virtue of which the braking fluid possesses the characteristic of being liquid. Does this mean that it is not the substance's being liquid, but its possessing structure $S$ that matters causally? The question is, in a certain way, misleading. Suppose, for instance, the braking fluid's being liquid were, in a particular instance, constituted by its possessing structure $S$. Although the property of being liquid and the property of possessing structure $S$ are distinct *properties*, the braking fluid's liquidity need not be something it possesses *in addition* to its possessing structure $S$. I shall say more about this possibility presently. First, it might be useful to look at a different sort of case.

Suppose that greenness supervenes on a family, $G$, of micro-

123

structural characteristics, $G_1$, $G_2$, $G_3$, . . . $G_n$, a family of characteristics possessed by the surfaces of green objects. Imagine, now, that you set out to build a 'green-detector', a Geiger-counter-like device that, pointed at suitably illuminated coloured surfaces, distinguishes those that are green from the rest: When a green surface is encountered, it clicks; it is silent otherwise. What might the causal story be in this case? Does the device function as it does in response to *greenness* or is it rather affected by the presence of one of the characteristics, $G_1$, $G_2$, $G_3$, . . . $G_n$?

If we suppose that greenness plays a part in the device's operation, it must do so obliquely, via an instance of $G$. This returns us to the trilemma we encountered earlier, however: (1) the operation of the detector is causally overdetermined, occurrences of greenness and G-ness independently causally suffice for its operation; (2) both the occurrence of greenness and an instance of $G$ are causally necessary, though neither, in the absence of the other, is sufficient, for the device to function; (3) greenness adds nothing to the causal capacities afforded by instances of $G$. There is, I have suggested, *some* reason to favour (3), to suppose that supervenient characteristics, though in an important sense distinct from their subvenient bases, contribute nothing to the causal capacities of those bases.[20] The present example might be thought to buttress this supposition. If our aim is to construct a device to detect instances of greenness, we must build it in such a way that it responds to occurrences of $G_1$, $G_2$, $G_3$, . . . $G_n$.[21] The operation of the device in registering instances of green depends on its basic physical makeup, a makeup that disposes it to click in response to occurrences of $G_1$, $G_2$, $G_3$, . . . $G_n$.

In considering examples of this sort, we may be pushed back in the direction of the view that the causal structure of the world is to be understood as at bottom depending on goings-on at some fundamental 'physical level'. From this perspective, it is not in virtue of their being mental, but in virtue of their being supervenient, or ontologically dependent, that mental characteristics might come to seem epiphenomenal, lacking in independent causal authority.

---

20 This claim will be qualified below; see § 7.
21 More accurately: We must build it so as to respond to $G_1$, $G_2$, $G_3$, . . . $G_n$ or to some equally basic physical characteristic that reliably covaries with $G_1$, $G_2$, $G_3$, . . . $G_n$. Because they do not affect the point at issue, I have ignored such complications here.

Does this mean that supervenient characteristics widely regarded as providing the subject matter of the special sciences must be stripped of the causal standing they have been presumed to possess? Perhaps not. A sensible account of the causal relevance of 'higher-level' characteristics might turn out to require neither a commitment to a species of causal relation grounded solely by ceteris paribus laws, nor a belief in 'downward' causal influences. Although I shall focus here only on intentional mental causation, the considerations I offer apply, mutatis mutandis, to the causal standing of supervenient characteristics generally. As a preliminary, I shall examine the account of mental causation advanced by John Searle. Searle's position is, I believe, closer to the truth than many philosophers seem to think. It leaves us short of our goal, however, in ways that will prove instructive.

## 5. SEARLE'S THEORY

In an epilogue to *Intentionality* (1983), John Searle advances a theory of the relation of states of mind to agents' physical conditions he baptises 'biological naturalism'. The theory promises to undercut the sorts of epiphenomenalist difficulty surveyed in § 4. A central tenet of biological naturalism is that 'mental states are both *caused by* the operations of the brain and *realized in* the structure of the brain' (p. 265). This, according to Searle, makes it possible to account for the 'real existence' of 'mental phenomena', and for the causal capacities of 'specifically mental aspects' of those phenomena.

> One of the assumptions shared by many traditional dualists and physicalists is that by granting the reality and causal efficacy of the mental we have to deny any identity relation between mental phenomena and the brain; and, conversely, if we assert an identity relation we have to deny any causal relations between mental and physical phenomena. . . . As a first step to removing the dilemma we have to show how mental phenomena can satisfy both conditions. (1983, p. 265)

Searle contends that the failure of materialist theories stems from an unnecessarily deflationary depiction of the mental: Mental phenomena are neither reducible to physical phenomena, nor eliminable. Dualists, in contrast, take mental phenomena seriously, but leave the causal efficacy of mental items unexplained and mysterious. According to Searle, dualists are right in regarding mental phenomena as irreducible and ineliminable, wrong in supposing

125

that mental phenomena are nonphysical; materialists are right in insisting that only physical phenomena possess causal clout, wrong in thinking mental phenomena are epiphenomenal or unreal: 'Mental states are as real as any other biological phenomena, as real as lactation, photosynthesis, mitosis, or digestion' (p. 264).

Searle frames his discussion as a response to an imagined challenge:

If the specifically mental aspects of mental states function causally as you claim, then the causal relation is totally mysterious and occult; if, on the other hand, you employ the notion of causation according to which the aspects of events which are causally relevant are those described by causal laws, and according to which all causal laws are physical laws, then there can't be any causal efficacy to the mental aspects of mental states. At most there would be a class of physical events which satisfy some mental descriptions, but those descriptions are not the descriptions under which the events instantiate causal laws, and therefore they do not pick out causal aspects of the events. Either you have dualism and an unintelligible account of causation or you have an intelligible account of causation and abandon the idea of the causal efficacy of the mental in favour of some version of the identity thesis with an attendant epiphenomenalism of the mental aspects of psychophysical events. (1983, pp. 264–65)

Searle proposes to 'demythologize the whole mind–body problem' (p. 265) by demonstrating that, despite appearances, a robust form of mental causation is utterly consistent with a sensible naturalistic, indeed *biological*, conception of the mind.

How, then, are states of mind related to the brain? Searle begins by examining a 'trivial and familiar' example that, he suggests, parallels the mind–brain case: the relation between 'the liquid properties of water' and 'the behaviour of individual molecules'. The liquid properties of water are, he supposes, both caused by the behaviour of individual molecules and realised in the collection of molecules so behaving.

The relation between the molecular behaviour and the surface physical features of the water is clearly causal. If, for example, we alter the molecular behaviour we cause the surface features to change: We get either ice or steam depending on whether the molecular movement is sufficiently slower or faster. Furthermore, the surface features of the water themselves function causally. In its liquid state water is wet, it pours, you can drink it, wash in it, etc. (1983, pp. 265–66)

The causal relation said to hold in this case between molecular behaviour and 'surface features' is difficult to assess. On the one hand, that relation might be taken to consist in a *vertical* dependence

126

relation holding between 'lower-level' molecular behaviour and 'higher-level' 'liquid properties'. The properties of the whole, as we might say, are caused by – just in the sense that they depend on or result from – the properties of its parts. More accurately, perhaps, the possession of certain characteristics by the whole is a contingent but nonaccidental consequence of the possession of certain characteristics by its parts.[22] On the other hand, Searle's example suggests that he means only to be singling out a *horizontal* causal relation: 'If . . . we alter the molecular behaviour we cause the surface features to change.' A certain event – my applying heat to a block of ice, for instance – brings about a molecular condition that turns out to realise the liquid properties of water. My applying heat, then, *obliquely* 'causes the surface features to change' by bringing about changes in the behaviour of individual molecules.

There is a third possibility, however, one that Searle may favour. The appearance of 'higher-level' liquid properties of water is obliquely caused by 'lower-level' molecular events, but only via an additional, sui generis vertical causal relation. Thus, Searle has in mind something more than the arrangement illustrated in Figure 4.6.[23] For Searle, the vertical arrow signifies *both* realising and causing (Figure 4.7).

If this *is* what Searle intends, it is hard to see how it is supported by his subsequent remarks. Thus, although it may be perfectly true that my altering molecular behaviour results in a change in 'surface features', this supports at most the notion that in heating a block of ice, I cause – that is, *efficiently* cause – a change in the behaviour of its constituent molecules, and, obliquely, a change in its 'surface features'. If Searle's vertical causal dependence relation is supposed to be anything more than this, it is not easy to imagine what this could be. Indeed, in the present case, although we may be disposed in advance to accept the existence of a vertical dependence relation between 'lower-level' molecular behaviour and 'surface features', the cause mentioned appears to be a cause of *both*: In causing the molecules to vibrate more rapidly, it causes (obliquely) the block of

---

22  For simplicity, I shall follow Searle and speak here of properties or characteristics causing and being caused, though, strictly, it is *instances* of properties or characteristics that have aetiological significance.

23  Figures 4.6 and 4.7 were inspired by Searle (1983, p. 269; reproduced as Figure 4.8 below).

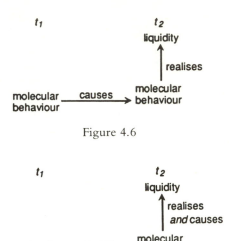

Figure 4.6

Figure 4.7

ice to become liquid. This, however, might simply be regarded as an instance of ordinary efficient – 'horizontal' – causation.

In discussing explosions in the cylinder of an internal combustion engine, Searle says that 'the explosion is caused by the firing of the spark plug even though both the firing and the explosion are caused by and realized in phenomena at a microlevel' (p. 269). The upshot is an arrangement resembling that depicted earlier in Figure 4.4 (Figure 4.8). Let us suppose, in what follows, then, that, in speaking of causes, Searle has in mind two distinct sorts of dependence relation: ordinary efficient causation and a kind of vertical, atemporal property dependence. The intended sense might be revealed by context.[24]

In addition to being caused (in whatever sense) by 'lower-level'

24 Although I find that, in most contexts in which one might take Searle to mean by 'cause' a vertical relation, as in the passage quoted above, it is possible to interpret him as referring to an unproblematic relation of efficient causation. Perhaps the best evidence that Searle has in mind something more than efficient causation is his remark that 'two phenomena can be related by both causation and realization provided that they are so at different levels of description' (p. 266), together with the diagrams on p. 269 (reproduced as Figure 4.8 here) and p. 270, where causal arrows run vertically as well as horizontally.

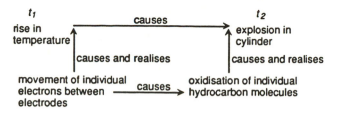

Figure 4.8

events, characteristics of a whole are *realised in* its parts taken collectively: 'The liquidity of a bucket of water is not some extra juice secreted by the $H_2O$ molecules. When we describe the stuff as liquid, we are just describing those very molecules at a higher level of description than that of the individual molecule' (1983, p. 266). The liquid characteristics of water, then, are caused by molecular behaviour and realised in collections of $H_2O$ molecules. Similarly, states of mind, mental occurrences, are caused by neurological events and realised in certain neurological conditions.

When we describe a substance as liquid and when we describe it as a collection of $H_2O$ molecules, we are, on this view, describing physical characteristics of a complex substance at two distinct 'levels': at the level of individual molecules, their properties, and their interactions, and at the level of the collection or system of molecules. This collection, like most collections, possesses properties not possessed by its constituents considered individually. Similarly, when we describe the brain at a 'low level', the items we mention – individual neurons, synapses, and neurological processes – exhibit no mentality. It does not follow that *brains*, or significant portions of brains, lack mental characteristics. Indeed, like liquidity, states of mind turn out to be caused by and realised in 'lower-level' physical – in this case, biological – features of brains. Mental characteristics are identified with these features described at a 'higher level'.

By way of reinforcing this point, Searle quotes an argument advanced by Leibniz against the possibility of mentality resulting from combinations of nonmental constituents. Leibniz says:

Supposing that there were a machine so constructed as to think, feel, and have perception, we could conceive of it as enlarged and yet preserving the same proportions, so that we might enter it as into a mill. And this

129

granted, we should only find on visiting it, pieces which push [one] against another, but never anything by which to explain perception. This must be sought for, therefore, in the simple substance and not in the composite or in the machine.[25]

Searle responds that an exactly parallel argument to Leibniz's would be that the behaviour of $H_2O$ molecules can never explain the liquidity of water, because if we entered into the system of molecules 'as into a mill we should only find on visiting it pieces which push one against another, but never anything by which to explain liquidity' (1983, p. 268). Leibniz's mistake, Searle thinks, is transparent. In seeking 'higher-level' characteristics by scrutinising 'lower-level' constituents, 'we would be looking at the system at the wrong level' (p. 268). Just as liquidity is not a feature of individual molecules, so states of mind are not states of individual neurons.

Let us suppose, with Searle, that my now thinking of Vienna is a 'higher-level' occurrence in my brain. What reason do we have to suppose that such 'higher-level' items could 'make a difference' causally? In Searle's terminology, what reason do we have to suppose that 'specifically mental aspects of mental phenomena' exhibit 'causal efficacy'? Consider again the 'higher-level' property of liquidity. Does a substance's *being liquid* add a causal capacity to the causal capacities possessed by individual $H_2O$ molecules? Searle contends that the answer is obviously, yes. Individual $H_2O$ molecules are not wet, and they cannot pour, for instance. These characteristics are possessed only by certain well-behaved *collections* of $H_2O$ molecules. Suppose, then, that the liquid properties of water just *are* these collective features. If we agree that wholes possess characteristics distinct from those of their individual parts, and we agree, as well, that these characteristics can be causally efficacious, we can allow that the liquid 'aspect' of water might itself possess significant causal authority.

Applying all this to an apparent instance of mental causation, the causing of a bodily movement by an 'intention in action': 'At the microlevel . . . we have a sequence of neuron firings which causes a series of physiological changes. At the microlevel the intention in action is caused by and realized in the neural processes, and the

25 G. W. Leibniz, *Monadology*, § 17, quoted in Searle (1983, pp. 267–68). Leibniz's argument is reminiscent of Searle's own 'Chinese Room' argument to the conclusion that intentionality is not a computational or functional property of the systems that possess it; see Searle (1980).

bodily movement is caused by and realized in the resultant physiological processes' (p. 270). Searle remarks that 'on such a model the mental phenomena are no more epiphenomenal than the rise in temperature and the firing of a spark plug' (p. 270; see Figure 4.8 above).

A view of this sort envisages the out-and-out identification of 'higher-level' characteristics with the collective features of 'lower-level' items. Thus, substances' being liquid might be identified with (and in that sense might just *be*) their having a certain dynamic molecular structure. Similarly, *being in pain* or *thinking of Vienna* might be identified with (might just *be*) the possessing by certain sorts of biological entity of certain sorts of organisation or structure. Searle's commitment to 'type identities' of this sort tends to be obscured by talk of 'higher-level' characteristics being caused by and realised in 'lower-level' conditions. This sort of causal talk, as Searle admits, carries with it the implication that cause and effect are distinct items. Yet the relation between 'higher-level' characteristics and the 'lower-level' conditions by which they are caused and in which they are realised is, as we have noted, a relation of atemporal dependence or determination, and not what is standardly thought of as a causal relation. Searle is at liberty to describe these relations as causal, but then we must guard against being taken in by the label.[26]

One might doubt that the 'higher-level' characteristics to which Searle appeals do uncontroversially possess causal relevance. Does a substance's *being liquid* endow it with causal capacities 'over and above' those possessed by the substance's constituent molecules? The question is off target. According to Searle, *being liquid* just *is* a characteristic possessed collectively by those molecules, a characteristic that might plausibly be taken to have straightforward aetiological significance. Collections of $H_2O$ molecules, molecular structures, *behave* very differently from individual $H_2O$ molecules, and they do so, in part, because collections possess characteristics not possessed by individual constituents of those collections.

Examples of this sort make it clear that Searle's guiding model for the relation of the brain to states of mind is the part–whole

---

26 Similarly, talk of 'higher-level' properties being *realised in* 'lower-level' conditions might naturally suggest the possibility of 'multiple realisation', a possibility Searle rejects; see below.

relation. Taking up that model, we might say that a wall is 'caused by and realised in' the bricks that make it up, though being wall is not something *in addition to*, not something *secreted by* collections of bricks: Being a brick wall just *is* being a particular sort of brick collection. Moreover, walls possess characteristics lacked by individual bricks. A particular brick wall might be ten feet tall, thirty feet long, and weigh more than a Buick. These properties endow walls with causal powers not possessed by an individual brick. A wall, but not an individual brick, shields us from the wind, blocks our view, and serves as a target for juveniles armed with paint in spray cans.

Searle's response to Malcolm's problem, then, involves an identification of mental characteristics with 'higher-level' physical properties – the collective properties of physical systems – he takes to have uncontroversial causal significance. In describing a substance as wet, and describing its collective molecular behaviour, we are picking out what is in fact the very same characteristic. If we have no objection to the notion that collective, 'higher-level' molecular behaviour has a legitimate causal standing, then we need have no hesitation in regarding the liquid 'aspect' of water as causally significant. This 'aspect' is 'caused by and realised in' the behaviour of molecular aggregates. Similarly, Wayne's thinking of Vienna is 'caused by and realised in' the collective activities of a particular assemblage of neurons. Thinking of Vienna is, in fact, nothing more than a 'higher-level' physical process of a sort that might occur in the brain of a human being. If 'higher-level' neurological characteristics possess causal significance, Wayne's thinking of Vienna *thereby* possesses causal significance.

If Searle is right, we should expect the relation between 'lower-level' characteristics and pertinent 'higher-level' characteristics to be a principled one.

If one knew the principles on which the system of $H_2O$ molecules worked, one could infer that [a substance] was in a liquid state by observing the movement of the molecules, but similarly if one knew the principles on which the brain worked one could infer that it was in a state of thirst or having a visual experience. (p. 268)

Mental characteristics of ordinary human agents are, on Searle's view, quite literally nothing but physical characteristics of brains. At the moment we do not understand the laws or principles that connect 'lower-level' neurological characteristics to 'higher-level' –

132

mental – characteristics. It is up to neuroscience, however, not philosophy, to fill in these gaps. Since mental characteristics are straightforwardly brain characteristics, our understanding of the brain will remain incomplete until we understand these principles – in precisely the way our chemical understanding would be incomplete without a grasp of the principles connecting liquidity and molecular behaviour.

In embracing type identity, Searle is able to accommodate mental causation, and defuse Malcolm's problem. Type identity, however, has a price few philosophers seem willing to pay. It is sometimes claimed, for instance, that type identity excludes the 'multiple realisability' of mental characteristics. In supposing that states of mind are *neurological* states, that mental characteristics are *brain* characteristics, we seem unwisely to exclude a priori the possibility of discovering conscious, intelligent agents whose biology differed radically from ours. It is surely imaginable, however, that there are intelligent creatures elsewhere in the universe whose 'physiology' differs dramatically from the physiology of *Homo sapiens* (perhaps their chemistry is silicon based), yet who harbour thoughts comparable to our own with respect to their causal roles and their intentional content. In fact, we need not go so far afield to find apparent counterexamples to type identity. Creatures on this planet to which we unhesitatingly ascribe a range of mental characteristics differ *biologically* from us in endless important respects. Forced to choose, then, between the 'multiple realisability' of mental characteristics and type identity, many materialist-minded philosophers have rejected type identity.

Searle, quite sensibly, offers a response to the charge that the prospect of multiple realisability excludes type identity.

The *a priori* arguments that I have seen against the possibility of type, rather than token, realizations tend to neglect a crucial point: What counts as a type is always relative to a description. The fact that we can't get type–type realizations stated in, for example, chemical terms, does not imply that we can't have type–type realizations at all. (pp. 271–72)

Searle justifiably leaves it open *which* neurological characteristics are relevant to the 'causing and realising' of states of mind. The relevant characteristics might turn out to be ones common to people and squids, indeed they might turn out to be common to people, squids, silicon-based creatures from Alpha Centauri, and computing machines. Were that so, states of mind would be multiply

133

realisable in one sense, but not in another. Is liquidity multiply realisable? Well, many different sorts of substances can be liquid. Yet, it might nevertheless be the case that they are all liquid in virtue of possessing one and the same 'higher-level' microstructural property.[27]

There is, I believe, a broader moral to be drawn here. Philosophers sometimes argue as though the prospect of multiple realisability automatically rules out type identities. It is in the nature of properties, however, that they are inevitably multiply realisable. If a given property, $P$, can be exemplified by objects of different sorts, objects possessing distinct properties, then $P$ is, in one clear sense, multiply realisable. Regarded in this light, it is difficult to think of a property that is *not* multiply realisable. Consider *being green*. Many different sorts of things can be green: plants, inanimate objects, beams of light. This by itself does not show, however, that being green must be a 'functional property', or that being green is not type-identical with some perfectly ordinary physical property shared by plants, inanimate objects, and beams of light.

The most serious threat to Searle's brand of type identity is not the prospect of multiple realisability, but, as we noted in Chapter 2, *externalism*. If we suppose that states of mind are 'caused by and realised in', not isolated brains, but in agents (or agents' brains) only in particular contexts, the prospect of there being compelling mental–physical identities is diminished. An externalist might think that intentional characteristics are characteristics of brains, of course, even that intentional characteristics are possessed by brains largely because of characteristics possessed by narrowly circumscribed *parts* of brains. The 'causing and realising' of mental characteristics, however, would depend, in part, on relations that brains or subregions of brains bear to external states of affairs and goings-on. The relevant types look, on the face of it, too ungainly to support interesting type identities.

Even if this were not so, the broad – that is, partly extrinsic – property base on which mental characteristics might be thought to depend seems to raise obvious difficulties for their possessing causal

27 Considerations of this sort have suggested to many theorists that mental characteristics might be identified with *functional* characteristics of intelligent creatures. The move is one Searle famously rejects, however; see Searle (1980).

efficacy. To take a crude example, it is one thing to imagine that a substance's *being liquid* encompasses a straightforward causal capacity possessed by the substance, but another matter entirely to imagine that the substance's *being Wayne's favourite drink* has a comparable sort of causal significance. In agreeing to take externalism seriously, however, we open up the possibility that intentional states of mind are related to the brains of intelligent agents in the way being Wayne's favourite is related to a particular sort of liquid substance. If the latter is irrelevant to the causal capacities of the substance, and if this irrelevance stems from its externalist character, then the causal clout of intentional attributes would seem to be similarly threatened. Searle's proposed solution offers little guidance here. It is scarcely surprising, then, that Searle has remained steadfastly opposed to externalist accounts of intentionality.

In what remains of this chapter, I shall advance a conception of mental causation designed to overcome these and other, related difficulties. My approach resembles Searle's in taking seriously the realising relation. I differ from Searle, however, in taking externalism seriously as well. In this regard, I have urged that externalism might be treated as a kind of 'worst case' possibility. In the absence of a convincing internalist theory of mentality, an account of mental causation that accommodates – without actually implying – externalism is preferable to one that does not.

## 6. THE REALISING RELATION

The parallel between Searle's conception of the causal place of supervenient characteristics as represented in Figure 4.8 and the conception portrayed in our earlier Figure 4.2 is striking. In both cases, causal relations put in an appearance at both 'higher' and 'lower' levels. Searle, as we discovered, assigns the vertical arrows a causal interpretation as well. Perhaps this is merely a terminological quirk, however. In any case, in the course of discussing the arrangement depicted in Figure 4.2, I observed that the upper arrow appears to be misplaced. Given the dependence of $\psi_2$ on $\varphi_2$, if $\psi_1$ is to bring about $\psi_2$, it must do so obliquely, that is, by bringing about $\varphi_2$. This led us to Figure 4.3. An arrangement of this sort, however, is apparently at odds with the conviction that the physical domain is causally closed. We were, in this way, pushed to something like the pattern in Figure 4.4. The worry engendered by such arrangements is that supervenient characteristics, here $\psi_1$ and $\psi_2$, appear to be causally superfluous, epiphenomenal.

Searle's solution is, I think, on the right track. 'Higher-level' items, $\psi_1$ for instance, are, according to Searle, 'caused by and realised in' 'lower-level' items like $\varphi_1$. This, as we have observed, may mean no more than that $\varphi_1$ realises $\psi_1$ – whatever that might come to: I have as yet said little to illuminate the realising relation. That relation, it would seem, resembles the causal relation, perhaps, in incorporating an element of determination. I prefer to distinguish realising from causing, however, for reasons that will emerge presently.

Let me preface my remarks with a reminder that discussions of mental causation are especially prone to type–token confusions. In considering events as participants in causal transactions, for instance, we are concerned, not with *types* of event, but with *token* events, dated, nonrepeatable, particular occurrences. If Wayne's striking a match causes it to light, the striking – and the lighting – are particular, concrete occurrences. It is all too easy to lose sight of this homely point. When we look over a diagram of the sort represented in Figure 4.4, it is natural to regard $\varphi_1$ and $\psi_1$ as types – certain *kinds* of thought or neurological process – as opposed to particular, concrete *instances* of various characteristics. This may lead us to focus on relations – type identity, say, or supervenience – holding among types or properties. In taking up the realising relation, however, we target property instances, not types.

In Chapter 3, supervenience was characterised as a relation holding between families of properties, characteristics, or types. If $\alpha$'s supervene on $\beta$'s, then anything that is an $\alpha$ is so in virtue of being a $\beta$; $\alpha$-characteristics in this respect depend on and are determined by $\beta$-characteristics. Supervenience relations, I contended, are ubiquitous. It is in light of these that our world presents itself to us as layered, its characteristics hierarchically ordered.

Supervenience is to be distinguished from the realising relation. Suppose that liquidity supervenes on molecular structure. Now consider a particular liquid substance, Clara's bowl of chicken soup. Given the supervenience of liquidity on molecular structure, we can say that the soup is liquid in virtue of its possession of a certain molecular structure. We can also speak of the soup's liquidity being realised in or by its molecular structure. The relation here is not a relation between types – properties or characteristics – but between instances or exemplifications of properties or characteristics, between the soup's liquidity and a particular dynamic distribution of its molecular constituents. If this particular arrangement of molecules realises the soup's liquidity, then the soup's being liquid is, I shall say, *constituted* by its molecular structure. More generally, $x$'s being $\alpha$ at $t$ is realised by $x$'s being $\beta$, just in case $x$'s being $\alpha$ is constituted, at $t$, by $x$'s being $\beta$ (see Boyd 1980; Pereboom and Kornblith 1991).

My desk is constituted by a particular arrangement of wood and metal parts, and, in this sense, my desk *is* a collection of wood and metal parts. The collection is not identical with my desk, however. There are worlds in which my desk is constituted by a different collection, that is, a collection of different constituents. Were I to replace some part of the desk, a screw that holds a drawer together, for instance, this collection, but not the desk, would cease to exist. There is, perhaps, a token or *contingent* identity relation between my desk and the collection of parts that constitutes it, a relation that need not hold across worlds. This is just to say that in this world, though not in certain other worlds, my desk is constituted by a particular collection of parts.

Realising relations are constrained by supervenience relations. Whether there is a world in which $x$'s being $\beta$ at $t$ realises $x$'s being $\alpha$ depends in part on whether $\alpha$'s supervene on $\beta$'s. The soup's liquidity is realised by its molecular structure only if liquidity supervenes on molecular structure. Further, if $\alpha$'s supervene on $\beta$'s, and some $\alpha$-characteristic is exemplified by $x$ at $t$, then $x$ must, at $t$, exemplify some $\beta$-characteristic that realises this $\alpha$-characteristic.

Return for a moment to my desk. Being a desk is a perfectly respectable supervenient characteristic, although its supervenience base is complex. Imagine a 'molecular duplicate' of the desk existing in a world containing no intelligent life; the molecules that make up the desk's twin have come together as they have purely by chance. Someone might deny – plausibly – that this duplicate is a desk. Suppose this were so. It does not follow that being a desk is not a supervenient characteristic, however, but only that, if being a desk is a supervenient characteristic, its supervenience base is 'broad'. The imagined 'desk' is only a 'narrow' molecular duplicate of my desk. A genuine desk must have a particular sort of causal history, perhaps, or bear certain relations to intelligent creatures. If the property of being a desk is 'broadly supervenient', then any collection of desk parts that realises a desk must have an appropriate causal history – or, at any rate, the collection must itself possess certain 'broad' characteristics.

Consider, now, Wayne's thinking, at $t$, of Vienna. We are supposing that intentional states of mind supervene on certain physical characteristics of agents. If that is so, then Wayne's thinking of Vienna is realised, in Wayne, by a certain physical condition, a particular pattern, $N$, of neuron firings, perhaps. At $t$, then, Wayne's thinking of Vienna is constituted by $N$. More long-windedly, the exemplification, by Wayne, at $t$, of the mental characteristic *thinking of Vienna* is constituted by the exemplication by Wayne, at $t$, of a certain neurological characteristic, $N$.

Realising, then, is a relation between property instances or exemplifications – Plato's 'moving forms', D. C. Williams's 'tropes' – whereas supervenience holds between families of characteristics or properties.[28] The liquidity of Clara's soup is realised by its molecular structure only if liquidity supervenes on molecular structure and the former 'trope' is constituted by the latter.

This conception of the realising relation is, I have insisted, consistent with externalism, consistent with the broad supervenience of mental characteristics. If thinking about Vienna is broadly supervenient, then, Wayne's thinking about Vienna is realised by $N$, only if $N$ possesses the right sort of causal history. A molecular duplicate of $N$ that lacked a causal history of this sort would not realise a thought about Vienna. Whether one 'trope' constitutes another, then, can turn on its circumstances or history.

Considered in this light, the realising relation is consistent both with fine-grained and coarse-grained ontologies. Suppose Clara's possessing some mental event characteristic, $\psi$, is constituted at $t$ by her possessing some neurological event characteristic, $\varphi$. On a fine-grained account of events, there are two distinct events here: Clara's $\psi$-ing and Clara's $\varphi$-ing. On a coarse-grained view of events, there is a single event that can be described as a $\psi$-ing and as a $\varphi$-ing. In neither case must we suppose that $\psi$ and $\varphi$ are 'type-identical', or that $\psi$'s are conceptually reducible to $\varphi$'s.

The step from the notion that intentional mental characteristics are physically realisable to a conception of mental causation might

28 See Williams (1966). For a discussion of the moving forms, see Morrison (1977).

now seem trivial. If Wayne's thinking, at $t$, of Vienna is constituted, at $t$, by a particular neurological configuration, $N$, the causal clout of Wayne's thought will be born by $N$. In a certain sense, Wayne's thinking, at $t$, of Vienna *is* his possessing this neurological configuration. If the latter exhibits causal clout, then so it would seem must the former.[29]

## 7. MENTAL CAUSATION

Have we solved the problem of mental causation, the venerable mind-body problem? Mental characteristics are realised by agents' physical characteristics, where realising is a matter of the exemplifications of those physical characteristics constituting the exemplifications of the mental characteristics. Furthermore, the physical characteristics in question seem to have an uncontroversial causal standing in the production of behaviour. Difficulties remain, however.

Return to Clara who, when we left her, was acquiring the intention to wave at Wayne. Suppose that Clara's acquiring this intention, $\psi_2$, is realised by a sequence of neuron firings, $\varphi_2$, in Clara's brain. This neurological occurrence leads Clara to move her arms in a way characteristic of waving. Is this a case of what might be called mental causation? Well, Clara's acquiring the intention to wave is realised by a given neurological occurrence – partly, perhaps, in virtue of its possession of a particular sort of causal history – and this neurological occurrence, as we are supposing, uncontroversially causes her behaviour. The trouble is that the occurrence in question may realise many characteristics that have no obvious *causal* bearing on Clara's behaviour. We need some way of establishing that $\psi_2$ is not among these causally idle characteristics.

An example originating with Fred Dretske neatly focuses the problem.

Something possessing content, or having meaning, can *be* a cause without its possessing that content or having that meaning being at all relevant to its causal powers. A soprano's upper register supplications may shatter glass, but their meaning is irrelevant to their having this effect. Their effect on the

---

29 An account of mental causation parallel in certain respects to the account recommended here may be found in Macdonald (1989), a work I discovered only after completing this chapter.

139

glass would be the same if they meant nothing at all or something entirely different. (1988, p. 79)

Imagine that Ella sings the phrase 'Break not my heart!' in such a way as to shatter a glass. Ella's singing shatters the glass, and Ella's singing a phrase with a certain meaning is constituted by her singing. In this case, we should not feel compelled to conclude that the meaning of what Ella sings contributed causally to the glass's shattering – that the glass shattered partly in virtue of that meaning. As Searle might put it, that 'aspect' of her singing is causally irrelevant to the glass's shattering.[30] Suppose that mental characteristics were invariably like this, suppose, that is, that in general an event's being mental made no causal difference to an agent's behaviour. How might we exclude this possibility?

The soprano problem leads us back into the thickets of epiphenomenalism by making vivid the fact that the realisation of $\alpha$'s by $\beta$'s is, by itself, insufficient to underwrite the causal relevance of $\alpha$'s, even when $\beta$'s enjoy unquestioned causal standing.

If we are to advance a sensible conception of mental causation, we shall have to find some way of distinguishing Clara and Ella, some way of solving the soprano problem. My suggestion is uncomplicated. It begins with the observation that a system or network of projectable counterfactual and subjunctive conditional truths of certain sorts holds in Clara's case, whereas nothing comparable holds for Ella. This network of truths is grounded in important facts about Clara and her circumstances. It is true of Clara, for instance, and people like Clara, that they more often than not do what they intend to do here and now. In the present case, it is true of Clara that were she to acquire the intention to gesture insultingly at Wayne, rather than the intention to wave, she would gesture insultingly. It is true, as well, that had Clara not acquired the intention to wave, then, her arm would not now be moving as it is.[31] In contrast, it is not the case that had Ella not sung a phrase meaning

---

30  This way of expressing the point is, as we have seen, potentially misleading. The event that is the shattering, when caused by Ella's singing 'Break not my heart', differs from a shattering caused by Ella's singing 'Doobie, Doobie, Doo'. The causes differ acoustically, for instance, and this could well affect (if only minutely) the way the glass shatters. The point, however, is not that features of causes might be causally inert *tout court*, but that they might have no bearing on features of effects in which we have a particular interest.

31  A reminder: In an effort to keep the discussion on track, I am excluding instances of overdetermination.

'Break not my heart!' the glass would have failed to shatter. Ella might have sung *anything* and shattered the glass provided only that she sang it at an appropriate volume and pitch.

To be sure, Ella *might* have deliberated over whether to sing the phrase 'Break not my heart!' at the appropriate pitch and volume, or the phrase 'Doobie, Doobie, Doo' softly, and at a lower pitch, and settled on the former course of action. In this case, had the phrase she sang not meant 'Break not my heart!' her singing would not have shattered the glass. Notice, however, that there is no *systematic, projectable* connection between singings that mean 'Break not my heart!' and glass-shatterings. There are nearby worlds in which Ella's singing has a different meaning, or, for that matter, no meaning at all, and still shatters the glass. There are no nearby worlds, however, in which Clara fails to acquire the intention to wave, yet waves.[32]

I think this is at least part of the story. We are entitled to regard Clara's intention acquiring as bearing causally on her behaviour, first, because her intention acquiring is realised by a particular physical occurrence that is itself uncontroversially causally implicated in her behaviour, and, second, because there is a network of counterfactual truths concerning Clara that link her intention to her subsequent behaviour. These truths rest in part on Clara's being the sort of creature for which there is a systematic, nonaccidental, projectable relation between the occurrence of physical conditions that realise intentions to $A$ and subsequent $A$-ings. There may be nomologically possible worlds in which Clara's arm moves just as it does in this world, yet Clara lacks the intention to wave. Here, one's thoughts turn to Twin Earth cases in which a molecular duplicate of Clara, Twin Clara, owing to her different circumstances, acquires an intention with a very different intentional content (or acquires no intention at all). Since Clara and Twin Clara are 'narrow' physical duplicates, and physical duplicates must move their bodies identically, we should suppose that their behaviour, at least in the 'narrow' sense, will be indistinguishable as well: The bodies of Clara and Twin Clara move identically.

The envisaged possibilities, however, are perfectly in keeping with the account of mental causation sketched thus far. The account implies that in a range of nearby worlds where Clara lacks the

---

32 On projectability, see Goodman (1965, chap. 4).

intention to wave, she does not wave. It does not exclude the possibility of remote worlds in which Clara lacks the intention in question, yet her arm moves just as it does in the actual world. In our world, a particular pattern of neuron firings in Clara's brain realises an intention to $A$; in these remote worlds, an intrinsically indistinguishable pattern of neuron firings, owing to differences in Twin Clara's circumstances perhaps, fails to realise an intention to $A$, yet produces the same arm motion.

Consider those nomologically possible worlds in which Clara is a 'narrow' physiological, but not psychological, twin of the actual Clara. Why should it be thought that these worlds are remote from the actual world? One might reason as follows. We have assumed that Clara possesses various intentional mental characteristics and that these are realised in her neurological condition. What is at issue here is only whether those characteristics bear causally on Clara's behaviour. In evaluating counterfactual and subjunctive conditionals that concern Clara's states of mind, then, nearby worlds are those in which Clara is most like the actual Clara with respect to her intentional attitudes. Perhaps Clara deliberated prior to acquiring the intention to wave, and elected to wave rather than to gesture insultingly. However, had she not decided to wave, Clara would have decided to gesture insultingly, acquired the corresponding intention, and subsequently gestured insultingly.

There is, perhaps, a deeper reason for ordering worlds as I have suggested. Consider, again, the possibility of worlds in which Clara is a physiological, but not psychological duplicate of the actual Clara. Given the supervenience hypothesis and the notion that mental characteristics are realised in the neurological conditions of agents, strictly speaking, any nomologically possible world in which Clara is a physical duplicate of the actual Clara is a world in which she is a mental duplicate as well. We can imagine a 'molecular duplicate' of Clara who differs from her mentally, only so long as we ignore the duplicate's circumstances and causal history. In conceding externalism, however, we are supposing that Clara might owe her mental constitution to her physical constitution partly in virtue of the history and circumstances of that physical constitution. Suppose, then, we imagine a world in which Clara, or her counterpart, physically *resembles* the actual Clara, but owing to differences in the causal history or circumstances of the replica, the replica lacks the intention to wave, an intention possessed by the actual Clara. A world of this sort is, I submit, *physically* remote from the actual world. More to the point, it differs from the actual world far more than a world in which Clara decides to gesture insultingly rather than wave. Any world in which Clara possesses the same intrinsic physical constitution she possesses in the actual world, but in which her causal history differs in such a way that she is, in that world, very different mentally, will differ from this world in endless physical respects.

Let me put the point slightly differently. In Chapter 2, I distinguished 'broad' from 'narrow' characteristics of objects. Broad characteristics are those that depend in part on an object's circumstances or causal history; narrow characteristics, in contrast, are possessed by an object irrespective of its circumstances and causal history. Two marbles might in this sense be narrowly indiscernible, but broadly discernible. They were produced at different times, from different batches of molten glass, perhaps, and their space-time trajectories differ. Clara in the actual world may be narrowly physically identical with Clara in some other world. If we are to suppose that the two Claras differ mentally, however, then we shall have to suppose that they differ broadly in certain important physical respects.

Now consider a world in which Clara is broadly discernible, but narrowly indiscernible, from the actual Clara. In that world, let us suppose, Clara lacks just those broad physical characteristics required for her biological condition to realise an intention to wave at Wayne, although she possesses the very same narrow physical characteristics possessed by Clara in the actual world. In any such world Clara would need a causal history different from her actual causal history, but one that results in her having the very same narrow physical characteristics she possesses in the actual world. Such worlds can be imagined perhaps, but they require endless fiddling with conditions in the actual world, more fiddling, certainly, than do worlds in which Clara elects to gesture insultingly at Wayne rather than wave.

A simple example will illustrate the point. Imagine a nomologically possible world in which Clara's neurological condition is narrowly indiscernible with her actual neurological condition but realises, not the intention to wave at Wayne, but the intention to signal Roman. In that world Roman resembles Wayne, at least to the extent that, at the time of her signaling, Clara's perceptual encounter with Roman produces in her a neurological reaction narrowly identical to the reaction produced by Wayne in the actual world. More seriously, in that world, Roman, in addition to being called 'Wayne', must have had a part in Clara's causal history comparable to the part played by Wayne in her actual causal history – otherwise, the content of Clara's intention would not have concerned Roman. Changes required to accommodate these differences – and of course we should have to postulate untold others – are significant. When we consider a world in which Clara is a narrow duplicate of herself but lacks any intention at all, the changes would need to be more extensive still. Compare these fiddled worlds with worlds in which Clara acquires the intention to gesture insultingly. Here we need envisage only tiny changes in Clara's mental or physical condition, changes resulting, perhaps, from incremental changes in her circumstances (she detects the trace of a smirk in Wayne's smile, for instance).

I do not want talk about possible worlds here to get in the way of an appreciation of the central issue. That issue concerns whether, given Clara's actual condition and circumstances, together with the condition of the actual world, certain subjunctive conditionals (for instance, were Clara to acquire the intention to gesture insultingly at Wayne, she would gesture insultingly) and counterfactuals (had Clara not acquired the intention to wave, she would not have waved) are true. We have every reason to think that they are true. Their truth is unaffected by the supposition that the intentional attitudes are 'broadly supervenient', that is supervenient on the broad biological conditions of agents.

It would be instructive at this point to recall Malcolm's observation, in a passage quoted earlier, that the possibility of providing a complete neurophysiological explanation of a man's climbing a ladder to retrieve his hat from a roof apparently preempts explanations that appeal to *reasons*.

We will recall that the envisaged neurophysiological theory was supposed to provide *sufficient* causal explanations of behavior. Thus the movements of the man on the ladder would be *completely* accounted for in terms of electrical, chemical, and mechanical processes in his body. This would surely imply that his desire or intention to retrieve his hat had nothing to do with his movement up the ladder. It would imply that on this same occasion he would have moved up the ladder in exactly this way even if he had no intention to retrieve his hat, or even no intention to climb the ladder. Given the antecedent neurological states of his bodily system to–

144

gether with general laws correlating these states with the contractions of muscles and the movements of limbs, he would have moved as he did regardless of his desire or intention. If every movement of his was completely accounted for by his antecedent neurological states (his 'programming'), then it was not true that those movements occurred *because* he wanted or intended to get his hat. (1968, pp. 52–3)

Malcolm is right in supposing that it is 'the antecedent neurological states of his bodily system' that provide the causal impetus for the man's behaviour. Agents, physically alike (and in comparable settings) will move their bodies, and so in one sense behave, identically. However, Malcolm's suggestion that an agent might have been just as he is physically, yet differ mentally, is correct only so long as we consider agents' narrow physical characteristics exclusively. The qualification is crucial. Malcolm thinks that it is 'not true that [the man's] movements occurred because he wanted or intended to get his hat'. The man's wants and intentions, however, at the time of his action, are constituted by his neurological condition, the same neurological condition that is causally responsible for his ladder-climbing behaviour. Further, it need not be true that 'he would have moved up the ladder in exactly this way even if he had no intention to retrieve his hat, or even no intention to climb the ladder'. If the man's wants and intentions *do* bear causally on his behaviour, then it is true of the man that, had he lacked those intentions and wants, and barring overdetermination, he would have behaved differently. To be sure, the behavioural difference would be traceable to neurophysiological differences. This, however, is exactly as it should be so long as we take the supervenience hypotheses seriously.

The possibility of intentional mental causation rests on the satisfaction of a pair of conditions. First, mental characteristics are realised by agents' physical characteristics, characteristics that might be thought to play an uncontroversial role in the production of behaviour. This is a straightforward consequence, I think, of the supervenience hypothesis together with plausible assumptions about the realising relation. Second, and barring overdetermination, it is true of particular agents at particular times that, were these mental characteristics to differ, were they *not* exemplified by those agents at those times, for instance, those agents would not be behaving as they are then behaving. They would not be so behaving because the pertinent physical mechanisms would not be operating as they are in fact operating. Further, these counterfactual and subjunctive conditional truths are grounded in features of agents for which it is possible to tell a systematic, projectable story.

I have located the causal authority of intentional mental characteristics in the physical – neurological, or biological, or quantum mechanical – conditions that realise those characteristics. Externalism can be accommodated by allowing that the physical conditions in question realise mental characteristics partly in virtue of their situations and the causal histories of the agents to whom they belong. Under the circumstances, it is fair to ask how these components of the account fit together. As we have noted previously, one may grant that the physical mechanisms responsible for behaviour also realise intentional mental characteristics, without thereby granting that the mental 'aspects' of those mechanisms are causally relevant to that behaviour. Indeed, it looks as though the historical features of an agent's physical condition must be irrelevant to its here-and-now causal standing. More generally, it would seem that the causal capacities of a given object depend exclusively on its narrow characteristics.[33] In supposing that Clara and a narrow molecular duplicate of Clara move their bodies identically, we have conceded as much.

The picture of mental causation I have been promoting denies none of this. Clara's intention inherits the causal authority of the physical condition realising it. That physical condition realises her intention partly in virtue of its having a certain sort of causal history, a history that is, we are supposing, irrelevant to its here-and-now bodily effects. Were we imaginatively to 'slice off' the history, its (narrow) effects would be the same. Considering an agent's physical condition independently of its history is, of course, to consider it abstractly. Every actual physical condition has some history or other. When mental characteristics have aetiological sig-

33 Or, at any rate, an object's *narrow* causal capacities might be thought to depend exclusively on its narrow characteristics; its *broad* causal capacities depend on its narrow capacities and its circumstances. (Broad and narrow causal capacities are discussed in Chapter 2, § 5.) Although the idea that narrow causal capacities stem from objects' narrow characteristics is certainly plausible, I do not endorse it unreservedly. Consider two narrowly identical billiard balls moving along different trajectories. Arguably, the balls possess different narrow causal capacities, though, considered at an instant, they contain nothing that could account for this difference. It is helpful, I think, to regard agents, no less than billiard balls, as possessing trajectories through the world.

nificance for behaviour (excluding cases of overdetermination) agents are such that, were they to differ mentally, they would behave differently. Given the supervenience hypothesis, this means that, were these agents to lack the historical features in virtue of which their physical conditions now realise these mental characteristics, those physical characteristics – narrowly conceived – would be different, and, in consequence, their narrow causal capacities would be different.

Clara's physical condition realises an intention to wave at Wayne partly in virtue of Clara's causal history. Suppose we alter that history with the result that Clara's physical condition no longer realises this intention. It might be thought that Clara's history could be changed in this way without affecting the narrow causal capacities of her physical condition: Her body would move just as before. This, Malcolm's picture, is precisely what the account of mental causation defended here calls into question, however. When mental characteristics are causally relevant to behaviour, physical changes, including changes in physical history, that would result in the absence of the mental characteristic in question would also affect the agent's here-and-now physical constitution in a way that would normally produce a clear-cut behavioural difference.

Again, this is not to deny that there could be nomologically possible worlds in which, by virtue of possessing a very different sort of causal history, Clara lacks the intention to wave, yet, owing to the character of her internal constitution, her arm moves just as the actual Clara's arm moves. As we have seen, however, such worlds are evidently remote from the actual world.

## 8. PSYCHOLOGICAL EXPLANATION

In appealing to mental characteristics in explanations of behaviour, we pick out causes by reference to aspects of those causes that are, for us, salient, manipulable, and that provide a reliable and systematic basis for the prediction of behaviour. The web of subjunctive and counterfactual truths on which an account of this sort rests, depends on assorted facts about agents *and* their circumstances. These facts are systematic in character. In consequence, psychological truths are lawlike: They are projectable, and they support counterfactual and subjunctive conditionals. Undoubtedly the underlying system itself has an explanation, one that hinges on some combination of fundamental physical law and contingent truths concerning entities and processes governed by physical law.

It is natural to suppose that the counterfactual and subjunctive conditional truths of the kind we are considering must be grounded in a mechanism of some sort. When I say that the clock would not have struck if the minute hand had not reached twelve, this counterfactual claim, if true, is grounded in further truths concerning the clock's workings. These latter truths are systematic in the sense that they range over, hence reflect, an orderly system. Familiar psychological truths exhibit a comparable pattern, and are grounded in a comparable mechanism. If externalists are right, the mechanism in question might be taken to include, not only agents, but agents together with their circumstances – their setting, social conditions, and biological makeup. In that case, the same truths may fail to hold for (narrow) molecular duplicates situated in different sorts of environment or for creatures with relevantly different sorts of causal history. Since these molecular duplicates inhabit worlds comfortably remote from our own, however, explanations of the behaviour of agents in the actual world framed in terms of familiar intentional mental characteristics reliably coalesce with 'lower-level', neurological or biological explanations ranging over simpler mechanisms that serve to realise those characteristics.

Although the pattern of explanation illustrated here is causal, it is not, I think, subsumptive. It does not depend on implicit appeals to causal *laws* connecting particular mental characteristics, even constellations of these, with particular nonmental, biological or behavioural characteristics. Twin Earth stories provide only the most vivid examples of ways in which such connections might hold locally, even though there are nomologically possible worlds in which they are broken. In explaining Clara's behaviour by appealing to her intentions, then, we are not invoking a law, even a ceteris paribus law, instantiated by her intention acquisition and subsequent behaviour. We are appealing, rather, to certain of Clara's salient features, features shared, in our world and in other nearby worlds, by intelligent agents generally. We can apparently extend this pattern of explanation to creatures that differ from Clara – to cats, chimpanzees, or blue-crested finches – or to creatures inhabiting very different sorts of environment – Martians, dolphins, inhabitants of Twin Earth – by making allowances for differences (but see Chapter 6). The pattern of explanation illustrated here is evidently widespread. A mechanic who understands the operation of an automobile engine can extend his understanding to more primitive engines on lawn-mowers, or to more exotic mechanisms, by adjusting for obvious differences. In such cases, as in the case of mental characteristics, causal explanation hinges, not on nomic subsumption, but on an appeal to distinctive patterns of counterfactual-supporting contingent truths (see Cummins 1983).

'Folk psychology', the system of concepts we employ in ascribing the intentional attitudes, provides us with a device that is remarkably, though certainly not infallibly, adept at picking out causes of behaviour on the basis of evidence to which we have ready access. Are there better systems? Malcolm's idealised neurophysiological theory comes to mind. Such a theory promises to provide a much finer-grained and far more accurate technique for the identification of behavioural causes. At the same time, it would be ungainly and wildly impractical in application. The evidence required by its concepts is rarely, if ever, available to most of us.

Reflections of this sort might be taken to encourage the view that the conceptual system that supports the application of intentional attitudes enjoys merely a pragmatic standing: It enables us to predict, and so to manipulate and coordinate behaviour; we are entitled, on that basis, and exclusively on that basis, to deploy it. Folk medicine might in this way be pragmatically warranted because it provides cures for a range of ailments. Were that so, it would not matter to us whether the categories of folk medicine had or lacked genuine application. What would matter would be only that it worked – or worked more often than not. If the account of mental causation advanced here is correct, however, explanations of behaviour couched in terms of beliefs, desires, and intentions work because they are, often enough, anyway, correct. In ascribing intentional attitudes to agents, we pick out internal causes of their behaviour. We do so, at any rate, so long as our ascriptions are true; like causal claims of any sort, explanations that refer to intentional attitudes are defeasible.

Does 'folk psychology' compete with Malcolm's envisaged neurophysiology? Both 'folk psychology' and neurophysiology pick out physical causes of behaviour. Neurophysiology is, from one perspective, far better at this. But that need not cast doubt on ordinary 'purposive' explanations of behaviour (or refinements of these of the sort found in cognitive psychology). Does an optical microscope lie because electron microscopes provide more powerful magnification? Few would say so. Just as we have no tendency to be eliminativists when it comes to optical microscopes, so I think we need have no qualms concerning the ascription of intentional attitudes in the explanation of behaviour. The system of concepts that empowers us to do this is a perfectly respectable, though certainly limited, instrument in the identification of causes of behaviour. Those causes can be identified more precisely and described more exhaustively by means of an appropriate (and as yet only imagined) neurophysiology. But this possibility by itself casts no doubt at all on 'folk psychology' or the intentional attitudes.

# 5

## *Privileged access*

### 1. DESCARTES REDUX

Recent work in epistemology and the philosophy of mind suggests that we may at last be putting our Cartesian heritage behind us. The notion that knowledge demands certainty, and that empirical knowledge, in particular, requires an agent–centred core of indubitable propositions, is out of fashion. Dualism is nowadays rarely espoused, and the Cartesian picture of minds as spectators monitoring an inner world that mirrors an outer world is under revision. Earlier, in Chapter 2, we surveyed arguments purporting to show that the contents of thoughts are fixed in part by historical or contextual features of thinkers, that what an agent thinks is determined, at least in part, by that agent's circumstances and causal history. A conception of this sort turns Cartesian internalism inside out. To possess a mind is not to occupy the place of a detached onlooker, but to be engaged in the world.

Although I am prepared to take externalism seriously, I have not officially endorsed any particular externalist programme. I have suggested only that, in general, externalist accounts of the mind promise to solve the problem of intentionality in a way that meshes with our impression of the world as layered, its characteristics hierarchically arranged. In particular, these accounts fit with the notion that agents possess mental characteristics in virtue of their possession of certain physical characteristics. An externalist twist is imparted to this doctrine if we suppose that the physical characteristics in question may be 'broad'; that is, if we suppose that they may include essentially historical and contextual elements.

In Chapter 4, I argued that, despite appearances, externalism leaves room for mental causation. In this regard, it is important to recognise that, although the 'supervenience base' for intentional

151

mental characteristics of agents may be broad, mental characteristics are not themselves 'spread out'. Clara's thought that there is chicken soup in her bowl may be realised in her neurological condition partly in virtue of that condition's possessing a certain sort of causal history. Still, Clara's thought is, if it is anywhere, 'in her head'. In this respect, Clara's thought is like the coin in my pocket, which *is* a quarter partly in virtue of its special causal history. The quarter is at this moment entirely in my pocket, however, and not somehow spread out over the world.[1] There is no mystery, then, in the notion that agents' states of mind incorporate causal capacities, or that these are realised in agents' physical conditions.

These are important results. They support externalism indirectly by removing conceptual ruts and impediments. My sense of the state of play in philosophy today is that, although few philosophers enthusiastically endorse internalism, most are suspicious of particular externalist programmes. Philosophical progress is signalled, however, not, as it seems to be in the sciences, by the triumph of particular theories, but in our transcending unproductive patterns of thought. In this milieu, a theory can endure, despite the erosion of positive reasons for holding it, so long as its advocates succeed in distracting attention by pitting their rivals against one another. In this chapter I hope to remove one such distraction.

## 2. EPISTEMIC PRIVILEGE, IMMEDIACY, AND DIRECTNESS

Descartes is often credited as a source of the doctrine of privileged access. The knowledge we have of our own states of mind is distinctive. I know all and only the contents of my mind *infallibly* and *completely*. Where *p* is a proposition ascribing a current thought to myself, it is necessarily true both that, if I believe that *p* then *p* is true, and that if *p* is true, I believe that *p*. Hume, a Cartesian in this respect at least, sums up this attitude: 'Since all actions of the mind are known to us by consciousness, they must necessarily appear in every particular what they are, and be what they appear' (Hume 1739/1964, I, iv, ii). To be sure, thoughts may misrepresent reality

---

1 The point is perfectly general. Every actual object has *some* causal history and stands in *some* relation to other objects. This does not mean that every object is 'broad', only that every actual object does possess 'broad' characteristics.

in one way or another. I think I see a puddle in the distance, but there is no puddle. Indeed, it is imaginable that *all* of our thoughts concerning contingent features of the external world are in this way mistaken. I cannot, however, be mistaken about my thoughts qua thoughts: If I entertain a thought of *F*, then I cannot err in taking this thought to be *of F*. The Method of Doubt Descartes recommends in the *Meditations* presumes as much. I am to consider all propositions doubtful, and accept as true only those that, on reflection, satisfy a certain standard. Were the contents of my own thoughts inaccessible or doubtful, the project could not get off the ground.

In *Meditation II*, on the heels of the *Cogito* argument, Descartes makes this commitment explicit.

Is it not one and the same 'I' who is now doubting almost everything, who nonetheless understands some things, who affirms that this one thing is true, denies everything else, desires to know more, is unwilling to be deceived, imagines many things even involuntarily, and is aware of many things which apparently come from the senses? Are not all these things just as true as the fact that I exist, even if I am asleep all the time, and even if he who created me is doing all he can to deceive me? Which of all these activities is distinct from my thinking? Which of them can be said to be separate from myself? The fact that it is I who am doubting and understanding and willing is so evident that I see no way of making it any clearer. But it is also the case that the 'I' who imagines is the same 'I'. For even if, as I have supposed, none of the objects of imagination are real, the power of imagination is something which really exists and is part of my thinking. Lastly, it is also the same 'I' who has sensory perceptions, or is aware of bodily things as it were through the senses. For example, I am now seeing light, hearing a noise, feeling heat. But I am asleep, so all this is false. Yet I certainly *seem* to see, to hear, and to be warmed. This cannot be false; what is called 'having a sensory perception' is strictly just this, and in this restricted sense of the term it is simply thinking. (1642/1986, p. 19)

It is usual nowadays to brush aside Descartes's professed certainty about mental functions – doubting, understanding, affirming, denying, imagining, sensing. Surely I can sense or doubt inattentively or even unconsciously, that is, without explicitly recognising that I am sensing or doubting. If that is so, it would seem that I could falsely believe that I am imagining, understanding, or sensing.

It is less easy to dismiss the Cartesian idea that the *contents* of my thoughts are necessarily certain for me. Suppose I sense a fallen tree in my path; that is, I go into a perceptual state the content of which is that there is a fallen tree in my path. Although I may err in thinking a fallen tree *is* in my path, it is less clear that I could err in my grasp of the content of this perceptual state, that I could be wrong in supposing that it concerns a fallen tree, for instance.

We *do* seem, in fact, to grasp the contents of our thoughts immediately and without effort. Admittedly, our thoughts may be confused in various ways. My conception of a 'rotator cuff' may fall short of the conception wielded by Dr. Frank Jobe. Such confusions may be reflected in my judgements. It is important, however, not to conflate the sort of grasp we have of the contents of our own thoughts and the adequacy of those thoughts as mirrors of nature.

In considering privileged access, it is natural to speak of *knowing one's own states of mind*.[2] The phrase, however, is, as is becoming evident, multiply ambiguous. Consider, first, the knowledge I have of my own current intentional attitudes. I may be ignorant of my beliefs or my desires, either because I fail to consider them or because I am prevented from doing so. It is unlikely that we enjoy any remarkable epistemic capacities when it comes to taking inventory of such things. True, I am typically in a rather better position than you to say what I do or do not believe, or want, or intend. I possess, after all, a quantity of information you lack. But this might signal no more than a contingent feature of my situation, not the brink of an epistemological chasm.

Second, consider a case in which I take myself to believe that *p*. In so doing, let us suppose, I believe myself to instantiate a particular attitude, belief, toward a proposition, *p*.[3] It would seem that my second-order belief could be wrong in at least three respects. First, I might be deluded, I might altogether lack this belief.[4] Second, I

2 Wittgenstein (1953/1968, § 246) holds that 'It can't be said of me at all (except perhaps as a joke) that I *know* I am in pain'. My assumption, on the contrary, is that it makes perfectly good sense to say that I have knowledge of, or beliefs about, my mental condition. I know, though you merely suspect, that my feelings have been hurt by Clara's slight. If I know this, then I believe it justifiably. I do not offer this as a refutation of Wittgenstein, but merely as an indication of where I stand.

3 Here and elsewhere, my use of the expressions 'proposition' and 'attitude' is intended only to signify distinguishable aspects of particular states of mind.

4 A qualification is called for here. If I take myself to have a certain attitude toward *p*, then it might seem that, although I may lack *that* attitude, I must nevertheless at least possess *some* attitude toward *p*, if only a taking-myself-to-believe attitude toward *p*. The point, however, is that it is possible for me to think that I believe

might be right about *p*, right about the content of my attitude, but wrong about the character of its attitudinal component. Perhaps I do not, after all, *believe* that *p*, perhaps I merely *want p* to be true, or *fear* that *p*, or merely *suspect* that *p*. In approaching a precipice, I might find myself in a state I should describe as *fearing* that I shall tumble over. I could be wrong, however. I might, in fact, secretly *want* to tumble over.[5] When I am wrong in this way, I am wrong, not about my intentional attitude as a whole, but wrong about one ingredient of that intentional attitude. I have an attitude toward *p*, only not *this* attitude.

There is a third respect in which it might seem that I could be wrong in taking myself to believe that *p*. Thus, I might be correct in supposing that I have a belief, but wrong about *p*, wrong about what my attitude concerns, wrong about its *content*. I recognise that I hold a certain belief, one I take to be the belief that *p*, when, as it happens, my belief is the belief that *q*. Were this a genuine possibility, we should be easy targets for an especially virulent form of scepticism, a form of scepticism that would, as we have seen, altogether undermine Descartes's project in the *Meditations*.

Is this an oversight on Descartes's part? That seems unlikely. For consider: Although I could be wrong, perhaps, in thinking I *believe* that *p*, it is not by any means obvious that (or how) I *could* be wrong in thinking that it is *p* my putative belief concerns. I know, it seems, with something approaching Cartesian certainty, the *content* of any of my thoughts or presumed thoughts I venture to consider, even if I am fallible when it comes to the identification of the *attitudes*, if any, I hold toward those contents. There appears to be no room for error in such matters, nothing on which to hang sceptical doubts.

Perhaps this assessment is hasty, however. We have agreed to take externalism seriously, after all, and externalism might be thought to provide an obvious opening for the sceptic. If the contents of my thoughts depend on conditions external to me, conditions about which I may remain blissfully ignorant, what is to prevent a sceptic from raising doubts about the character of those

---

that *p* even though I do not *believe* that *p*, but harbour some other attitude toward *p*.

5 It might be that my desire causes my fear, a different case. It certainly seems possible that I could confuse my genuinely *accepting* a certain proposition, *p*, and my merely *hypothesising p*.

conditions, hence, it would seem, doubts about the contents of my thoughts?

I shall approach this question in two stages. First, I shall argue that an externalist conception of intentional states of mind is at least no worse off than competing – internalist, even dualist – conceptions of mind in respect to the phenomenon of privileged access. Second, I shall recommend an account of the distinctive character of (what I shall call) Cartesian thoughts, those to which the notion of epistemic privilege most readily applies. First, however, a word is in order concerning this presumed privilege.

The notion of privileged access, like much else in philosophy, is an agreeable one, so long as we keep our distance. When we move closer, when we try to spell out, explicitly and in detail, what privileged access amounts to, complexities and caveats proliferate.[6] Very strong – Cartesian – conceptions of privileged access occupy one end of a continuum of possibilities. A Cartesian holds that agents' knowledge of their own states of mind is complete and infallible in the sense that it is *conceptually* impossible for agents to err in assessing their current mental condition. At the other end of this continuum lies the notion that, *just as a matter of fact*, one's assessments of one's own mental condition are, on the whole, more accurate than assessments made by others.[7] I shall not attempt to locate some preferred position along this continuum; my aim is not to defend a particular conception of privileged access. Instead, I shall focus on whether externalism and privileged access – *however* conceived – are reconcilable. Having professed indifference as to the precise character of privileged access, I shall proceed to recommend some broad, independently plausible constraints on the notion. The discussion would otherwise remain at an uncomfortably elevated level of abstraction.

The crucial ingredient in our preanalytical conception of privileged access is that of *epistemic asymmetry*: My assessment of my own mental condition is nonaccidentally epistemically superior to assessments I might make of 'external' states of affairs. These encompass the condition of material bodies generally, including my own body, and the mental lives of others. One way of explicating the asymmetry is via the Cartesian notion that agents possess a *direct* awareness of

6 William Alston (1971) provides an admirable discussion of the topic.
7 This perhaps is close to a position defended by Ryle (1949). See also Bem (1972).

156

the contents of their own minds, in virtue of which they are infallible and omniscient with respect to judgements about those contents. In contrast, our access to matters outside our minds is indirect, mediated by inferences that render us fallible, less-than-omniscient concerning such things. My knowledge of material bodies is founded on inferences I make from the character of my sensory experiences. And, although my knowledge of *your* thoughts is based on observations of what you say and do, the knowledge I have of my own thoughts is unmediated, direct.

It is unclear, however, what directness or immediacy of this sort involves. One might take the proximity metaphor literally, and suppose that the directness in question is *causal* directness: Whereas my access to material objects and to your states of mind is invariably causally circuitous, I am in direct and immediate contact with my own thoughts. Shorter causal chains, it might be imagined, afford fewer possibilities of error. Self-awareness is a limiting case: There is *no* causal gap between my mental condition and my appreciation of that mental condition, hence literally no room for error.

Causal immediacy is a difficult notion to evaluate. It is reasonable to wonder, for instance, what sorts of causal processes underlie self-consciousness. In reflecting on my own condition, I am unaware, perhaps, of any sort of complexity, but I am equally oblivious, when I look about the world, of the complexity of causal sequences that occur in the course of ordinary visual or auditory perception. In the absence of anything more interesting to say on the matter, we seem left with the idea that, owing to causal *proximity* – my thoughts are, after all, *in my head* – I am less likely to err over the character of my own mental condition than I am to misapprehend goings-on in the 'outside world'. This is not much on which to build a conception of privileged access.

Suppose, however, we take the notion of directness or immediacy, not causally, but epistemically. Whatever their causal background, assessments of my mental condition are *epistemically* immediate for me in a way my assessment of another's mental condition is not. I believe that Clara is now thinking of a bowl of chicken soup. This belief is based on other beliefs I have concerning Clara. I believe that Clara is fond of chicken soup, that there is a bowl of chicken soup in the vicinity, and that Clara has noticed this bowl. Suppose, in contrast, I take myself now to be thinking about Vienna. My self-assessment seems not to depend on any *additional*

157

information I have about myself. I am directly or immediately justified in taking myself to have the thought in question, in the sense that the warrant I possess for my regarding myself as I do does not depend epistemically on my having additional evidence, further warranted beliefs, or knowledge. In the case of my belief about Clara's thoughts, you might reasonably ask *why* I believe what I do. In the case of my self-assessment, such a request seems out of place.[8]

The idea here might be expressed more generally. Consider cases in which I assess my own 'occurrent' mental condition and entertain a particular Cartesian thought: I take myself now to be thinking that $p$. In so doing, I accept a proposition to the effect that I am now thinking that $p$, one that ascribes – to me – certain intentional characteristics. Call propositions of this sort self-ascriptive propositions. With this as a background, we can formulate a principle of epistemic privilege:

EP Necessarily, (1) if any agent, $S$, holds true a self-ascriptive proposition, $p$, where $p$ concerns some current, conscious thought, $S$ is epistemically warranted in holding $p$ true; (2) $S$ is, in this respect unique – no agent other than $S$ is so related to these propositions.[9]

I shall suppose that when $S$ is warranted in holding true some self-ascriptive proposition, $p$, and $p$ is true, $S$ *knows* directly or immediately that $p$. There are, I realise, well-known counterexamples to accounts of knowledge framed in terms of justified true belief. These do not obviously apply in the present case, however (see Alston 1971, p. 229). Allowing for complications, then, I shall in what follows speak both of immediate justification or warrant and of immediate knowledge.

Principle *EP* implies neither infallibility nor omniscience. In this regard, *EP* belongs somewhere toward the deflationary end of the continuum of possible conceptions of privileged access. *EP* does, however, provide us with a notion of epistemic privilege that turns

8 Which is not to say that the request *lacks sense*. If, after years of analysis, I reach the conclusion that I regard my Yugo as a rival for the affections of my mechanically minded wife, I may do so on the basis of considerable evidence. You are well within your rights in challenging this evidence and any beliefs based on it.

9 Excluding God, perhaps, or the omniscient interpreter. Principle *EP* is close to Alston's *T6* (1971, p. 235). Different versions of *EP* result from different interpretations of the modal operator. Here, and elsewhere in this chapter, 'thought' signifies a generic intentional attitude.

on an important asymmetry between first-person and other-person ascriptions of intentional characteristics.

I suspect that *EP*, or something close to it, is probably true. In one sense, however, what matters is not whether the principle is true, but whether it provides us with a coherent, reasonably plausible notion of privileged access against which to measure externalism. It should, in any case, be noted that the focus of *EP* is on a salient epistemic asymmetry. *EP* does not imply that *only* one's own states of mind are immediately warranted. I may be immediately warranted in beliefs about the disposition of my body, that my feet are now resting on the floor beneath my desk, for instance. Although I could certainly have evidence that my feet are so placed – they might cast a shadow visible from where I sit – my belief about them need not be *based on* any evidence. Even so, that belief might be warranted for me. Perhaps its warrant depends on its having been caused in a certain way. Or perhaps it is warranted in virtue of its possession of a certain feature, its resulting from a clear and distinct apprehension, for instance.

This is not the place to attempt a solution to the long-standing problem of epistemic warrant. Still, it certainly seems that any conception of immediate warrant that might be thought to capture the sort of warrant enjoyed by Cartesian thoughts, could be extended to other domains as well. My belief that the bird outside my window is a blue-crested finch is based in part on evidence I have just acquired from my *Audubon Guide*. If my belief is warranted, then, its warrant is not immediate. What of Wayne, the ornithologist across the garden, who can tell in a glance the bird is a blue-crested finch? If Wayne's seeing the bird leads to his believing that it is a blue-crested finch, and if this belief is warranted for Wayne, must it be based on evidence? Perhaps not, perhaps in Wayne's case this belief, under these conditions, is immediately justified. I differ from a blind person, in part by the fact that certain beliefs that have at least prima facie immediate warrant for me – beliefs about colours, for instance – are only warranted for such a person on the basis of evidence. If mute creatures can be said to possess justified beliefs, then some of these – pigeons, for instance, or honeybees – are immediately justified in believing things I am justified in believing exclusively on the basis of evidence.

Reflections of this sort deposit us on a slippery slope. Consider my beliefs about *your* thoughts. These are not, in typical cases,

159

immediately warranted. They are based, rather, on evidence I gather by observing what you say or do. Nevertheless, it is certainly conceivable that I could come to be immediately justified in beliefs about your states of mind. This might happen were I wired to you in such a way that I share a portion of your nervous system. Less fantastically, we all learn to read the thoughts of colleagues and family members, just as a botanist learns to read the flora of the surrounding countryside. Given a measure of ignorance about my own thoughts, then, it seems to follow that I might know your mind better than my own.[10]

We seem left with an unsatisfactorily anaemic notion of privileged access: I know some of my thoughts, perhaps, immediately (but I know some of them only by inference); I know a few of your thoughts by inference (although there is no obvious epistemic barrier to my knowing some of them immediately). Asymmetry, then, might seem to survive only quantitatively: The proportion of my thoughts that I know immediately appears invariably to be greater than the proportion of yours I know immediately. Prodded by a sceptic, however, I might be brought to wonder why there could not be cases in which the proportion is reversed.

Does this mean that we must drop *EP*, and seek some deeper principle? I do not think so. I began the discussion by noting that, although the notion of privileged access enjoys considerable pre-analytical appeal, capturing that notion by means of our usual stock of epistemological concepts is another matter altogether. Perhaps this shows something about the notion of privileged access, or perhaps it shows something about the conceptual repertoire available in epistemology.[11] The question at hand, however, is whether externalist accounts of intentional characteristics square with some ordinary notion of privileged access. We can evaluate that question only by first saying what privileged access might plausibly involve, then inquiring as to whether this is at odds with externalism. We are entitled, I think, to suppose that *EP* provides at least a rough approximation of the ordinary conception of privileged access. If *EP* turns out to be consistent with externalism, then, that is an

---

10 Thus breathing new life into the old joke about two behaviourists meeting on the street: One says to the other, 'You're fine, how am I?'

11 Or perhaps it is just that I have not been clever enough in my deployment of that repertoire. That goes without saying.

interesting result. More importantly, if it turns out that an argument that demonstrates this consistency can be generalised straightforwardly to other, perhaps more astute, characterisations of privileged access, then I can rest my case. We can, in this way, deploy *EP* as a stalking horse, while recognising that *EP* may not represent the last word on the matter.

## 3. EXTERNALISM AND COGNITIVE ALIENATION

Let us pretend, then, for the sake of argument, that externalism is right, that the content of the intentional attitudes depends, not solely on intrinsic features of agents, but in some measure on agents' histories and circumstances. Imagine, now, that I am thinking that $p$, that is, entertaining a thought the content of which is $p$. My thinking that $p$, is, we are supposing, realised in my neurological condition. More particularly, my thinking that $p$ is, on this occasion, constituted by my being in neurological condition $N$, and that $N$ realises my thinking that $p$ partly in virtue of the obtaining of a complex state of affairs, $A$. In addition to certain of my intrinsic features, $A$ includes features of my context: various environmental and historical circumstances. To fix the discussion, let us imagine a simple externalist theory according to which $N$ realises my thinking that this is a tree in virtue of having been caused by a tree. In that case, $A$ will include $N$'s having been caused by a tree, and $p$ will be the 'content', *this is a tree*. Different versions of externalism, of course, will provide different accounts of $A$, different accounts of whatever it is in virtue of which $N$ on this occasion realises a thought with this particular content. For the moment, all that matters is that we take the content of my state of mind, my thought, to depend essentially on something distal, something outside my body.

Imagine now that I entertain the thought that I am thinking that $p$. I have labelled thoughts of this sort, thoughts that themselves concern the contents of thoughts, *Cartesian thoughts*. Cartesian thoughts are, at bottom, second-order attitudes, intentional attitudes the content of which itself includes the content of some attitude. On this occasion, I am thinking that $p$ and thinking that I am thinking that $p$. Let $p*$ designate the content of this Cartesian thought. Thus, if $p$ is *this is a tree*, then $p*$ is something like *I am thinking: This is a tree* (see Burge 1988). My harbouring this second-

161

order attitude, my taking myself to be thinking $p$, is realised in neurological state $N*$, and it is so realised partly in virtue of the obtaining of some state of affairs, $A*$, the constituents of which include, in addition to $N*$, items not included among my intrinsic features. We might suppose that, at least in typical cases, $A*$ in some fashion depends on or includes $A$: Whatever it is in virtue of which $N$ realises the thought that this is a tree also contributes to the circumstances in virtue of which $N*$ realises the corresponding Cartesian thought.[12]

Given this picture, it is easy to imagine that externalism *distances* us from the contents of our own thoughts. This impression might arise from a line of reasoning of the following sort. So long as the content of my first-order thought depends on the obtaining of $A$, my coming to appreciate that thought's content requires my discovering that $A$ obtains. In our simplified example, this would mean that, for me to recognise that I am thinking *this is a tree,* I should first have to ascertain that my thought was *caused by* a tree.[13] But this is not something I could plausibly discover simply by reflection. I should need, it seems, *evidence* about the circumstances under which my thought was produced, evidence that could easily fall short of conclusiveness.

Thus, even if I happened to be right about what caused my thought, hence right about that thought's intentional content, my *access* to the thought would hardly be immediate. It would be based on clues amassed, and on inferences drawn from those clues. In general, my beliefs about the content of my own thoughts might depend on my being right about matters the knowledge of which would hinge on the results of delicate empirical tests and experiments. It goes without saying that, under these circumstances, I might err in identifying the cause of my thought, hence err in my assessment of that thought's content. In cases where I did not take the trouble to investigate the aetiology of my thoughts, beliefs

12 I leave open the possibility that there are cases that fail to satisfy these conditions. My aim is not to give an exhaustive account of Cartesian thoughts, but merely to show that there is nothing in the nature of self-consciousness that conflicts with externalism.

13 *Or* that $N$, the neural condition that realises that thought was so caused (though not necessarily under the description '$N$'). Perhaps I should need to know as well that certain of $N$'s characteristics, including $N$'s being caused by a tree, are sufficient for $N$'s realising a thought with the content *this is a tree.*

about their contents would be scarcely more than shots in the dark (see Leon 1988; Georgalis 1990; Noonan 1992).

This line of reasoning exhibits an initial intuitive plausibility. Perhaps that plausibility is only apparent. Suppose, for instance, one reasoned that, since the thought that $p$ depends on the obtaining of $A$, one must know that $A$ obtains if one is to know that one is thinking that $p$. An argument of this sort hinges on a principle of the form:

$P$ Necessarily, if $p$ depends on $q$, then $q$ must be known if $p$ is known.

Principle $P$, however, seems clearly false. Descartes's existing might depend on the existence of DNA, yet surely Descartes can know that he exists without knowing that DNA exists (see McKinsey 1991).

Still, even if we reject principle $P$, something may remain of the original worry. That worry stemmed from a consideration of the externalist notion that the contents of my own thoughts are radically underdetermined by my current internal condition. I might be ('narrowly') indistinguishable in this respect from a twin who, owing to a very different causal history, is now thinking some very different thought. The *information* for what thought I am now entertaining is unavailable to me *except* via my access to $A$.

This prospect is doubly unsettling. First, it seems to oblige us to suppose that beliefs about the contents of our thoughts are epistemically mediated, based on empirical evidence. This flies in the face of the conviction that our knowledge of such things is, on the whole, epistemically direct.[14] Second, if beliefs we entertain about our own states of mind depend in this way on evidential backing, then we might, with fair frequency, *make mistakes* about those states. I might have evidence, for instance, that a particular be-

---

14 Earlier, I suggested that one might have immediately warranted beliefs, hence immediate knowledge, about things other than one's mental condition. If that is so, it might be possible to know the contents of one's thoughts immediately even if the warrant for beliefs about one's own thoughts depended on the obtaining of $A$. This apparent loophole, however, is of no help to one hoping to reconcile externalism and privileged access. Suppose that my assessment of my own mental condition were immediately warranted in the manner suggested. It would nevertheless be reasonable for you to require that I produce evidence for my assessment, evidence for the obtaining of $A$. If this is implausible, as it surely seems to be, then any theory that implies it is implausible.

lief I harbour is the belief that $p$, the belief, say, that snow is white. But I could be wrong. My belief *might*, for all *I* know, be a belief about something altogether different – that Tarski is Swedish, or even that snow is *not* white. My getting its content right apparently requires my getting the determinants of that content right, and, so long as my access to these is epistemically mediated, I could easily fail to do so. I seem vulnerable to bizarre sceptical worries about whether I am *ever* right about the content of my thoughts. As a reaction, I might seek solace in antirealism or religion.

We have reached an apparent impasse. On the one hand, when we consult our own experience, it is patent that we have something like a Cartesian entrée to the contents of our thoughts. This need not be taken to imply that we are infallible or incorrigible concerning the mental, only that our assessment of the contents of our own states of mind exhibits an epistemic immediacy apparently at odds with externalism. We seem bound, then, to reject externalism as a plausible account of intentional content. On the other hand, there are powerful considerations favouring externalism, favouring the notion that the content of a thought depends partly on complicated features of a thinker's circumstances. We seem, then, to be faced with a choice: Either we revert to Cartesianism, thereby preserving our intuitions about privileged access, or we accept some version of externalism and abandon those intuitions. Neither option is especially inviting.

Before venturing a solution to this dilemma, I shall consider an argument advanced by Michael McKinsey (1991) to the conclusion that externalism and privileged access are indeed irreconcilable. If McKinsey is right, the attractiveness of the externalist programme would be seriously diminished.


## 4. PRIVILEGED ACCESS AND A PRIORI KNOWLEDGE

McKinsey accepts the idea that the mark of privileged access is not incorrigibility: 'Surely one can make mistakes about what one believes, intends, or desires' (1991, p. 9). Rather, the core ingredient in our ordinary conception of privileged access is that 'we can in principle find out about these states in ourselves "just by thinking",

164

without launching an empirical investigation or making any assumptions about the empirical world' (p. 9). Knowledge of this sort, 'knowledge obtained independently of empirical investigation', McKinsey calls 'a priori knowledge' (p. 9). An agent, Oscar, who entertains the thought that water is wet and knows 'independently of empirical investigation' that he is entertaining this thought *knows a priori* what he is thinking.

One way to understand what it means to describe Oscar as knowing that *p* 'independently of empirical investigation', is to suppose that Oscar's knowledge that *p* is *epistemically unmediated*. Epistemically unmediated knowledge, however, what is sometimes called 'direct knowledge', need not be a priori in one familiar sense of 'a priori'. In that sense, if *p* is knowable a priori, *p* does not entail any empirical proposition. To say that Oscar knows *p* directly, however, is just to say that Oscar's knowledge that *p* does not epistemically depend on some other belief. Oscar may 'know directly' that his tooth aches or that there is a blue-crested finch in the garden, but neither case is plausibly regarded as a case of a priori knowing. I shall bracket these considerations for the moment, and return to them presently.

McKinsey invites us to suppose that externalists are right, that Oscar's entertaining the thought that water is wet 'depends on' the truth of some proposition, *E*, 'the "external proposition" whose presupposition makes Oscar's thought that water is wet a wide state' (p. 12). (In this context, a 'wide state' is a thought the propositional content of which depends at least in part on the thinker's circumstances.) McKinsey contends that the following three sentences are inconsistent (p. 12):

(1) Oscar knows a priori that he is thinking that water is wet.
(2) The proposition that Oscar is thinking that water is wet necessarily depends upon *E*.
(3) The proposition *E* cannot be known a priori, but only by empirical investigation.

Externalists, McKinsey argues, or at any rate externalists who hope to accommodate some plausible conception of privileged access, must hold that (1), (2), and (3) are consistent. I can know 'a priori' that I am thinking that *p*, my thinking that *p* might depend on *E*'s being true, yet the truth of *E* need not be knowable a priori.

According to McKinsey, so long as we permit the dependence relation mentioned in (2) to signify 'metaphysical dependence' – as

165

distinct from 'logical' or 'conceptual' dependence – there is no inconsistency. 'Since metaphysical dependencies are often only knowable a posteriori, propositions that are knowable a priori might metaphysically depend upon other propositions that are only knowable a posteriori' (p. 13). Descartes might know a priori that he exists, for instance, without knowing a priori that DNA exists, even though Descartes's existence might depend metaphysically on the existence of DNA.

McKinsey argues that externalists require something stronger than metaphysical dependence in premise (2). Externalists are committed to the view that the dependence relation in question logically or conceptually *suffices* for Oscar's thought about water, his 'water-thought', to be a 'wide' thought. But if a thought's metaphysically depending on the obtaining of some external state of affairs logically or conceptually suffices for its being wide, then *all* thoughts must be wide – or at least they must be wide given the reasonable assumption that their existence metaphysically depends on the obtaining of endless external states of affairs. My thinking 'I exist', for instance, or Oscar's thinking that water is wet, might metaphysically depend on the existence of DNA. But it is implausible to suppose that this suffices for these thoughts' being wide.

Let us suppose that McKinsey is right: Externalists are committed to the view that Oscar's thinking that water is wet 'conceptually implies' some proposition, $E$, 'whose presupposition makes Oscar's thought that water is wet a wide state'. We interpret 'necessarily depends on' in (2), then, to mean 'logically or conceptually implies'. This yields

(2b) The proposition that Oscar is thinking that water is wet conceptually implies $E$. (p. 15)

As a result, 'it is easy to see' that (1), (2b), and (3) are inconsistent.

Suppose (1) that Oscar knows a priori that he is thinking that water is wet. Then by (2b), Oscar can simply deduce $E$, using only premises that are knowable a priori, including the premiss that he is thinking that water is wet. Since Oscar can deduce $E$ from premises that are knowable a priori, Oscar can know $E$ itself a priori. But this contradicts (3). . . . (p. 15)

More generally, if I know a priori that I am thinking that $p$, and if 'I am thinking that $p$' implies $q$, then $q$ is knowable a priori (just by deducing $q$ from 'I am thinking that $p$' alone, or from 'I am thinking that $p$' together with other propositions knowable a priori).

166

This means that, for any proposition $p$, if I can know a priori that I am thinking that $p$, where $p$ logically depends on – implies – the truth of some empirical proposition, it follows that I should be able 'to know a priori that the external world exists' (p. 16). McKinsey concludes that 'since you obviously *can't* know a priori that the external world exists, you also can't know a priori that you are in the mental state in question. It's just that simple' (p. 16).

*Is* it that simple? I have noted that, on one reading, 'a priori' in the argument above might be taken to mean 'epistemically unmediated' or 'epistemically direct'. If we substitute 'epistemically direct' for 'a priori' in that argument, (1) and (2b) do *not* appear to imply anything obviously inconsistent with (3). Suppose that Oscar knows directly that he is thinking that water is wet, and suppose that 'the proposition that Oscar is thinking that water is wet conceptually implies $E$'. If $E$ is 'conceptually implied' by premises that are directly knowable, does it follow that $E$ is directly knowable? This seems unlikely for two reasons. First, what is or is not directly knowable may depend as much on characteristics of doxastic agents as on internal features of propositions. Oscar may hold $p$, and $p$ may 'conceptually imply' $q$, without its being true that $q$ is directly knowable by Oscar. To the extent that Oscar's belief that $q$ depends epistemically on his other beliefs, his belief that $q$ is epistemically mediated. Indeed, if Oscar holds $q$ in part because he recognises that $q$ is a deductive consequence of $p$, then his knowledge of $q$ is *not* direct. Thus, $q$ might be known by Oscar on the basis of deductive reasoning from premises that are themselves directly known, yet $q$ not be known directly. Second, if 'directly knowable' simply means 'in principle knowable directly', then it is hard to see how *any* proposition, including the proposition that the external world exists, could fail to be directly knowable – if only by God.

This may be unfair to McKinsey, however. Suppose the argument is rephrased in such a way that a priori knowing is taken in the sense mentioned earlier: A proposition is knowable a priori only if it does not logically imply any empirical proposition.[15] So construed, (1) and (2b) imply that $E$ is knowable a priori, and thus are inconsistent with (3). Suppose this is so, suppose we cannot consistently hold (1), (2b), and (3). Which of these assertions should we

15 Of course if we do this, it is less clear that we ought to accept McKinsey's claim that the knowledge we have of our own states of mind is a priori.

abandon? McKinsey's suggestion is that the offending assertion is (2b). If we give up (2b), we could continue to hold (1) and (3), continue to accept the Cartesian notion that the epistemic access we have to the contents of our own conscious thoughts is privileged. If, in contrast, we cling to (2b), we should have to give up (1), the possibility of privileged access; (2b) and (3) are inconsistent with (1).

It is also possible, however, to maintain consistency by rejecting (3), the claim that $E$ cannot be known a priori. Whether an externalist is entitled to disavow (3) depends on what exactly $E$ is supposed to be. Recall that McKinsey describes $E$ as 'the "external proposition" whose presupposition makes Oscar's thought that water is wet a wide state' (p. 12). Unfortunately, McKinsey does not say what this 'external proposition' is. Were $E$ the proposition that water exists, for instance, then, since this proposition is straightforwardly empirical, we should be stuck with premise (3). No sensible externalist would hold that Oscar is thinking that water is wet conceptually implies that water exists, however. (Compare: Oscar is thinking that unicorns are white conceptually implies that unicorns exist.) So what might $E$ be? This will depend on details of particular externalist theories. The important question is whether, on any plausible externalist account of intentional content, $E$ must express an empirical proposition. If not, then premise (3) is false and the alleged inconsistency vanishes.

If McKinsey is right in regarding externalist theories as advancing purported conceptual truths, it would seem unlikely that $E$ *could* express an empirical proposition. The situation would parallel that in epistemology. We might insist on causal conditions for empirical knowledge without thereby taking these to entail empirical truths. Imagine, then, that $E$ expresses a principle of the form

$E_1$ Necessarily, the content of a thought is fixed in part by its causal history.

Although $E_1$ 'makes Oscar's thought that water is wet a wide state', $E_1$ is not obviously empirical in McKinsey's sense, nor does it, together with the proposition that Oscar believes that water is wet imply any empirical proposition.

Is $E_1$ too weak? $E_1$ suffices for Oscar's thought's being 'wide', and so satisfies McKinsey's stipulation. A critic of externalism might nevertheless insist that actual externalist theories are committed to principles of the form

$E_2$ Necessarily, an agent's thought that $p$ concerns a putative natural kind, $K$, only if the agent is in causal contact with instances of $K$.

If Oscar's thought concerns water, and if both 'Oscar is thinking of water' and $E_2$ are knowable by Oscar a priori, then it would seem that Oscar could know a priori that his thought about water is caused by water and, in consequence, that water exists. If it is impossible to know such things a priori, McKinsey's contention would be vindicated.

This reply is unsatisfactory, however. First, so interpreted, $E_2$ is implausibly strong. Thoughts concerning phlogiston bear no causal relation to phlogiston, and this is something recognised by any sensible externalist theory.

Second, imagine that an externalist *were* committed to something like $E_2$. Would it follow that Oscar is thereby in a position to infer from $E_2$, together with the proposition that he is thinking that water is wet, that his thought is partly caused by water, that water exists, hence that the external world exists? Would Oscar be in a position to advance an a priori refutation of scepticism?

We have seen that an externalist need not accept (3), need not grant that $E$ is knowable only on the basis of empirical investigation. The worry now is that, if we construe $E$ along the lines of $E_2$, then (1) and (2b), in concert with $E_2$, might imply some other empirical proposition. To be sure, if (3) is false, if $E_2$ is knowable a priori, one might wonder how (1), (2b), and $E_2$ *could* imply any empirical proposition unless either (1) or (2b) – or both (1) and (2b) – were themselves empirical propositions. Let us ignore this complication, however, and consider just premise (1). Given $E_2$, the contents of Oscar's thoughts are partly determined by their causal histories: When Oscar thinks a thought he would express by an utterance of the form 'water is wet', his utterance and the thought it expresses concern water only if Oscar stands in an appropriate causal relation to instances of water – that is, to instances of $H_2O$.[16] Oscar's circumstances could be such that his thinking 'I am thinking that water is wet' does not, in concert with $E_2$, imply that

16 To streamline the exposition I shall speak of Oscar's thinking '$p$' in order to designate the thought '$p$' would express were it uttered by Oscar, thereby leaving open what proposition, if any, *is* expressed by $p$. The argument here owes much to Putnam 1981, chap. 1; see also Heil 1987. My intention is not to defend Putnam, however, but merely to show that externalism does not obviously have the remarkable consequences Putnam and McKinsey envisage.

water exists. This might be so were Oscar a brain in a vat or were he an inhabitant of a Cartesian demon world. Assuming that Oscar is like us, however, it is true both that, in thinking 'water is wet', Oscar is thinking that water is wet and that Oscar is in a position to know a priori (in McKinsey's sense) he is thinking that water is wet. From this, together with $E_2$, *we* could deduce a certain empirical proposition, namely the proposition that water exists in Oscar's world. This proposition is one to which we have only a posteriori access. What about Oscar?

Consider the sentences Oscar might use to express his thought. When Oscar says 'water is wet', he expresses a thought about water. In contrast, Twin Oscar's utterance of 'water is wet' expresses a thought about twin water. When *we* say that Oscar's utterance of 'water is wet' expresses a thought about water, we express a certain empirical proposition, one we are in a position to know only a posteriori. Is this proposition the same proposition that Oscar expresses in uttering the sentence 'when I utter the sentence "water is wet", I am expressing a thought about water'? And if it is, is the proposition one Oscar might come to know a priori? Suppose the answer to both questions were yes. Then Oscar could know something a priori that we can know only a posteriori. Could Oscar know a priori that the external world exists, then? Consider the following argument:

Argument X

(1) $E_2$ is true.
(2) $E_2$ is knowable by Oscar a priori.
(3) Oscar can know a priori that his 'water' thoughts concern water.
(4) Oscar can know a priori that water exists [from (2) and (3)].
(5) Oscar can know a priori that the external world exists [from (4)].

Would Argument X afford Oscar a convincing proof that the external world exists, a refutation of scepticism?

Note that Argument X is *formally* identical to an argument a deluded Oscar might advance in a demon world. In such a world, Oscar's 'water' thoughts would not concern water; nor would his 'external world' thoughts concern an external world. It does not follow, of course, that, in the demon world or in the actual world, Oscar is in the dark about the contents of his thoughts. Granting $E_2$, then, and assuming the right conditions are satisfied, it seems to follow that Oscar in our world would be in a position to know a priori that the external world exists. Does this mean that Oscar is in possession of a stunning refutation of scepticism? That is unlikely.

Consider an epistemological analogue. Imagine that some epistemic principle of the following form were correct:

> K S knows that p if and only if S believes truly that p, and S's belief that p has property F (where F is some property in virtue of which p is epistemically warranted: *being supported by adequate evidence*, for instance, or *being reliably produced*, or *being self-evident*, or *being perceived clearly and distinctly*).

Principle K is, if it is knowable at all, knowable a priori. Imagine that Oscar knows some empirical proposition, p, the proposition that water exists, and suppose that Oscar could know a priori – solely on the basis of reflection, 'independently of empirical investigation' – that he knows that p: Oscar might introspect, and form the true belief that he knows that p. So long as this introspective belief had property F, Oscar would know that he knows that p. Now it might seem that Oscar is in a position to infer the existence of the external world a priori. How? Consider an analogue to Argument X:

Argument X'

(1') K is true.
(2') K is knowable by Oscar a priori.
(3') Oscar can know a priori that he knows that water exists.
(4') Oscar can know a priori that water exists [from (2') and (3')].
(5') Oscar can know a priori that the external world exists [from (4')].

One might have qualms about premise (3'). Bearing in mind that we are following McKinsey here and using 'a priori' to mean 'independent of empirical investigation', it might still be doubted that Oscar could know solely on the basis of reflection that he knows some empirical proposition. Imagine, however, that Oscar believes that water exists on the basis of a sensory experience that he is now drinking water, and pretend that his believing on this basis satisfies F. As he forms this belief, Oscar might reflect on his epistemic situation. In so doing, Oscar recognises that his belief that water exists is based on a certain sort of sensory experience, and, on this basis, comes to believe truly that he knows that water exists. Oscar's belief that water exists might have been based on a reliable process, or on self-evident beliefs, or on clear and distinct beliefs. That it was so based is, in some cases anyway, knowable by Oscar

171

without recourse to independent empirical investigation. If this is so, it would seem that Oscar can know a priori that he knows that water exists, and premise (3') is vindicated.

Does Argument $X'$ provide Oscar with a satisfying response to scepticism? I think it does not. Imagine that we are eavesdropping on an Oscar inhabiting a demon world. In that world, Oscar reasons in a way formally indistinguishable from Oscar in our world, yet fails to know (or to know that he knows) that the external world exists. This is something we are in a position to appreciate, though Oscar is not. In setting out to refute scepticism by proving that there is an external world, we seem obliged to step outside ourselves, to observe ourselves from the same transcendental perspective from which we observe Oscar. By the nature of things, that is impossible.

The parallel between Argument $X$ and Argument $X'$ suggests that the respect in which some version of externalism might be thought to imply that we can know a priori that the external world exists is not a respect that poses a threat either to scepticism or to common sense. Even if these observations were off base, however, they concede rather more to McKinsey than necessary. As we have seen, there is no particular reason for externalists to endorse $E_2$ or any principle like $E_2$. In either case, McKinsey's argument fails, and externalism is vindicated.

## 5. SELF-CONSCIOUSNESS

The failure of McKinsey's argument points the way to a solution to our dilemma. Consider again the Cartesian thought that I am thinking that $p$. That second-order thought, recall, is realised in neural condition $N^*$, while my thinking that $p$ is realised in neural condition $N$. The content of the first-order thought depends on the obtaining of some state of affairs, $A$, that includes $N$'s standing in an appropriate causal relation to a particular tree. What, then, prevents our simplified theory (and, mutatis mutandis, *any* viable externalist theory) from providing an exactly parallel account of the content of my second-order belief? Bluntly put: If the content of my first-order thought (*this is a tree*) is fixed by a state of affairs, $A$, that includes the realising basis of that thought's being caused by a tree, then the content of my second-order thought (*this is the thought: This is a tree*) is fixed by the obtaining of a state of affairs,

$A*$, one that might (though it need not) include $A$, hence include the determinants of the content of my first-order thought. Even more bluntly: If we are willing to grant an externalist account of first-order intentional content, we have no particular reason to balk at an externalist account of second-order intentional content.

It is important to keep in mind that externalist theories of the sort under scrutiny hold that the content of thoughts is fixed by the *obtaining* of certain states of affairs. They do not, or certainly need not, require in addition that agents know or believe that these states of affairs obtain. On our simplified externalist theory, my thought concerns a tree because it was prompted by a tree, not because I know or believe it was so prompted. If we grant this much, the same account can evidently be extended to second-order, Cartesian thoughts. When I take myself to be thinking: *This is a tree*, the content of my reflection is fixed in part by its having been caused in an appropriate way (or whatever), *not* by my discovering it to have been so caused.

Such cases are especially interesting because the *content* of the first-order thought is itself *part of* the content of the second-order thought. Not all inner-directed thoughts share this feature. It is perfectly possible to take oneself to be thinking a thought that is a thought that $p$, without thereby comprehending that thought as *of* $p$.[17] Indeed, one might worry that, were externalism true, the access we have to our thoughts might *inevitably* have this character.

The contents of ordinary thoughts, according to externalism, depend on the obtaining of states of affairs that can include components distinct from the purely intrinsic features of the agents to whom the thoughts belong. Contents, so fixed, need not, and almost certainly will not, include important aspects of those external components. If my thought about a tree is a thought about a tree in part because it was caused by a tree, its being caused by a tree need not, and in this case certainly will not, be reflected in its content.[18]

---

17 Suppose I don an autocerebroscope, a helmet-like device that displays, on a small hand-held screen, a record of the thoughts that pass through my mind. Unfortunately, the model I have chosen displays this information in Portuguese, a language I do not know. Even so, I can tell by looking at the screen that the thought I am now thinking exactly resembles a thought I entertained before lunch.

18 Searle may disagree (see Searle 1983, pp. 48–50). Of course, even if my thought that this is a tree included in its content its having been caused by a tree, it would *not* include in its content a host of other arcane factors that would, if externalists are right, figure, no less than the tree, in the determination of its content.

Similarly, my taking myself to be thinking that $p$ can incorporate $p$ without this second-order thought's thereby including (as part of *its* content) the conditions ultimately responsible for fixing the sense of the original thought. In *both* cases – in my thinking that $p$, and my taking myself to be thinking that $p$ – the content of my thought is fixed by the obtaining of states of affairs concerning which I may remain largely ignorant.

I have been discussing externalist theories of intentional content as though only these could motivate doubts about the possibility of privileged access. We imagine that, if content were not, or were not exclusively, fixed by goings-on 'in the head', our access to the contents of our own thoughts would be a chancy thing. But why should bare *proximity* be considered relevant? If the contents of one's thoughts depended entirely on the state of one's brain, for instance, why should that fact alone render our access to those contents any less indirect or problematical? Were it assumed that, in order to grasp the contents of our thoughts, we must ascertain the conditions that fix those contents, we should be out of luck if those conditions included complex neurological goings-on. Even if one insisted only on the obtaining of those conditions, it is by no means obvious why conditions that depend solely on instances of characteristics or events inside one's head should be taken to have an *epistemological* priority over those that depend partly on items or events occurring elsewhere. Nor is it obvious that a traditional Cartesian dualist is in any better position to account for epistemic privilege. A thought's realisation in a nonphysical substance does not, by itself, afford a reason for supposing that one's apprehension of its content is immediate and certain.[19] Considerations of this sort suggest that worries about access to mental contents associated with externalism are misplaced. Precisely analogous worries can be generated for nonexternalist, even dualist, theories. Difficulties arise, if at all, not from the 'broad' or external character of whatever happens to fix intentional content, but from some other source.

---

19 Of course we could, following Hume and Descartes, stipulate that occurrences in a mental substance 'must necessarily appear in every particular what they are, and be what they appear'. Then, however, privileged access is accommodated by stipulation, and we need not be impressed.

## 6. THE MIND'S EYE

The source, perhaps, is a certain philosophically persistent conception of the mind, one according to which awareness of our own thoughts is taken to be based on inward glimpses of representational entities. It is tempting to model in this way the access we have to the contents of our own thoughts after our perceptual awareness of states of affairs in our environment. The temptation stems from a seductive picture of the mind as a container of (in Ryle's phrase) *phosphorescent* mental items – ideas, in one tradition, mental sentences, in another. We introspect these interior items in something like the way we observe objects and events in our studies. If introspection seems, by comparison, less fallible, this is due to our intimacy with introspected items or to the fact that those items are quite literally *unmistakable*. We err in our assessments of ordinary perceptual objects, perhaps, because those objects are distant, or badly illuminated, or unfamiliar. Comparable problems cannot arise in the case of mental objects. These, we imagine, are encountered in a way that squeezes out the possibility of error.

Epistemic privilege does not – and, I think, *could not* – rest on the inward perception of a special class of *object*. Once we rid ourselves of this picture, we may be in a position to make sense of the phenomenon. Having done so, we shall have at the same time removed whatever grounds that might remain for supposing that externalism poses a threat to our ordinary conception of privileged access.

As a preliminary, it will be helpful to consider a kind of intentional occurrence that, at first blush, might seem an excellent candidate for the inward perception model: the entertaining of visual images. According to Stephen Kosslyn,

Visual images might be like displays produced on a cathode ray tube . . . by a computer program operating on stored data. That is, . . . images are temporary spatial displays in active memory that are generated from more abstract representations in long-term memory. Interpretive mechanisms (a 'mind's eye') work over ('look at') these internal displays and classify them in terms of semantic categories (as would be involved in realizing that a particular spatial configuration corresponds to a dog's ear, for example). (Kosslyn et al. 1979, p. 536)

An account of this sort, whatever its empirical credentials, exudes an aura of implausibility (see Heil 1982).[20] That is due, I think, at least

20 It is not, of course, that we cannot entertain mental images or describe their

in part, to its making explicit an unlikely conception of the sort of access one has to one's mental condition. Were the conception apt, then whatever asymmetry we find in the access you and I have to the contents of your states of mind would be epistemically fortuitous.

I say to you, 'Form an image of your grandmother', and you comply. Suppose now I ask, 'What makes you think the image is of your *grandmother* – and not, say, someone *just like* her?' The question is ill-conceived. It is not that you cannot be wrong about what you imagine. If the person whom you had been brought up to regard as your grandmother were an impostor, for instance, then you would be wrong in supposing that the image you have just formed is of your grandmother. It is an image of the impostor. This, however, seems not to be a mistake you make about the image, but a mistake of a different sort, one that concerns, not the image, but its target.

Imagining, in this respect at least, resembles *drawing* – as distinct from *observing* or 'interpreting' – a picture or a diagram. In the course of a lecture on the battle of Borodino, you make $X$'s on a large map to mark the location of Napoleon's forces and $O$'s to mark the disposition of Kutuzov's armies. I inquire, 'What makes you think the $X$'s stand for Napoleon's troops and not Kutuzov's?' The question misfires no less than the corresponding question about the image of your grandmother. You may be wrong in many ways about Borodino, of course, in which case you could be wrong in supposing that the diagram you have drawn represents things as they were at the time of the battle. It is possible, for instance, that Russian regiments in fact occupied the places on the battlefield indicated by your $X$'s. Perhaps the diagram more accurately depicts Austerlitz, or perhaps you slipped and drew, by mistake, a diagram of Austerlitz. (Compare: In the course of your lecture you say 'Napoleon' intending 'Kutuzov'.) Your knowledge of the diagram's significance, however, is not something separable from your constructing it with a certain sense, not something that emerges from your *inspection* of the diagram. As an observer, my situation is very different. I could well be wrong or confused about the significance of your $X$'s and $O$'s.

contents. The question is, what this comes to. *One* possibility is that favoured by Kosslyn et al. To doubt that possibility is not to doubt the phenomenon.

The asymmetry here is instructive. I am an observer and, like any observer, may err in understanding or describing what I see. You, however, are not, or at any rate, not essentially, an observer. I am obliged to take your word concerning what you have drawn, not because you have a *better view* of it, or because the drawing reveals its sense to you in some especially luminescent way, but because the drawing is *yours*. You may err, to be sure, but not in the ways I may err about the drawing.

This point may be obscured by superficial linguistic similarities in the ways in which we describe representational errors. I can be wrong about what your diagram depicts, but so can you. I see the diagram, but misinterpret it. This suggests a corresponding error on your part: You misinterpret your own diagram. Although this can happen – you might misinterpret a note you have left for yourself on the refrigerator door – most often such errors are errors of misconstruction, not misinterpretation.[21]

The privileged status we enjoy with respect to the contents of our own thoughts is analogous. In reporting the contents of our thoughts, we need not be taken to be describing properties possessed by objects or episodes scanned by our mind's eye. Were that so, we should, I think, be at a loss to account for the privileged status such reports are routinely accorded. The access we enjoy to our own mental contents would be superior to what is available to others, perhaps, but only contingently so. Its superiority would be epistemically on all fours with the epistemic superiority I enjoy with respect to the contents of my trouser pockets.

## 7. THE SIGNIFICANCE OF THOUGHTS

There is perhaps a lingering worry. The literature on externalism is replete with examples of agents who seem, in one way or another, confused about the contents of their own thoughts.[22] Is it plausible

21 Imagine that drawings expressed unconscious thoughts or hidden 'social meanings'. Then you might need to consult an expert to recover these hidden meanings and in that sense to interpret your work. Deconstructionists make much of such possibilities.
22 Burge (1979) contends that cases of the sort to be described are common; see also Chapter 2 above.

to suppose that such agents possess anything approximating Cartesian access to what they are thinking? Consider three representative examples.

(1) Alison, who has seen television commercials touting dandruff treatments, now suspects that she has contracted dandruff on her knee. On many externalist accounts of intentional content, it will turn out that, although Alison is confused about what dandruff is – a condition of the scalp – her thoughts nevertheless concern dandruff.

(2) A beginning philosophy student, Henry, has no beliefs about Aristotle except that he was Plato's teacher. Externalism encourages us to describe Henry's thoughts as thoughts about Aristotle, yet surely his conception of Aristotle is muddled.

(3) Leif, a physicist, reflecting on the possibility that electrons carry observers with them into superposition, realises he has no satisfactory conception of what this comes to.

Examples like these suggest that externalism must be, after all, at odds with privileged access.

A parallel worry arises from a consideration of Twin Earth cases. There is, we have supposed, no difference in subjective 'feel' between Earth and Twin Earth. Were my twin and I instantaneously to exchange places, for instance, neither of us would notice the slightest difference in our respective experiences. Given that, according to externalism, the thoughts my twin and I entertain nevertheless diverge, how could it be supposed that each of us knows the contents of our respective thoughts? These contents are alleged to differ, but apparently not in any subjectively detectable way.

It is important, in evaluating such cases, to distinguish (1) our entertaining thoughts with a certain content and knowing of those thoughts that they have this content, from (2) our being in a position to *characterise* that content, or define it, or provide an analysis of it. The former need not be thought to entail the latter. Were that not so, few of us would know much at all about our thoughts. Alison's thoughts, then, may concern dandruff, and she may recognise that they do, despite her confusion about what dandruff *is*. Henry's false beliefs about Aristotle need no more prevent him from thinking about Aristotle self-consciously, than from thinking about Aristotle *tout court*. And, although Leif, in common with most physicists, may be unable coherently to spell out what it is for an observer to be carried into superposition, it would be excessive to deny that Leif's thoughts, self-conscious and otherwise, concern that notion.

In a Twin Earth case, Wayne's thoughts might concern water, while his twin Dwayne's do not. But neither Wayne nor his twin is thereby barred from thinking self-consciously about, respectively, water and twin water. If the twins exchange places, on most versions of externalism, their thoughts about water and twin water will remain, at least for a time, unaltered. Again, there is no special problem about the access of either twin to the contents of his thoughts. Wayne, for instance, will believe (falsely, of course) that there is water in the glass in front of him, and this is precisely what he would take himself to believe were he to reflect on it. After a time, we should, perhaps, begin to describe Wayne's thoughts differently. Once that happens, once it becomes appropriate to describe Wayne as thinking that there is twin water in the glass in front of him, it would also be correct to describe him as taking himself to have this thought, that is, as having a thought about twin water. All of this is consistent with Wayne's remaining forever oblivious to the fact that he has been transplanted to Twin Earth.

These reflections return us to a consideration of the internal character of Cartesian thoughts. I have presumed that Cartesian thoughts like Wayne's are reducible to the having of second-order thoughts. It is natural to suppose that these second-order thoughts are entirely distinct from the first-order thoughts they concern. We might, it seems, have thoughts about *second*-order thoughts, and, in general, $n+1$-order thoughts about $n$-order thoughts. This conjures a picture of thoughts piled on top of thoughts. Without going so far as to deny that this is possible, I do want to suggest what seems to me a more felicitous model for the phenomenon.

In possessing a capacity to entertain the thought that $p$, I possess, as well, the capacity to entertain that thought *self-consciously*. In exercising this capacity, I recognise myself to be thinking that $p$.[23] Although I may stumble in assessing the place a thought occupies in my overall mental condition, I cannot similarly err in respect to its content. This 'self-intimating' character of thought underlies our ground-level conception of privileged access (see Ryle 1949).

Most of the thoughts I entertain run through my mind unremarked. I take explicit note of them only very occasionally. When I do, my awareness that I am thinking those thoughts, thinking that

23 Burge (1988, pp. 658–62) speaks of 'thinking $p$ self-ascriptively'. The position endorsed here is close to Burge's.

179

*p*, for instance, is partly induced by and partly constituted by my thinking that *p*: My awareness *includes* the original thought by virtue of being a self-conscious thinking of that thought. The having of Cartesian thoughts is not, or not fundamentally, a matter of my entertaining a pair of distinct thoughts, a target thought and a detached, second-order thought. The original – contained – thought is itself an essential ingredient in the containing thought. Self-consciousness, on this model, is fundamentally *reflexive*.

In thinking that *p*, I am in a certain mental condition. In taking myself to be thinking *p*, however, or in entertaining the thought that *p* self-consciously, I need not be entertaining a thought about an inwardly observed mental object. Were this the source of my knowledge of the content of my thought, then, I should be in the position of an observer, an interpreter of items present on an internal stage or television screen. If this is the model, then to preserve the notion that there is an interesting and important epistemological gulf between my grasp of the contents of my thoughts and your understanding of those same thoughts, we must suppose that mental items possess a remarkable property: Their significance is *transparent*, they wear their meanings on their sleeves.

We are moved to postulate objects of this sort, however, only so long as we are in the grip of a certain picture. Once we abandon the picture, the postulated items lose their charm. Davidson expresses the idea this way:

Many attempts have been made to find a relation between a person and an object which will in all contexts hold if and only if the person can intuitively be said to know what the object is. But none of these attempts has succeeded, and . . . the reason is clear. The only object that would satisfy the twin requirements of being 'before the mind' and also such that it determines . . . the content of a thought, must, like Hume's ideas and impressions, 'be what it seems and seem what it is'. There are no such objects, public or private, abstract or concrete. (Davidson 1987, p. 455)

We understand ourselves, but not as we understand others.[24] The capacity to entertain thoughts, no less than the capacity to form an image of one's grandmother or sketch a diagram of the battle of

---

24 I do not deny that we can take up an attitude toward ourselves very like the attitude we commonly take toward others. We can engage in various forms of self-analysis. My claim is just that this is an inappropriate model for the explication of Cartesian thoughts, ordinary self-conscious thinking.

Borodino, essentially *includes* the capacity to grasp their content. I appreciate what I am thinking, in the sense of grasping the contents of my thoughts, not by observing those thoughts and reading off their content, but by entertaining them in a particular way: self-consciously. My being in a self-conscious condition is a matter of my being in a condition that both includes and is partly induced by my entertaining a thought with a particular intentional content. My being in this self-conscious condition constitutes my recognising that content. If the content of my thoughts depends on goings-on outside me, then I may recognise that content, in the sense of recognising what I am thinking, despite being mostly ignorant of those external goings-on. My thoughts have their content, perhaps, in virtue of the obtaining of certain complex states of affairs. My recognising that content, however, need not consist in my knowing about those complex states of affairs.

Just as your capacity to produce a map of your neighborhood is not in general separable from your capacity to grasp the significance of that map, so your capacity to entertain thoughts is inseparable from your capacity to grasp the significance of those thoughts. We might, perhaps, construct a device (or imagine a creature) that could produce maps – or inscriptions we could interpret as maps – yet lacked understanding. The explanation of the behaviour of such a device, however, would be very different from the explanation of the behaviour of an intelligent map-maker. Were we to set out to endow a mechanical mapping device with understanding, we should not succeed by simply adding a module that 'scanned' the inscriptions and computed an 'interpretation' for each. A mechanism of this sort would resemble, not a self-conscious agent, but a pair of agents encompassing a single body, one an interpreter, the other a producer of interpretable inscriptions (see Chapter 6).

Theories of intentional content posit conditions agents must satisfy if they are to be counted as possessing thoughts. An agent's satisfying these conditions, however, need not be a matter of that agent's recognising them to be satisfied. This, I think, is, or ought to be, uncontroversial. Anyone who questions it is immediately faced with the spectre of a regress: If my thought's possessing a particular content requires that I recognise that certain conditions are satisfied, then it requires my having some *other* thought with a particular content, one, namely, corresponding to this recognition.

181

But, of course, *this* thought would require its own corresponding recognition of the satisfaction of appropriate conditions for *its* content, and we are off to the races.

How does all this square with externalism and the supervenience hypothesis? Intelligent agents have the capacity to go into states that exhibit intentional characteristics partly *because* they exhibit these characteristics. Thoughts occur to us out of the blue, but they need not. Typically the thoughts we entertain are explicable, in part, by reference to their content: They occur to us, in part, *because* of what they are about. Directed thinking of this sort resembles sketching or map-making in this respect. In each case we *create* something with a particular significance in part *because* it possesses that significance. In so doing we may, though we need not, be copying or reproducing some independently significant item. An artist may form an image and use this as the basis of a sketch, but the artist may also allow the significance of the sketch to emerge with the sketch. Much of our thinking is like this. Indeed were it not so, we should be faced with another sort of unpleasant regress.

If I give someone the order, 'fetch me a red flower from the meadow', how is he to know what flower to bring, as I have only given him a *word*?

Now the answer one might suggest first is that he went to look for a red flower carrying a red image in his mind, and comparing it with the flowers to see which of them had the color of the image. . . . But this is not the only way of searching and it isn't the usual way. We go, look about us, walk up to a flower and pick it, without comparing it to anything. To see that the process of obeying the order can be of this kind, consider the order '*imagine* a red patch'. You are not tempted in this case to think that *before* obeying you must have imagined a red patch to serve you as a pattern for the red patch which you were ordered to imagine. (Wittgenstein 1958, p. 3)

I take Wittgenstein's reflections here to encourage a sensible conception of privileged access, one that reinforces the notion that there is an apparent conceptual connection between one's capacity to entertain thoughts and one's capacity to recognise the contents of those thoughts. It makes no difference that the contents of our thoughts might be fixed by the obtaining of some state of affairs about which we are largely ignorant. Granted, the character of our thoughts could depend on some as yet unconsidered intrinsic feature they possess. But the evident fact that we can know immediately and with certainty what we are thinking is not a reason to think that this is so, not a reason to prefer internalism to externalism. Externalism might prove to be misguided. Certainly, we can find fault with particular externalist doctrines and programmes. We have, however, reached the point in philosophy where it is no longer possible to regard internalist proclivities as philosophically innocent.

# 6

# *Talk and thought*

## 1. LANGUAGE AND THOUGHT

How are language and thought related? In the case of *Homo sapiens*, the capacity for thought and a capacity for linguistic expression develop apace. The linguistic repertoire of children mirrors their conceptual development in a way that could scarcely be accidental. Attempts to impart linguistic sophistication to creatures – apes, dolphins, and the like – that would altogether lack it otherwise, have been inhibited by these creatures' cognitive limitations (see Premack 1986). It is tempting to suppose, on the basis of such reflections, that thought and language go hand in hand. At the same time, we may find ourselves pulled in the opposite direction. We routinely impute apparently sophisticated thoughts to infants, pets, and creatures in the wild by way of explaining their behaviour. Spot barks at the front door because he thinks Wayne is outside. When Wayne enters, Spot greets him enthusiastically, before returning to his place in front of the fire. Such explanations, and the predictions they license, seem not merely *convenient* but entirely *appropriate*. Perhaps, then, thought and language are manifestations of distinct, though in the case of human beings, developmentally linked talents.

Although it is easy to imagine thought occurring in the absence of linguistic expression, it is natural to suppose that a capacity to use language presupposes a certain level of conceptual finesse and intelligence. Indeed, it is precisely this that distinguishes the use of language from lesser forms of communicative behaviour. The actions of a mute creature may provide useful information about that creature's internal condition and, indirectly, about the world.[1]

---

1 'Mute creatures' are those lacking a capacity for genuine linguistic expression – whatever exactly *that* is. So far as we know, terrestrial creatures other than human beings are in this sense mute.

When these actions are stereotyped and systematic, and when their presence is explained by reference to the information they afford conspecifics, we often describe them as 'linguistic'. Honeybees are language users in this attenuated sense. One might argue that systems of communication like those of the honeybee are not genuinely linguistic on the grounds that they are markedly impoverished in their capacity for expression when compared with familiar natural languages. Although it is certainly true that there is a vast gulf between the 'linguistic' repertoires of nonhuman species and those of human beings, purely quantitative differences of *this* sort are arguably inessential. The communicative ingenuity of some species of bird could well outstrip that of a two-year old child, yet there might be good reason to regard the two-year old's communicative behaviour, but not the birds', as 'genuinely linguistic'. What is important, it would seem, is not the complexity or range of reputed linguistic behaviour, but its *explanation*. Human beings produce utterances for reasons of certain sorts, nonhuman creatures apparently do not.

There is an essential difference between a creature's engaging in behaviour because that behaviour is (in some sense) meaningful, and a creature's engaging in behaviour in part because the creature *recognises* that the behaviour expresses some particular meaning and regards this as providing a reason for so behaving (see Grice 1957; Bennett 1964). Honeybees engage in information-conveying dances in part *because* those dances are information-conveying (von Frisch 1950/1971). In this case, however, the 'because' does not seem to point toward reasons the honeybees have for dancing as they do, but toward a connection between information-conveying features of honeybee dances and adaptive advantages for the honeybees of engaging in dances of this sort. Part of the reason honeybees dance as they do is that their dances are in a certain way informative. The 'reason' here, however, is not the honeybees', but Mother Nature's.

My reluctance to regard honeybee dances as genuinely linguistic is not due to the fact that honeybee dances are apparently 'wired-in', whereas human linguistic behaviour is 'learned'. Imagine that the dances of a particular honeybee were, owing to a genetic deficiency perhaps, systematically 'misleading'. Other honeybees might 'learn' that when *this* bee dances in a way that, for a normal honeybee, would indicate a food source at a certain distance and direction relative to the hive, they must adjust their flight in a particular way. When a normal honeybee performs a dance of type $T$, this provides observer bees with information that a food source is in direction $c$ and at distance $d$ from the hive. When the 'mendacious' honeybee, $M$, performs a dance of type $T$, observers have learned to fly in direction $c + 45$ for distance $d$ to locate a food source. Again, we might explain the honeybees' behaviour by reference to the 'meaning' of $M$'s dance. Yet there is no temptation to suppose, either that $M$ has reasons for dancing in a particular manner, or that observer bees who learn to respond adaptively to these nonstandard dances do so for reasons that include beliefs about what the dances indicate.

Learned communicative behaviour, then, need not be linguistic. Similarly, 'wired in' responses need not, solely on account of being wired in, fail to count as linguistic. A human being might exploit a wired-in response because – that is, for the reason that – it communicates something he wants to communicate. Wayne might, for instance, be wired in such a way that his belches sometimes come out sounding like the English sentence, 'A magnificent meal!' Having just enjoyed a meal at Clara's table, Wayne resists suppressing an impending belch, in part because he can count on her taking that belch as the expression of a compliment. A wired-in response may, in this way, be *recruited* to play the role of a response that would, under other circumstances, be voluntary. What matters, it seems, is not the physiology of the response, but relations the response bears to the agent's reasons.

There is, then, prima facie plausibility in the notion that the use of language requires thoughts of a certain sort: 'Genuine linguistic behaviour' is behaviour engaged in by creatures for particular sorts of reasons. 'Genuine languages' might be identified with widespread patterns of behaviour so motivated.

The suggestion that language *requires* thought is, of course, intended as a suggestion concerning a presumed *conceptual* relation. The point is not simply that it would be surprising or unlikely for creatures lacking a capacity for thoughts of a certain sort nevertheless to begin conversing. It is rather that behaviour, even systematic, informative, 'intelligent' behaviour, would not count as *linguistic* behaviour unless it were pursued by a creature with certain aims.

I have described the notion that language is dependent on thought as plausible, and I have tried to indicate briefly and schematically what this dependence might come to. I shall not dwell on the matter, however. My concern, rather, is whether language and thought might somehow be *inter*dependent. Thus, suppose we grant that the use of language presupposes a capacity to entertain thoughts of certain sorts and ask whether the capacity to entertain the required sorts of thought might not itself require a facility with language so that, as Davidson puts it, 'only creatures with a language can think' (1982/1985, p. 474, n. 1).

A conception of this sort is to be distinguished from the notion that thought is conceptually *reducible* to linguistic activity. A behaviourist, for instance, might imagine that thinking is a kind of 'subvocal speech', or that the ascription of a thought to an agent amounts, in Quine's words, to 'something like quotation of one's own imagined verbal response to an imagined situation' (1960, p. 219). The ascription of thoughts to mute creatures, on such a view, has no literal force.

We find ourselves attributing beliefs, wishes, and strivings even to creatures lacking the power of speech, such is our dramatic virtuosity. We project ourselves even into what from his behavior we imagine a mouse's state of mind to have been, and dramatize it as a belief, wish, or striving, verbalized as seems relevant and natural to us in the state thus feigned. (1960, p. 219)

Since, according to Quine, ascriptions of intentional attitudes are eliminable, language, in one respect, outstrips thought.

In the strictest scientific spirit we can report all the behavior, verbal and otherwise, that may underlie our imputations of propositional attitudes, and we may go on to speculate as we please upon the causes and effects of this behavior; but, so long as we do not switch muses, the essentially dramatic idiom of the propositional attitudes will find no place. (1960, p. 219)

Although there is much to be said about an eliminativist stance of this sort, I mention it here simply in order to set it to one side. My concern is with the view that language and thought are interdependent, not the notion that thought *is* talk, or a disposition to talk, imaginatively projected.

I shall set to one side, as well, views of the sort defended by Jerry Fodor (1975, 1987), according to which thinking is conducted in a biologically engineered 'language of thought'. Thoughts, Fodor contends, have an 'internal structure . . . they constitute a language; roughly, the syntactic structure of mental states mirrors the semantic relations among their intentional objects' (1987, p. 138).

The picture is a seductive one. Thoughts demand a *medium*. This is afforded, in ordinary human agents, by the brain. Thoughts, then, are realised as neurological inscriptions that possess a syntax (in virtue of which they exert influence over other thoughts and over behaviour) and a semantics (in virtue of which they are describable as 'mental representations'). The mirroring of semantics by syntax turns the brain into what John Haugeland (1981) calls a *semantic engine*, a device that subserves intentional ends by means of formal operations over symbols in an 'internal code', a language of thought.

According to Fodor, then, thinking trivially implies a capacity for language, though not necessarily a capacity for anything identifiable as overt linguistic behaviour. This is an interesting empirical hypothesis. It has little bearing on the question I want to address here, however. That question most directly concerns, not the medium or vehicle of thought, but the connection between an agent's thoughts and that agent's capacity to produce and understand utterances.[2]

In what follows, then, I shall use 'language' to mean something like 'natural language or overt communicative behavioural pattern'. I am not entirely happy with this form of expression, but my immediate aim is merely to set to one side the notion of a language of thought. The expression 'overt communicative behavioural pattern' is intended simply to capture the possibility of there being patterns of behaviour that, while perhaps falling short of those that exemplify the use of a fully developed natural language, nevertheless might deserve to be called linguistic. I leave open what these might be (see Bennett 1964, 1976 for some suggestions).

We may begin to focus the discussion by considering the idea that the power of thought might be entirely independent of the power of linguistic expression. Such a view is associated with Locke: We find ourselves entertaining thoughts and invent language as an efficient means of conveying these to others.[3] An agent's words 'stand

---

2 I prefer to put the matter this way rather than by reference to natural languages. It is, I think, important to leave open the possibility that thought is linked in some important way to the communicative behaviour of thinkers, even when this behaviour could not be said to constitute, or even approximate, a natural language like English.

3 The thesis I am ascribing to Locke may or may not be his. My concern is conceptual, not historical.

as marks for the *Ideas* within his own Mind, whereby they might be made known to others' (Locke 1690/1978, III, i, 2; here, and in the passage quoted below, the italics are Locke's). Thoughts, on this conception, need not themselves be sentential or language-like. Once we have acquired a facility with language, of course, we may entertain linguistic thoughts. These are in no way special, however. They are merely silent utterances, animated, not by any connection they might bear to outward speech, but by ideas they express. Language, on this view, enjoys no privileged status. Inscriptions and utterances are simply objects in the world arranged so as to induce ideas effectively. 'The *ends of Language in our Discourse with others*, being chiefly these three: *First, To make known* one Man's Thoughts or *Ideas* to another. *Secondly*, To do it *with* as much ease and *quickness*, as is possible; and *Thirdly*, Thereby *to convey* the *Knowledge* of Things' (Locke 1690/1978, III, x, 23).

What of *ideas*? What bestows on *these* the power to represent? They stand, it seems, outside the linguistic order; they incorporate whatever it is in virtue of which inscriptions – covert or overt utterances, for instance – come to function as meaningful signs. Ideas breathe life into what otherwise is semantically inert. They reflect our capacity to deploy images, gestures, diagrams, and utterances representationally. Ideas enable us to make some bits of the world, whatever bits we take up as signs, *transparent*. In using signs, we peer through them to their referents.

One attraction of a conception like Locke's is that it promises to account for an intuitive asymmetry between thought and speech. We seem able to imagine mute creatures, creatures lacking linguistic abilities, who nevertheless enjoy intricate and diverse mental lives. It is another matter, however, to envisage a creature, fluent in some language, yet thoughtless. Thoughts can, but need not, be expressed. An articulate creature, then, one who apparently lacked an inner life but one whose words suited its deeds, would be a creature we should be inclined to regard as possessing the peculiar habit of thinking aloud.

## 2. THOUGHT AND ITS EXPRESSION

Locke's view occupies one end of a continuum of views the opposite end of which encompasses conceptions of thought that emphasise its *social* dimension. On some such conceptions, language is primary, thought derivative.[4] In mastering a natural language, we acquire a capacity to express meanings. This is not a matter of redirecting what is meaningful already, of making public what has heretofore been available only privately. Inner episodes, just in themselves, have no more significance than do marks on paper. In either case, items empty of meaning achieve significance by being suitably embedded in a community of language users. Having got hold of meanings publicly, speakers can invoke these privately, perhaps. But the possibility of meaningful thought rests on thinkers' responsiveness to public conventions and norms. And this responsiveness itself requires the medium of a public language.

Factors motivating views of this sort provide a source of inspiration for behaviourist and other reductionist conceptions of thinking. It is possible, however, to regard them in a rather different light. Suppose we are convinced already that a facility with language demands a capacity for certain distinctive sorts of thoughts. Considerations that point to a dependence of thought on language might then be taken as evidence, not for the possibility of reduction, but as providing support for the notion that language and thought are, at bottom, sides of a single coin. This, at any rate, is how I shall interpret such considerations here.

An uncomplicated route to the establishment of a conceptual link between thought and language is via thought-manifesting *behaviour*. One might reason as follows. There is a nonaccidental connection between the capacity to *entertain* thoughts and the corresponding capacity to *express* those thoughts. Thus, thoughts are sensibly ascribable only to agents who possess the wherewithal to evidence those thoughts in some fashion. The expressive repertoire of nonlinguistic creatures, however, is notably limited. When Spot barks at the foot of a tree, we may feel no compunction in crediting him with the belief that there is a cat in the tree. Even here, however, matters are scarcely straightforward. What, it may be asked, warrants us in describing Spot's belief as a belief about a *cat* and not, say, as a belief about a small animal, or a furry object, or a potential meal? What could lead us to prefer one of these characterisations to another? And why should we imagine that there is any ascriber-independent 'fact of the matter' in such cases?

Even if Spot's behaviour did not immediately give rise to worries

---

4 Stanley Fish (1980, 1989) seems to defend an extreme version of this view.

of this kind, it might be argued that simple beliefs about particulars of the sort we are comfortable attributing to mute creatures ultimately require embedding within a rich assemblage of general beliefs. Davidson, for instance, contends that

we identify thoughts, distinguish between them, describe them for what they are, only as they can be located within a dense network of related beliefs. If we really can intelligibly ascribe single beliefs to a dog, we must be able to imagine how we would decide whether the dog has many other beliefs of the kind necessary for making sense of the first. It seems to me that no matter where we start, we very soon come to beliefs such that we have no idea how to tell whether a dog has them, and yet such that, without them, our confident first attribution looks shaky. (1982/1985, p. 475)

Might Spot, for instance, reasonably be credited with a belief that a cat is in the *tree*?

This would seem impossible unless we suppose the dog has many general beliefs about trees: that they are growing things, that they need soil and water, that they have leaves or needles, that they burn. There is no fixed list of things someone with the concept of a tree must believe, but without many general beliefs there would be no reason to identify a belief as a belief about a tree. (1982/1985, p. 475)

Perhaps indeterminacies of the sort envisaged bother us only when we take to our studies and reflect on them. They are symptoms, however, of a more serious difficulty. We are not inclined, for instance, to ascribe thoughts about the future, or the distant past, or thoughts about spatially remote states of affairs, or thoughts expressing modalities or mixed quantification to a mute creature like Spot. It is unclear, however, that we can coherently regard a creature incapable of such thoughts as capable of 'simpler' thoughts. A belief about the *current* whereabouts of the cat might be thought possible only for a creature equipped to distinguish the present from the past and the future. Beliefs about what is *here*, might make sense only for a creature capable of entertaining thoughts concerning what is *not* here. Belief about what *is* the case might seem out of the question for creatures lacking a full complement of modal concepts. Indeterminacies, present in any case, pile up and threaten altogether to overwhelm the practice of ascribing thoughts to such creatures in any but a metaphorical or 'extended' sense.

We can, of course, make up stories in which it seems credible to attribute beliefs with particular contents to mute creatures on the basis of their behaviour, but these may strike us, on reflection, as

191

unconvincing. Consider just tensed beliefs – beliefs the intentional content of which is most naturally expressed by means of a tensed sentence. What could Spot do *here and now* to evidence the belief that Wayne will return home the day after tomorrow? In accord with a suggestion of D. M. Armstrong's, Spot might behave in a 'restless and expectant' manner the day after tomorrow when Wayne's arrival is imminent (Armstrong 1973, p. 32; cf. Wittgenstein 1953/1968 § 650; Heil 1983, chap. 8). Such behaviour, however, seems at most to express a belief that Wayne's arrival is imminent. Our original question concerned what Spot might do *here and now* to manifest a particular *tensed* belief.

Perhaps such considerations show only that our *evidence* for the presence of a thought, though not the thought itself, depends on a creature's possession of a language. This leaves the thought itself untouched. Granted, so long as Spot remains speechless, we might never have the slightest reason to suppose he believes that master will return in a fortnight or that two is the only even prime. This need not be taken to show that Spot could not secretly harbour these beliefs anyway.

This line of response, however, runs the risk of detaching thoughts from deeds more than seems fair. Thus, it might be thought that creatures without a language would not just be creatures who kept opinions to themselves, but creatures altogether lacking the power to do otherwise, at least for large classes of opinion. Considerations of this sort push in the direction of the view that linguistic ability is a condition on the capacity to enjoy mental states determinate enough to merit our calling them thoughts. If we conjoin such reflections with our previous supposition that linguistic ability itself is founded on a capacity for certain sorts of thought, we are on the way to an appreciation of Davidson's conjecture that thought and language are conceptually interdependent.

This conjecture, it is important to recognise, is that language and thought are mutually dependent, neither is reducible to, or explicable in terms of, the other. The character of the dialectic here makes the point worth emphasising. Most theorists readily accept the notion that a capacity for language entails a capacity for thought. Against this background, anyone hoping to establish an interdependence thesis is bound to focus on the complementary relation. The state of play is analogous to that in which we set out to establish the

192

truth of a biconditional, $p$ if and only if $q$, in circumstances in which 'if $p$ then $q$' is widely accepted: Naturally enough, we concentrate on establishing 'if $q$ then $p$'. This may leave the false impression that we have no interest in the complementary conditional. Similarly, it is easy, amidst Davidson's efforts to demonstrate a conceptual dependence of thought on language, to lose sight of the fact that he is not defending a form of reductionism, but the very opposite. In what follows, then, although I shall concentrate on considerations supporting the notion that thought requires talk, we should not lose sight of the broader thesis of which this is but a single component.

## 3. HOLISM AND 'SEMANTIC OPACITY'

Davidson's conjecture is articulated and defended primarily in two papers, 'Thought and Talk' and 'Rational Animals', published seven years apart (1975/1984, 1982/1985). In both papers assorted considerations are advanced in support of the conclusion that language and thought are conceptually interdependent, although in neither case does Davidson represent these considerations as decisive. Allowing for a certain looseness that an approach of this sort involves, I shall endeavour to reconstruct a line argument from Davidson's hints. Unsurprisingly, the argument, though suggestive, will prove inconclusive. This, in itself, does not show that Davidson is wrong, of course. My own view – to lay my cards on the table – is that, making allowances for an ineliminable softness of focus, the picture Davidson sketches is on the whole apt.

As a preliminary, let us be clear on what Davidson has in mind in linking thought to speech. The thesis is *not*

that each thought depends for its existence on the existence of a sentence that expresses that thought. My thesis is rather that a creature cannot have a thought unless it has a language. In order to be a thinking, rational creature, the creature must be able to express many thoughts, and above all, to be able to interpret the speech and thoughts of others. (1982/1985, p. 477)

This reinforces a point on which I have already insisted, namely, that an attempt to establish the interdependence of language and thought is to be distinguished from eliminativist or reductionist programmes that seek to derive the one from the other: 'Neither language nor thinking can be fully explained in terms of the other, and neither has conceptual priority' (1975/1984, p. 156).

193

Davidson notes that ascriptions of propositional (or as I prefer, intentional) attitudes – belief, desire, intention, and the like – exhibit 'semantic opacity'. 'One way of telling that we are attributing a propositional attitude is by noting that the sentences we use to do the attributing may change from true to false if, in the words that pick out the object of the attitude, we substitute for some referring expression another expression that refers to the same thing' (1982/1985, p. 474). In ascribing to Spot the belief that a cat is in the tree, we might wonder whether the propriety of this ascription would be affected were we to substitute for 'the tree' some other expression that refers to the tree. If not, this would be evidence that our attribution of belief to Spot falls short of literalness. Suppose, for instance, we substitute 'the tallest object in the yard', or 'the only oak on the block', or 'Spot's favourite source of shade', for 'the tree' in our original ascription. How would that affect its truth-value?

A natural first reaction might be that it is just uncommonly difficult to *tell* in such cases. We can be confident that some substitutions are inappropriate ('the object planted in May of 1929'), but there remains an alarmingly spacious range of possibilities within which any choice might seem as good as any other. That being so, perhaps the imputation of belief to Spot in cases of this sort is *de re*, not, as we had assumed, *de dicto*. Perhaps we ascribe to Spot a belief *about* a particular tree while remaining neutral as to how Spot himself 'conceptualises' the tree. Spot, we may now say, believes *of the tree* that it contains a cat. *De re* attributions are semantically transparent, so the substitutivity test does not apply. Supposing that spontaneous attributions of belief to Spot are inevitably *de re*, however, merely represses the original worry. A *de re* ascription presumes the aptness of *some de dicto* ascription. If Spot harbours a belief about the tree, he must do so 'under some description' or other (Davidson 1982/1985, p. 475). We are back, then, with the difficulty of envisaging a sensible description of Spot's mental condition that honours the requirement of semantic opacity. The prospects of success, Davidson contends, are slender.

I intend to take seriously Davidson's formulation of the requirement of semantic opacity. A sentence used to ascribe an intentional attitude '*may* change from true to false' when co-referring terms are substituted for those indicating 'the object of the attitude'. Thus, although I shall equate semantic opacity with *fine-grainedness* or *definiteness* of content, I shall leave open the question whether an opaque content must be in any respect *perfectly* definite, *absolutely* fine-grained. It is unlikely, I think, that all of our thoughts, or even very many of them, are utterly definite in the sense that they could not be captured by distinct but extensionally equivalent propositions or sentences. This is intended, I should add, as a comment on the character of intentional content, not an observation on the indeterminacy of ascription.

To concede the 'intensional test' is, in any case, not to concede very much. Indeed, if we suppose that intentional attitudes, like belief, invariably possess some definite content, it is just a way of sharpening the question at hand. We must still decide whether there is any reason to doubt that a mute creature like Spot could entertain thoughts, thoughts satisfying the requirement of semantic opacity.

Davidson's position is that semantic opacity can be had only by connecting thoughts to utterances. He advances two distinguishable, though ultimately convergent, lines of argument to this conclusion. The first appeals to holistic considerations of the sort introduced already, and moves from these to the contention that, since we could never have grounds for ascribing the requisite *background* beliefs to mute creatures like Spot, we could never be warranted in ascribing to such creatures any thoughts at all.

The argument, as applied to the case of belief, has the following form. Ascriptions of belief exhibit semantic opacity. This requires that we regard beliefs as possessing some definite intentional content. The possession of a belief with a definite content, however, presupposes 'endless' further beliefs. If we are entitled to ascribe any belief to a creature, then, it must be true, as well, that we are entitled to ascribe to that creature these further beliefs. As Davidson puts it, 'the intrinsically holistic character of the propositional attitudes makes the distinction between having any and having none dramatic' (1982/1985, p. 471). A creature to whom we should be warranted in ascribing the relevant background beliefs, however, is one possessing a sophisticated behavioural repertoire. Only linguistic behaviour exhibits the sort of complex pattern that might warrant such ascriptions. We could never have reason, then, to ascribe thoughts to a mute creature, to a creature lacking a language. Schematically, the argument looks something like Figure 6.1.

Suppose Davidson were right. Suppose that, if it makes sense to ascribe to Spot a belief about some tree, it must make sense to

$$\text{Semantic Opacity} \rightarrow \text{Definite Content} \rightarrow \text{Holism} \rightarrow \text{Complex Patterns of Behaviour} \rightarrow \text{Language}$$

Figure 6.1

ascribe to him general beliefs about trees ('that they are growing things, that they need soil and water, that they have leaves or needles, that they burn'). And suppose such beliefs could be manifested only via linguistic utterances. Even if we grant all this, we are left, not with the conclusion that Spot, or any creature like Spot, necessarily lacks thoughts, but only that, if Spot has thoughts, he has lots of them, and this is something for which we are unlikely ever to have decisive evidence.[5]

Davidson, however, appears to draw a much stronger conclusion:

> From what has been said about the dependence of beliefs on other beliefs . . . it is clear that a very complex pattern of behavior must be observed to justify the attribution of a single thought. Or, more accurately, there has to be good reason to believe there is such a complex pattern of behavior. *And unless there is actually such a complex pattern of behavior, there is no thought.* (1982/1985, p. 476; emphasis added)

The italicised sentence in this quotation seems obviously unwarranted. We can agree on the need for 'complex patterns of behavior' for the justification of belief attributions, without agreeing that, in the absence of this behaviour, there is no belief. Even if we granted the stronger conclusion, however, it requires another argument to show that the 'complex pattern of behavior' must be *linguistic* behaviour.

Leaving aside the latter point for the moment, it is tempting here to imagine that Davidson is mistakenly — or perhaps deliberately — conflating an epistemic claim about what we could know or have reason to believe, with a substantive claim concerning what might be the case. I think it unlikely that Davidson has slipped up here, nor is it likely that he is opting for some form of verificationism or for any other antirealist conception of the intentional attitudes. The

5 Or, at any rate, evidence in excess of whatever evidence we have for the target ('foreground') belief.

Intentional Attitudes → Belief → Concept of Belief → Membership in a Speech Community

Figure 6.2

quoted passage represents only one strand of Davidson's argument, a strand, as I shall suggest later, for which a plausible, nonverificationist, realist reading can be given. Meanwhile, I shall concentrate on a second, more tortured, line of argument that follows on the heels of the first.

A recurring theme in Davidson's writings is that 'belief – indeed *true* belief – plays a central role among the propositional attitudes':

Not only does each belief require a world of further beliefs to give it content and identity, but every other propositional attitude depends for its particularity on a similar world of beliefs. In order to believe the cat went up the oak tree I must have many true beliefs about cats and trees, this cat and this tree, the place, appearance, and habits of cats and trees, and so on; but the same holds if I wonder whether the cat went up the oak tree, fear that it did, hope that it did, wish that it had, or intend to make it so. (1982/1985, p. 475)

A creature's possession of intentional attitudes, on this view, depends on its harbouring 'endless interlocking beliefs'. These create 'a logical and epistemic space' within which thoughts are located, and with reference to which they exhibit an identifiable content (1975/1984, p. 157). Since 'without belief there are no other propositional attitudes'(1982/1985, p. 478), we may safely concentrate on 'conditions for belief' in assessing the relation of thought to language. If belief is possible only for a creature endowed with a language, then, given the pivotal character of belief, only creatures possessing a language could entertain any thoughts at all.

The structure of the ensuing argument is deceptively linear. Intentional attitudes require a 'dense network' of beliefs. 'In order to have a belief, it is necessary to have the concept of belief', however. And 'in order to have the concept of belief one must have language', that is, one must be a member of a 'speech community' (1982/1985, p. 478). This progression of ideas is represented schematically in Figure 6.2. The progression is, I believe, best approached at a simple level, then elaborated.

197

## 4. REPRESENTATION AND
## SELF-CONSCIOUSNESS

Davidson contends that 'in order to think one must have the concept of a thought, and so language is required' (1982/1985, p. 478).

This is not to claim that all thinking is self-conscious, or that whenever we think that $p$ we must be aware that $p$, or believe that we believe that $p$, or think that we think that $p$. My claim is rather this: In order to have any propositional attitude at all, it is necessary to have the concept of belief, to have a belief about some belief. (1982/1985, p. 479)

What conceivable reason could Davidson have for this remarkable claim? Why should anyone think it likely that belief is possible only for creatures that possess – and deploy – a concept of belief?

Imagine a device capable of registering aspects of its surroundings. The device might be a scientific instrument, a computing machine, or a sentient creature. We may think of such a device as 'representing' states of affairs in its vicinity at least in a certain weak sense: Various of its internal states are nonaccidentally correlated with worldly goings-on, and the device is arranged so as to exploit these correlations.[6] The thermostat in my hallway might serve as an example of a simple mechanism that satisfies these conditions. Certain of its internal states – changes in the alignment of a bimetal strip – are reliably correlated with changes in air temperature. A thermostat is designed to capitalise on this correlation by incorporating a switch capable of turning the furnace on and off in response to variations in ambient temperature.[7]

It should be clear that in describing a thermostat as *representing*,

---

6 See Dretske (1981, 1988); Millikan (1984, 1989). Again, the correlations are non-accidental, lawlike. We could describe a device of the sort envisaged as *containing* representations of its surroundings, though this need only mean that it represents those surroundings – and not, for instance, that inside the device there are bits or items identifiable as representations. Martin and Pfeifer (1986) argue that representation or 'directedness' of this sort, indeed representation that satisfies the traditional conditions on intentionality, is abundant in natural objects and artifacts. It is, they hold, a common feature of our world, not a distinctive feature of intelligent creatures.

7 One might worry that an appeal to an artifact designed for a certain purpose by intelligent agents begs important questions here. The worry is misplaced. Thermostats might grow on trees like coconuts. We might then play the part of Mother Nature in selecting and cultivating only those naturally occurring specimens featuring components that reliably covaried with air temperature and installing them in our houses.

say, air temperature, we need only imagine that (1) its states are appropriately correlated with air temperature, that they reflect temperature changes, and that (2) they serve some control function or other that exploits this correlation. This is not to say that thermostats possess intentionality, much less that they think or have beliefs and desires. Nor is it, however, merely to note that thermostats are representational *for us*. In this respect, at least, they differ from purely conventional significatory devices: numerals, alphabetic inscriptions, symbols on maps, the gestures of an aggrieved motorist. Their representational characteristics, such as they are, depend exclusively on the existence of perfectly natural mechanical regularities. We say unselfconsciously that dark clouds mean rain, smoke means fire. But this is just to say there is a certain relation, a particular sort of correlation, between dark clouds and rain, smoke and fire, in virtue of which these things point beyond themselves in ways we can easily appreciate.

A word is in order concerning the role of requirement (2) in the characterisation above. The aim here is not to advance a theory of representation. Nevertheless, it is possible to say something about plausible constraints on any such theory. Without (2), or something like it, we should be obliged to count too many things as instances of representation. The metal bell on my telephone, for instance, expands and contracts minutely with changes in temperature of the air in the vicinity of my desk. Does this expansion and contraction *represent* changes in local air temperature? Does the bell's being in a certain state now represent the air's being at a certain temperature now? We might be prepared to say so, but only if we discovered that the bell's minuscule expansions and contractions somehow played a role in the mechanism of which it is a component, that the mechanism in some way took advantage of – exploited – the correlations between the condition of the bell and the temperature of the air.

The liquid in an ordinary alcohol thermometer is said to represent temperature because *we* make use of the correlations it exhibits in judging the temperature. The equally systematic correlations exhibited by the water in my neighbor's birdbath are not so used; hence there is no reason to regard the changing water levels as representational. The moral is not that, to count as a representation, something must be a representation *for* some intelligent observer. Rather, it is that we seem inclined to regard something as represen-

199

tational even in the weak sense intended here only if it plays a representational role of *some* sort, only if it functions in the system of which it is a part – a system that may include *us* as an essential component – representationally. And we can describe a thing as functioning representationally if at least part of the explanation for its role in the system appeals to its representational character.[8]

Suppose, then, that we permit this line of representational talk even for lowly thermostats. What, if anything, entitles us to resist the ascription of *thoughts* to such devices? There are various possibilities. Perhaps creatures to whom thoughts are ascribable are not merely those harbouring representational states, not even those whose behaviour is largely controlled by such states. An ordinary thermostat might plausibly be thought to satisfy both these conditions. The having of thoughts is not merely a matter of representing, however, but of *appreciating* in some way that this is what one is doing, of exhibiting the capacity to manipulate and act on representations qua *representations*. An appreciation of this sort is involved, for instance, in one's comprehending a distinction between representations and represented states of affairs, between one's subjective impression of the world and the world as it is independently of that impression, between *opinion* and *truth*.

A thermostat fails to have thoughts, though perhaps not because it fails to represent its surroundings, but because it altogether lacks the capacity to recognise that this is what it is doing, the capacity, that is, to grasp a distinction between the world, or an aspect of the world, as it is *taken* to be and the world, or that aspect of it, as it *is*.[9] The capacity to appreciate that one's thoughts are in this sense representational enables one to act not merely on the basis of representations but also to act on the basis of these representations *being representations*. The actions of thinking creatures reflect, perhaps, not merely *what* they think but also that they *think* it – and that those

---

8 Thus, although we feel no compunction in saying that dark clouds mean rain or that smoke means fire, we do not takes clouds and smoke to *represent* rain and fire, respectively.

9 A thermostat is excludable from the class of thinkers on holistic grounds alone if Davidson is right. Bennett (1976, §§ 21–22), too, would exclude thermostats, though for somewhat different reasons: Intentional properties are ascribable to systems only when those systems exhibit *patterns* of behaviour not capturable via 'lower-level' generalisations (cf. Dennett 1987). Part of what I hope to show here is that such considerations are, at bottom, connected with the requirement of self-consciousness.

thoughts may be, in various ways, infelicitous. You believe that the ice is safe, but you are in a position to recognise, as well, that this is *a belief*, something you could easily be wrong in thinking.

We have a distinction, then, a potentially important distinction, between creatures or systems the behaviour of which is partly determined by, hence partly explicable in terms of, representational characteristics, and creatures or systems capable of appreciating representational characteristics qua representational. Why should we imagine that only creatures of the latter sort, only those capable of self-consciousness, are properly described as having thoughts? Consider ordinary honeybees. Honeybee behaviour is explicable partly by reference to internal, behaviour-controlling states that are (1) at least weakly representational and (2) function as they do in part *because* of their representational character. Do the honeybees have thoughts? If we follow Davidson and suppose that thoughts exhibit semantic opacity, we should be hard-pressed to pin down honeybee representings to some particular intentional content. Do honeybee 'thoughts' concern food, possible food, the source of a particular sort of odor correlated with food, the presence of a chemical substance of type $F$, or *what*? A decision here may reflect features of honeybees' circumstances salient to us, but not to the honeybees.

The more we learn about honeybees, of course, the more we narrow the class of plausible candidates for what might count as the intentional content of their 'thoughts'. In the end, however, there may remain scores of options, and no particular reason to fasten on any one of these while excluding the rest. If we take seriously the intensional test, the requirement of semantic opacity, we must suppose that thoughts feature some definite content, however, a content constrained by facts about honeybees or their circumstances.[10] This is just what honeybee representational states seem to lack.

Imagine now that a certain species of honeybee were discovered to have a capacity for self-consciousness: Honeybees of this species sometimes reflected on the contents of their own representations and adjusted their behaviour accordingly. Were that so, our representational ascriptions would be constrained, not merely by honeybee-states-to-world correlations, but by the honeybees' own

10 A reminder: Definite content is content the description of which satisfies the test for semantic opacity as formulated in § 3 above.

second-order representations. The consequences of this shift to second-order representations are, I think, momentous. Suppose that, on encountering a food source, a honeybee goes into state $R$, a state we should regard as representational. Following Davidson, let us grant that the content of $R$ is essentially indefinite; ascriptions of $R$ to honeybees fails the intensional test. Once we suppose that a honeybee reflects on its own representational states, however, definite content is forced into the picture. Reflections on thoughts about food sources differ – semantically, of course, but also in their epistemic and behavioural implications – from reflections on thoughts about the presence of a chemical of type $F$. The idea is not that $R$ features some determinate content all along, content that is revealed only once the honeybees acquire a capacity for reflection. The idea is rather that $R$ functions as a state with a definite content only insofar as it belongs to a *system* in which its having a definite content plays some identifiable role or other. Only in such systems does intentionality blossom.

This idea extends our earlier observations concerning the character of representational states generally. I contended that a state could be regarded as weakly representational only if it subserved one or another control function partly in virtue of its representational character. This brings representational content into the picture in the sense that an explanation of a particular system's operation might advert to the representational character of certain of its components. Descriptions of these components need not satisfy the requirement of semantic opacity, however. The explanations we offer of the system's operation require only that representational states covary nonaccidentally with represented features of the world however these are 'conceptualised', 'described', or picked out. This is all that is required for a system of the sort in question to work properly, or to behave adaptively. It is only when we introduce second-order representational capacities into a system that anything approximating the fine-grained character of intentionality is achieved.

What would it take to provide my thermostat with self-consciousness, with an appreciation of its representational states *as* representational? Not, it would seem, merely the addition of a further representational mechanism sensitive to – capable of monitoring – the first. A thermostat might register fluctuations in ambient air temperature by means of changes in a bimetal strip, and an added sensor might register the state of this strip. In doing so, however, the sensor would not thereby incorporate a second-order representation. It would register the states of something that happened to have a representational role, to be sure, but it would not register those states qua representations. The condition of the bimetal strip represents ambient air temperature, and the sensor's condition represents the state of the bimetal strip. But we should, on this basis alone, have no reason to include the 'content' of the state of the bimetal strip in a description of the 'content' of the sensor's representational condition.

The representational character of the imagined sensor, if any, depends not merely on the holding of correlations between its states and the condition of other components in the system, but on the system's *use* of these correlations. The sensor might be deployed, for instance, merely to monitor changes in the bimetal strip as a way of keeping track of the system's level of activity. A more interesting possibility arises if the sensor is attached to a switch that controls an auxiliary device, an air-humidifier, for instance, designed to operate in concert with the furnace. Since changes in the sensor covary with changes in the bimetal strip, they covary as well with fluctuations in air temperature. Might an arrangement of this sort give us reason to regard states of the sensor as possessing representational content that includes the representational content of states of the bimetal strip?

I doubt it. It is more plausible, surely, to regard a sensor so arranged as simply registering air temperature. The sensor's condition is correlated with air temperature, and it is this correlation that is exploited by the system to which it belongs. Admittedly, the correlation is achieved via a link to the bimetal strip. More is required, however, if the sensor is to register the 'content' of states of the bimetal strip. Its registering that content, and its thereby endowing the system with a measure of self-consciousness, must figure appropriately in the operation of the system. We would be entitled to regard states of the sensor as having a second-order representational character, I think, only if we had reason to believe that the system possessed a capacity to exploit *fine-grained* representations, representations exhibiting semantic opacity. Against this background, Davidson may be seen as offering the conjecture that only a system capable of interpreting speech could satisfy this condition.

Despite the examples above, one might wonder how the addition of second-order representational capacities is supposed to advance matters. After all, if first-order representations by themselves fail the intensional test, why should the addition of representations of *these* representations make any difference? Why should second-order representations be any less prone to semantic indefiniteness?

I have suggested that there is a vast difference between a second-order representational capacity and a capacity merely to 'monitor' some first-order representational condition. A genuine second-order representation includes in its content first-order representational *content*. In this respect a second-order representation *settles* the issue of definiteness. A representational state that failed to do so would not be a *second*-order state, a representation *of* a representation. A system that incorporates second-order representations, then, necessarily possesses fine-grained intentional capacities, capacities that reflect the 'intensional' character of its representational components.

Consider again the representational character of my thermostat's bimetal strip. We are supposing that this is semantically transparent, that, while weakly representational, it lacks a definite content. We can, of course, *describe* the bimetal strip as registering air temperature, but we might, with equal justice, describe it as registering mean molecular kinetic energy. The distinction is one to which the system incorporating the bimetal strip is oblivious. In introducing a second-order representational capacity, however, matters change dramatically. A second-order representation necessarily assigns a *content* to some first-order representation. In the present case, that would mean *pinning down* content exhibited by the condition of the bimetal strip. Providing the system with this capacity is not merely a matter of providing it with more elaborate or more finely-tuned sensors, but of providing it with a capacity to *make use of* fine-grained, semantically opaque representational characteristics. A system with this capacity might, of necessity, turn out to be complex indeed.

I shall say more about such systems presently. First, however, it will be useful to examine a second, related reason to be sympathetic to the view that genuine thought requires a capacity for self-reflection. In Chapter 5, I suggested that our ability to entertain thoughts includes a capacity for self-consciousness. We do not, as it were, first produce thoughts then set out to discover what these concern. Davidson's contention that thought requires second-order representational capacities could be reexpressed in terms of this observation. Any creature to which we have reason to ascribe thoughts with a definite content, semantically opaque thoughts, is a creature we should have reason to regard as self-conscious.[11]

## 5. SUBJECTIVITY, OBJECTIVITY, AND TRUTH

Let us suppose that something like this is at least approximately correct. The having of thoughts, the possessing of representational states exhibiting semantic opacity, includes a capacity for self-consciousness, second-order thought. We are still only half way to Davidson's conclusion that thinking presupposes language. Earlier, I suggested that the reasoning exhibits this structure set out in Figure 6.2. We are granting, at least provisionally, that the intentional attitudes require the having of beliefs, and that these, in turn, require second-order thoughts – 'beliefs about beliefs'.

The move from second-order belief to the concept of belief is, in this context, transparent. In possessing a concept, one possesses a capacity of a certain sort. If I possess the concept of a tree, I possess the capacity to entertain thoughts in which trees figure. I possess, as well, in concert with other capacities, a capacity to distinguish trees perceptually, to produce utterances about trees, and so on. One may believe something *of* a tree, without having the concept of a tree, perhaps, but then one must represent the tree under some *other* concept – the concept of an object, a living thing, an obstacle, a provider of shade. Davidson's position as I am construing it does not, at bottom, require that creatures capable of thought possess the concept of belief per se, only that they possess a generic concept of *representation*.[12] The difference is, for present purposes, inessential. What *is* important is the move between the claim that the concept of belief (or the concept of a thought or representation) is a prerequisite of thought, and the contention that the possession of this con-

---

11 Although I have expressed it epistemically – in terms of reasons one might have for ascriptions – the point is not exclusively, or even primarily, an epistemic one. It is intended to bear on what might be required for a creature to *be* a thinker, a possessor of semantically opaque representational characteristics. For a different, though related, defense of the requirement of self-consciousness, see Van Gulick (1988).

12 Davidson also states the requirement by reference to 'the concept of a thought' (1982/1985, p. 478). I take 'thoughts' to be generic intentional states.

cept is possible only for creatures with a capacity for language, indeed only for members of a linguistic community.[13]

Davidson's reasoning, I think, leans on the idea that representations in general, and beliefs in particular, include in their concept the possibility of *mis*representation, error. The concept of representation incorporates some notion of fitting, satisfying, *being true*. Such notions, in turn, find application only in concert with their complements: failing to fit, failing to be satisfied, being false. Consider, then, what is involved in a conception of truth and falsehood. Such a conception presumes some notion of *objective* correctness, some standard of aptness transcending one's subjective impression of correctness. According to Davidson, however, a conception of this sort is possible only for members of a speech community, only for interpreters. In this way we might connect the idea that thinkers necessarily possess a belief concept and the seemingly unrelated idea that thinkers must be interpreters, hence members of a speech community. How might such a connection be established?

First, the possibility of belief, or thought generally, is taken to depend on the concept of belief, the concept, that is, of a representation that might be true or false. A conception of truth and falsehood includes some notion of an objective, public domain.[14] And this notion, according to Davidson, is possible only for an interpreter.

Someone cannot have a belief unless he understands the possibility of being mistaken, and this requires grasping the contrast between truth and error –

13 Although Davidson formulates it this way ('a creature must be a member of a speech community if it is to have the concept of belief', 1975/1984, p. 170), I am construing the requirement in an especially weak sense. Possession of the concept of belief need not presuppose membership in a community that *shares* a language, but only membership in a community of speakers who sometimes interpret one another's utterances. I leave open (for now; see § 6 below) the question whether a single individual might, under appropriate circumstances, count as a limiting instance of a 'speech community'. In any case, Davidson holds that 'what is essential . . . is the idea of an interpreter, someone who understands the utterances of another' (1975/1984, p. 157).

14 One might distinguish the requirement of *objectivity* from a requirement of *publicity*. Worlds containing solitary individuals, or those comprising individuals aware only of their own conscious states, apparently leave room for objectivity but not publicity. Suppose that what I know is limited to my own conscious experiences. It is nevertheless 'objectively' true of me that I have or lack this or that conscious experience, though these truths need not be public in the usual sense. At any rate, an argument is needed to show that these apparent possibilities are *only* apparent. I shall, for the moment, bracket such considerations.

true belief and false belief. But this contrast . . . can emerge only in the context of interpretation, which alone forces us to the idea of an objective, public truth. (Davidson 1975/1984, p. 170; cf. Bennett 1985, pp. 623–25)

Why should we agree? Again, it is a long, and somewhat gappy, story. Consider once more the phenomenon of self-consciousness, a system's appreciation of its own representational character. What is included in such an appreciation? To simplify matters, consider what might be involved in a case in which I reflect on the content of a map. In recognising that the map *has* a content, that it is *representational*, I perforce acknowledge a distinction between the map's content, what it *says*, and the situation it purports to represent. My grasp of a representation qua representation depends on my grasping it as potentially inappropriate; and my having a conception of correctness or error requires that I distinguish in some fashion between the way things are and the way they are represented as being.[15]

Given that belief is possible only for creatures possessing the concept of belief, then, our having beliefs might plausibly be thought to entail our having the capacity, at least in typical cases, to recognise that we have got it wrong, to have some conception of truth and error. What might this encompass? At the very least it seems to require that we apprehend a distinction between the way things are and the way we *take* them to be, between an independently persisting domain onto which our thoughts are projected, and the character of those thoughts. The distinction in question is involved in the very *conception* of representation. Such a conception incorporates a distinction between *what* is represented, represented states of affairs perhaps, and their representation, a distinction that brings with it the notions of potential correctness and incorrectness, truth and falsehood. Although ordinary representations are satisfied or not, true or false, a representation or representational state, considered just in itself, affords no distinction between truth and presumed truth. A representation says only, 'This is how things

15 One worry about such a view is that it seems not to apply to patent necessary truths. My belief that $2 + 3 = 5$, for instance, may be one I recognise *as* a belief, *as* a representational state, without thereby recognising that the proposition $2 + 3 = 5$ might be false. One who hoped to defend a strong connection between our concept of a representation and a concept of truth and falsity might insist that a creature whose representational repertoire consisted entirely of obvious necessary truths would not be in a position to develop a concept of representation. I am grateful to Alfred Mele for the example.

stand' (Wittgenstein 1921/1960, § 4.022). In the case of belief, for instance, my belief that $p$ is, as it were, the belief that $p$ is true. The 'as it were' here is important. That $p$ is true is not part of the *content* of the belief that $p$ – the belief that $p$ differs from the belief that $p$ *is true* – but simply a feature of its mode of presentation. 'A creature may react to the world in complex ways without entertaining any propositions. . . . Yet none of this, no matter how successful by my standards, shows that the creature commands the subjective-objective contrast as required by belief' (Davidson 1982/1985, p. 480).

Bearing in mind these admittedly impressionistic remarks, we might describe systems capable only of simple, first-order representations or representational states as being 'truth-blind'. Their being representations, hence being true or false, is, in the case of systems that possess representational characteristics but lack self-consciousness, *invisible* to those systems. We have supposed that thermostats lack beliefs, not because they fail to contain, and perhaps even 'act' on, representations of their surroundings, but because their operation in no way depends on their appreciating that this is what they are doing. The representational character of the bimetal strip coiled inside the thermostat mounted on the wall in my hallway is invisible to the thermostat itself.

Davidson suggests that the self-consciousness requisite for genuine thought manifests itself in the phenomenon of *surprise*.

Suppose I believe there is a coin in my pocket. I empty my pocket and find no coin. I am surprised. Clearly enough I could not be surprised (though I could be startled) if I did not have beliefs in the first place. And perhaps it is equally clear that having a belief, at least one of the sort I have taken for my example, entails the possibility of surprise. If I believe I have a coin in my pocket something might happen that would change my mind. But surprise involves a further step. It is not enough that I first believe there is a coin in my pocket, and after emptying my pocket I no longer have this belief. Surprise requires that I be aware of a contrast between what I believe and what I come to believe. Such awareness, however, is a belief about a belief: If I am surprised, then among other things I come to believe my original belief was false. (1982/1985, p. 479)

Whether every instance of surprise involves second-order beliefs is debatable. Nevertheless, Davidson insists that 'one cannot have a general stock of beliefs of the sort necessary for having any beliefs at all without being subject to surprises that involve beliefs about the correctness of one's own beliefs' (Davidson 1982/1985, p. 479).[16]

Surprise requires familiarity with the distinction between truth and error, between how one *takes* things to be and how they *are*. Reflect for a moment on what is included in the capacity to employ the concepts of truth and error. So long as I consider only my own case, the idea of error, or its complement, truth, need never occur to me. My representational states present themselves to me in a 'truth-blind' mode. They *possess* truth-values, perhaps they *are* true or false, but their possession of truth-values, hence their functioning for me as representations, might remain invisible to me. It is only when I begin observing others and ascribing thoughts to them in the course of interpreting their utterances that space is created for the concepts of truth and error. Only in such circumstances does the notion of an objective domain make an appearance, only in such circumstances am I obliged to distinguish false from true representations. This, at any rate, is one way Davidson's reasoning might be thought to go. What can be said in its favour?

Consider a case in which I falsely represent some state of affairs, the strength of the ice on a frozen pond, for instance. Partly as a result of my representing the ice in this way, I attempt to skate on it, and it gives way beneath me. As a result of this misfortune, my representation of the strength of the ice no doubt changes. It may do *that*, however, without my having to reflect on my former representation. I can, in this way, like the thermostat, be guided by representations, even modify the content of those representations intelligently in response to changes in my surroundings, without ever considering those representations for what they are, without ever considering them qua representations. Their representational character might remain, as it does in the case of a thermostat or a honeybee, invisible to the system that exploits it.

At this juncture a connection could be made with the representa-

---

16 Davidson goes on to conclude that 'surprise about some things is a necessary and sufficient condition of thought in general' (1982/1985, p. 479). This is unlikely. It is possible to imagine an agent – Mr. Magoo comes to mind – whose beliefs, even when false, never result in the sort of calamity that might induce surprise. It seems possible as well to conceive of an omniscient being – an 'omniscient interpreter', perhaps – whose beliefs are invariably true and who, in consequence, is incapable ever of being surprised; see, e.g., Davidson (1986).

tional states of others. There is no question, it might be urged, of my finding a distinction between truth and error, hence any notion of representation, just by attending to my own case. It is only when I turn to *others* that a *concept* of representation necessarily comes into play. If, subsequent to my mishap, I observe *you* venturing onto thin ice, I can make sense of your behaviour only by taking you to be falsely representing its strength. (The ice is thin. What accounts for your stepping out onto it, then? One possibility: You mistakenly represent the ice as being safe.) Once in place, the concept of representation can be applied to my own case. But the concept will only come to *be* in place if I have a conception of an objective world, a *shared,* intersubjective domain concerning which my beliefs, like yours, might be true or false. The concept of such a domain is the concept of something objective capable of being represented from distinct subjective perspectives. In recognising that I occupy one such perspective, I recognise the possibility of others. This, Davidson holds, is imaginable only for one capable of the ascription of representations to others, and *this* ultimately hinges on a capacity for understanding another's speech.

A deeper point lurks in the background of this discussion. It might be argued that my possession of a conception of myself is impossible in the absence of a conception of others, a conception of representers distinct from myself who share with me an objective world. In the *Tractatus,* Wittgenstein remarks that 'solipsism, when its implications are followed out strictly, coincides with pure realism. The self of solipsism shrinks to a point without extension, and there remains the reality co-ordinated with it' (1921/1960 § 5.64). A concept of self includes, perhaps, the conception of a world distinct from the self in which the self is located and concerning which the self reflects. If Davidson is right, then the conception of an objective world is the conception of an intersubjective domain, a realm capable of being represented by others. Our concepts of the I, the other, and a shared world are of a piece, a relationship mirrored in our concept of representation.

## 6. WHAT HAS LANGUAGE TO DO WITH IT?

This, or something like it, may be a part of what Davidson has in mind, but it cannot be the whole story. Perhaps it is plausible to suppose that, in setting out to interpret another's utterances I must have recourse to the notion of a shared, objective world, a domain to which I take those utterances to refer. Perhaps Davidson is right in claiming that a concept of representation cannot be detached from the concept of a shareable intersubjective world. Still, questions remain. First, why should we imagine that the latter concept requires my *actually interacting* with agents like myself? What would prevent me from arriving at the notion of an objective world by reflecting on *possible* agents, for instance, or on my own case over time? Second, even if we must have other agents in the picture, why should we grant that my only access to their representational condition is via *language*? I may discover what you believe by interpreting your utterances, but I can also come to appreciate those beliefs by observing your nonlinguistic behaviour – or so it seems.

I shall postpone discussion of the first of these questions and concentrate on the second. This, I think, obliges us to reconsider our earlier assessment of belief manifestation. If we accept broad holistic constraints on belief and consider, in light of these constraints, what might license the ascription of belief to a given creature, we may be persuaded that only linguistic behaviour could exhibit a sufficiently fine-grained structure: 'Unless there is behaviour that can be interpreted as speech, the evidence will not be adequate to justify the fine distinctions we are used to making in the attribution of thoughts' (1975/1984, p. 164). Davidson provides an example in the case of someone who expresses a preference 'by moving directly to achieve his end, rather than by saying what he wants' (1975/1984, p. 163). The difficulty in a case of this sort is to constrain the possibilities.

A man who takes an apple rather than a pear when offered both may be expressing a preference for what is on his left rather than his right, what is red rather than yellow, what is seen first, or judged more expensive. Repeated tests may make some readings of his action more plausible, but the problem will remain how to determine when he judges two objects of choice to be identical. (1975/1984, p. 163)

In § 3 I noted that even if we accept the notion that we must rely on linguistic utterances in deciding on agents' states of mind, this might be thought to be no more than an epistemic point about what could count as evidence that someone believes or prefers something. In the present context, however, this is precisely what is at issue. We are supposing that a conception of objectivity requires that we be in a position to ascribe thoughts – representational

211

characteristics – to others. The question now is whether this might be possible only via the interpretation of utterances, so that 'the concept of intersubjective truth depends on communication in the full linguistic sense' (1982/1985, p. 480).

The notion that only utterances could afford the fine-grained structure required for the attribution of thought, might suggest that there must be some intrinsic structural difference between linguistic and nonlinguistic behaviour. This, however, is unlikely. Non-linguistic activities are often complex and highly structured; utter-ances can be structurally unremarkable. If Davidson's contention were that utterances, considered just as instances of behaviour, pos-sess a built-in complexity and organisation absent from nonlinguis-tic stretches of behaviour, he would certainly be wrong. Regarded purely as behaviour, utterances are nothing special. How, then, are we to understand the emphasis on linguistic deeds?

In delivering an utterance, I set out to produce something that possesses a definite sense, one that I can reasonably expect my audience to recover. The recovery of sense, interpretation, is, ac-cording to Davidson, a matter of bringing to bear a 'theory of truth' (see, e.g., Davidson 1973/1984). A theory of truth provides, among other things, a systematic, projectable mapping of sentences uttered onto sentences understood. You understand my utterances, then, only if you possess a theory of truth that assigns a meaning, not merely to utterances I have thus far produced within your hearing, but to utterances I would or might produce under widely different circumstances.

We need not, or at any rate I shall not, pursue the details of Davidson's theory of interpretation.[17] The line of reasoning we are now considering does not depend on those details. Davidson could be wrong about meaning and truth, but right about the relation of speech to thought. I shall, then, try to motivate Davidson's claims about utterances while remaining neutral as to particular concep-tions of meaning.

The production of an utterance is the production of something in part because – for the reason that – it expresses a definite, recover-able intentional content. There are, as we have seen, grounds for supposing that productive capacities of this sort go hand in hand with interpretive capacities. We have seen, as well, that there is

17 The interested reader should consult Davidson (1984).

some reason to think that only a creature with the capacity for self-consciousness, a capacity to reflect on the contents of its own representations, is capable of thought. This is so, at least, if we grant that thoughts necessarily exhibit semantic opacity. We noted that a system's capacity for self-conscious thought must be reflected somehow in the system's operations. What sort of system is one in which semantically opaque representings have a part?

Davidson's answer is that any such system is one capable of generating and interpreting utterances, a system possessing *linguistic* prowess. This is not a matter merely of producing and reacting to gestures or sounds.[18] It is a matter of being disposed to produce and react to gestures or sounds in accord with something like a theory of meaning, a scheme that allocates definite, semantically opaque, intentional content to utterances. The idea is not that we extract intentionality by endowing intelligent creatures with theories of meaning that they then apply in sensible ways. Presumably the possession of a theory is possible only for a system already capable of sophisticated representational feats. The idea rather is that only a system the operation of which exhibits the kind of structure implied by such a theory is a system in which semantically opaque representations make an appearance. On Davidson's view, a system of this sort is necessarily capable of producing and interpreting utterances.

Suppose we grant that a capacity for semantically opaque representation itself requires the ability to ascribe representations. Why must these ascribed representations themselves exhibit semantic opacity? True enough, in taking an apple, you might be expressing any one of many distinct preferences. Still, I can grasp your behaviour as expressing some definite preference or other even when I am in no position to say what precisely that preference is. Similarly, so long as you remain silent, I may be unable to discover exactly what you think, but this need not prevent me from regarding you as harbouring some determinate thought or other. My status as a thinker may hinge on my having a capacity to ascribe representations, but it is not obvious that these ascriptions must themselves be fine-grained. Indeed, it might seem that our ascriptive talents could be confined to the identification of the representational characteris-

---

18 I do not mean to limit utterances to gestures and sounds; I use these merely as examples. See Vonnegut (1973, pp. 58–59).

tics of thermostats or honeybees. Thermostat representations may lack the definiteness of thoughts, but if all we require is the possession of the concept of representation, something capable of truth or falsehood, this might be enough.

The envisaged possibility rests on a confusion, however. The concept of representation we apply to thermostats and honeybees is not conceptually detachable from a fine-grained concept of representation. The concept of a representational state that lacks semantic opacity is simply a degenerate or recessive version of the concept of representation that includes this property. I should be in a position to ascribe representations to thermostats only insofar as I am in a position to consider belief-like, semantically opaque representations. If Davidson is right, I am in this position only if I am an interpreter, an agent equipped to understand the utterances of others. Once I have a relatively comprehensive grasp of your intentional attitudes, of course, I may be able to decipher your actions without interrogating you. This is possible, however, only given a sufficiently rich conceptual framework, one that includes as an essential component a theory of meaning for your utterances. Such a theory, Davidson holds, requires my associating the meanings of actual and possible utterances with sentences I understand. My capacity to ascribe representational states to you presupposes my use of a language, a representational system with determinate meanings.

## 7. INTERPRETATION, TRIANGULATION, OBJECTIVITY

Pet owners are apt to be put off by the suggestion that thoughts are ascribable only to interpreters. Such a view apparently obliges us to withhold the ascription of beliefs – and thoughts generally – to mute creatures, to pets and infants, for instance. This looks on the face of it unreasonable. We find it perfectly natural, after all, to describe Spot as believing there is a cat in the tree, Tabby as believing there is food in her dish, baby Mark as believing his mother is absent.

Reactions of this sort, however, miss the point – and the force – of the line we have been pursuing. In the first place, Spot, Tabby, and baby Mark, like thermostats, may be steered by representations of their surroundings. Indeed, it is scarcely imaginable that they are

214

not so steered (cf. Ramsey 1978, p. 134). This, however, as we have seen, need not by itself be sufficient for the possession of thought. Second, we may well find it both natural and convenient to employ the vocabulary of belief, desire, and intention in explanations and predictions of the behaviour of mute creatures – or even in explanations and predictions of the behaviour of artifacts like computing machines and thermostats. Indeed, it is consistent with the discussion thus far that what Dennett (1987) calls the 'intentional stance' is not merely useful, but practically indispensable. It is important, however, to distinguish instances in which the practice of ascribing thoughts is warranted on pragmatic grounds from those the warrant of which stems from the possibility that they are literally and objectively true. I am, and I take Davidson to be, rejecting 'antirealist' accounts of the intentional attitudes: Some creatures have them, and some creatures lack them, though some creatures that lack them can nevertheless fruitfully be regarded as if they did have them.

It is still far from clear that we ought to accept Davidson's conjecture, however. Significant lacunae remain in the line of reasoning as I have reconstructed it. I shall, in the present section, focus on two matters that appear particularly troubling. First, a point raised earlier, why should we agree that one's possession of the concept of representation requires that one actually be an ascriber of representations to others? Why should it be thought impossible for me to arrive at a conception of representation, or of truth and error, by attending to my own case? Second, can Davidson possibly be right in pushing the holistic character of belief as far as he does? Does Spot's having a belief about an object really necessitate Spot's having 'endless' general beliefs about objects of that sort and untold related matters?

First, then, why should we think that a creature's possession of the concept of representation requires the exercise by that creature of a capacity to ascribe representational states to other, distinct creatures? Davidson, as we have seen, ties the concept of representation to the notion of objective truth and falsehood, a notion that, he contends, arises only when we go about the business of interpretation. He says this:

If I were bolted to the earth I would have no way of determining the distance from me of many objects. I would only know they were on some line drawn from me toward them. I might interact successfully with objects, but I could have no way of giving content to the question where they were. Not being bolted down I am free to triangulate. Our sense of objectivity is the consequence of another sort of triangulation, one that requires two creatures. Each interacts with an object, but what gives each the concept of the way things are objectively is the base line formed between the creatures by language. The fact that they share a concept of truth alone makes sense of the claim that they have beliefs, that they are able to assign objects a place in the public world.' (1982/1985, p. 480)

I do not pretend to understand these remarks completely. Since they seem to hold the key to Davidson's approach to the intentional attitudes, however, I shall offer some suggestions as to how we might take them.

Consider my registering the presence of some object in the world, a nearby iceberg, and producing an appropriate utterance, 'Iceberg!' My registering the iceberg's presence might be taken to result in an imaginary line of projection running from me to the iceberg. More accurately perhaps, the line runs between me and some state of affairs of which the iceberg is a component. I shall ignore this complication here, however, and pretend, with Davidson, that the objects of our thoughts are, typically anyway, *objects*. In any case, from *my* perspective this line of projection collapses into a point. I have no sense of there being an object, the iceberg, 'out there' at the end of the line.[19] Now imagine an interpreter, Clara, introduced into the scene. Clara's relation to the iceberg resembles mine. If we imagine that relation taking the form of a line projecting from Clara to the iceberg, that line is, from Clara's perspective, and echoing Wittgenstein, 'a point without extension' (*Tractatus* 5.64, quoted near the end of § 5 above). In interpreting my utterance, however, Clara constructs, via a 'base line' created by her interpretation, my original line of projection to the iceberg. In this way she is in a position to 'triangulate' an object, to locate it in an intersubjective space. If I am removed from the picture, the possibility of triangulation vanishes.

The story is suggestive, but uncomfortably metaphorical. It is possible, nevertheless, to see how it might apply in the present case, and, at the same time, to tie up a number of loose ends.

Earlier, I sought to motivate the idea that the concept of an objective world, hence that of representation, is possible only for an

---

19 This is not a remark about the phenomenology of visual perception, but a comment on one aspect of our concept of objectivity.

interpreter by imagining a case in which I, a solitary being, represent the ice as being safe, a representation that turns out to be false. I attempt to skate on the ice and fall through, as a result of which I no longer represent the ice as being safe, but represent it as being *unsafe*. For this to occur, I need not reflect on – that is, represent – the former representation as being false. Indeed, I need represent no *representation* at all. In contrast, when I endeavour to understand *your* actions, I should need to credit you with representations, some of which, by my lights, may well be false.

This shows, perhaps, that it is possible to suppose that a creature is, on occasion, led to revise its assessment of the facts, without thereby supposing that the creature appreciates its representations of those facts as representations. But it scarcely follows that a creature *could not* otherwise acquire the concept of representation. An argument to *that* conclusion requires that we locate a conceptual link between my possessing a notion of the possibility of truth and error, the way things are as distinct from the way they are taken to be, and my actually engaging in interpretation. Thus far we have only something weaker. There is no conceptual barrier to the supposition that I might somehow stumble on or find myself in possession of the requisite concepts just by minding my own business. I do, after all, make mistakes, and I sometimes discover that I have done so. I take the ice to be safe and discover that it is not. Is there any reason to think that I might not, then, come to distinguish true from false representations of an independent world – thereby arriving at the concept of a representation, hence the concept of belief – just on my own? For that matter, what rules out the possibility that I acquire the relevant concepts as a result of a fortuitous blow to the head or the effects of Q-rays emitted by a malfunctioning toaster?

Consider a creature equipped to take account of its activities *over time* and in that way to 'triangulate' and arrive at a concept of an intersubjective world. I might, for instance, at $t$, represent the iceberg, then later, at $t'$, represent it again, this time, however, from a distinct spatial location. I might then notice that I can take up distinct points of view on objects, and so 'triangulate' on my own. The envisaged possibility may seem question-begging. After all, it looks as though I should have to be in a position to appreciate representations qua representations in order to carry out the project of triangulation. Triangulation, however, was supposed to *yield* a concept of representation via the concept of an objective domain.

This, I think, is to take the metaphor of triangulation in the wrong way. We do not first triangulate, then subsequently arrive at a conception of a persisting world with respect to which we and others have a point of view. The metaphor does not support a genetic interpretation. The concepts of representation and objectivity, rather, are supposed to be part of a package, no ingredient of which could occur in the absence of the rest. In evaluating possible counterexamples, then, we must evaluate the entire package at once. If we do this, it certainly looks as though the possibility of 'self-triangulation' is both coherent and satisfies the remaining conditions Davidson lays down.

Despite appearances, however, it may be that the imagined possibility is at bottom actually *consistent* with Davidson's picture. Davidson speaks of speech *communities*, and of cases in which I ascribe thoughts to *another*, or meanings to *another's* utterances. This suggests that thought requires at least two thinkers. Now, Davidson may well believe that this is so, but perhaps he need not. Perhaps observations I make of myself over time are all that the reasoning requires. If that were the case, if a single agent might, under the right circumstances, count as a limiting instance of a 'speech community', then appeals to solitary thinkers would not, after all, undermine Davidson's conjecture.

This suggestion, I think, saves Davidson's thesis from certain prima facie implausible consequences. Suppose that thought does require an interpreter distinct from the thinker, and imagine that I am thinking about the iceberg in the company of Clara. Now remove Clara from the scene. The possibility of triangulation vanishes, and with it my thought.

One might think that the counterintuitive character of such examples is only apparent. After all, I have been inordinately tolerant of doctrines that appeal to Twin Earth cases in which agents, indistinguishable with respect to their intrinsic physical characteristics, diverge mentally. Why, then, should I be put off by the idea that my thoughts might depend somehow on the presence of Clara. Resemblance between the example above and Twin Earth cases, however, is only superficial. Agents on Twin Earth differ from their Earthly counterparts with respect to the causal relations they bear to their surroundings. These causal relations are taken to figure essentially in the determination of the content of their thoughts. The relation Clara bears to me, however, is not causal, but interpretive. If we imagine that Clara, or someone like Clara, *must* be in the picture, we move in the direction of an antirealist construal of mind, a construal I have resisted. If my having thoughts does not depend on others ascribing those thoughts to me, however, it is not easy to see how my having thoughts could be taken to depend on my actually ascribing thoughts to others.

I am not, incidentally, supposing that Davidson imagines that thoughts occur only during those moments when thinkers are actively scrutinised by interpreters. My assumption is that, if Davidson believes that thought requires the existence of interpreters other than the thinker, it is enough that the interpreters are *available*. Their availability gives bite, perhaps, to the normative, 'rule-governed' dimension of language.

I shall say more about language below. For the present, however, it is important to be clear about the role of interpreters in the having of thoughts. It is one thing to suppose that I have thoughts only when someone else ascribes them to me, and another matter altogether to suppose that my thoughts depend only on their being potentially ascribable. If the latter is what Davidson has in mind, then it is hard to see why we should have to imagine that thinkers must invariably share settings with other interpreters. Of course, it may be *unlikely* that, left to my own devices, I would acquire on my own the concepts I need in order to entertain complex thoughts. But that is another matter. Davidson's thesis is conceptual, not empirical.

Perhaps I have missed something. Perhaps we must have others in the picture, not as ascribers or potential ascribers of thoughts, but as *ascribees*, agents to whom *I* ascribe thoughts. Again, it is impossible to take seriously the idea that I could have thoughts only in the presence of others, so we need suppose only that ascriptive targets are *available* to me if I am to have thoughts. This, however, returns us to our earlier musings on the possibility of self-ascription, self-triangulation. My capacity to ascribe thoughts might be put to work in ascriptions of thoughts to myself over time. Such ascriptions might be based on recollection or on physical records ('traces') I have left behind. If the thought of a distinct 'other' is required, then we could imagine that I *hallucinate* Clara and interpret her hallucinatory utterances. These are ways in which I might, to all appearances anyway, operate with the concepts Davidson takes to be necessary but in the absence of actual interlocutors.

I conclude that, though we may agree that thought requires a range of capacities, including the capacity to interpret the utterances of others, we need not suppose that thinkers must actually exercise these capacities socially, in a setting that includes other speakers. I have carefully avoided comparing Davidson's suggestions in this regard with Wittgenstein's strictures against 'private languages' (1953/1968). I should be surprised, however, if the positions are entirely unrelated. I should be surprised, as well, if either is intended to exclude the possibility of a solitary, thoughtful Crusoe.

A second sticking point in the picture Davidson sketches is its ironclad holism. Davidson contends that the content of every thought, every belief is fixed largely by its place within 'a world of further beliefs'. Many of these beliefs concern general propositions. For Spot's belief about this cat to be a belief about a *cat*, then, we must be prepared to imagine Spot harbouring a host of general beliefs about cats – that they are thought to be finicky, that they are mammals, that they are related to tigers, that they bear their young live. Each of these beliefs, in turn, owes *its* content partly to relations it bears to still other general beliefs – and so on and on. In this way we are led from uncomplicated singular beliefs we are comfortable in ascribing to Spot, to complex general beliefs requiring concepts of a sort Spot is unlikely to comprehend. To the extent that we lack grounds for ascribing such beliefs to Spot, then, we thereby lack grounds for ascribing to him the original, simple belief.

The ease with which we ascribe beliefs to mute creatures without bothering about an elaborate background of general beliefs might be regarded as evidence against the sort of all-or-nothing holism Davidson espouses. Our confidence that Spot believes that a cat is in the tree might lead us to doubt that such a belief does, in fact, require a world of further beliefs. I have suggested already that a sensible response to an appeal to practices of belief-ascription to mute creatures is to concede the practices, but to insist on a distinction between truth and utility. The intentional stance may be justified in all sorts of cases for reasons that have nothing to do with the truth of the attributions it yields.

Still, there is something right about the suspicion that the holism invoked by Davidson is excessive. Suppose, then, we grant the holistic character of the intentional attitudes, but opt for holism on a more modest scale. If Spot has beliefs, then, he must have many beliefs. We need not, however, suppose that the doxastic background characteristic of a creature like Spot approaches in detail and specificity the doxastic background of a literate adult human being. Thus, we might initially leave open the precise content of Spot's beliefs, and leave open, as well, the content of whatever general beliefs with which we should be willing to credit him. If the content of a belief is determined partly by its niche in an edifice of further beliefs, then, we should be obliged to admit that the contents of Spot's beliefs about trees and cats differed importantly from the contents of our corresponding beliefs.

In an important sense, then, the words we use to describe Spot's beliefs, if indeed he has any, will be inadequate.[20] But whoever thought otherwise? My grounds for ascribing a belief about a *cat* to Spot may be shaky, but it does not follow that Spot could not, even so, harbour a representational state with a perfectly definite, semantically opaque intentional content. I might, for instance, have difficulty finding the right *words* to capture Spot's putative thought, or I might be hard-pressed to find some reason to prefer one description of that thought to another. If we suppose that the contents of intentional states are fixed at least in part by a creature's circumstances, I might be insufficiently in touch with Spot's distinctively canine lifestyle, hence unable to proclaim with confidence what he is thinking.

In advancing a scaled-down holism here, I am not challenging the notion that the possession of thought requires the concept of thought, nor am I going back on the suggestion that systems capable of thought are those with a capacity to ascribe thoughts. If Spot has thoughts, then, he possesses the requisite concepts and enjoys the associated capacities. We can expect these to be reflected in what Spot does, in his behaviour. There is reason, perhaps, to be pessimistic about Spot's capacities in this regard.[21]

It is this aspect of intentionality, the capacity for deployment or

---

20 I do not mean that we *could not* express such beliefs in our own words, only that the words we are apt to use in ascribing beliefs to Spot – assuming for a moment that Spot might have beliefs – are likely to be, in various ways, inadequate. Here we should appeal to those who study animal behaviour.

21 The matter is, however, an empirical one, not something to be decided by philosophers. Of course, should it turn out that Spot lacks the requisite capacities, we need not give up the notion that Spot is guided by representations. Perhaps this is all we should want.

*use*, that accounts for the vague intuition that the possession of thoughts, and not just our evidence for their presence, is tied to creatures' expressive capacities. Thus, in introducing the topic, I suggested that even the simplest, most rudimentary sorts of representational state – those discoverable in thermostats, for instance – owe their representational standing in part to their *role* in the system to which they belong. A particular state *counts* as a representational state of the system to which it belongs only if it could be harnessed by that system in a way that exploits its representational features. This enables us to see why it is natural to regard with suspicion that idea that a creature could harbour thoughts of a certain sort yet remain altogether incapable of expressing those thoughts. Particular thoughts, of course, might be inexpressible for a given creature owing to a variety of factors. A thought may be, in this way, *idle*. What is less obvious is that there is sense to be made of the notion that a creature might harbour thoughts that are, for that creature, *necessarily* idle (Heil 1983, chap. 8). This is not to say that every thought must be expressed behaviourally, or even that it must be expressible. The components of a system can have important roles within the system without ever announcing those roles in overt deeds of any sort.

If anything is to *count* as a thought, it must contribute – even if only potentially – to the operation of the system to which it belongs. A state or event that contributes to the operation of a system, one that is deployed by the system, might be expected to have a distinguishable effect on the system's output. A thought, then, ought to find *some* reflection in overt behaviour – or so it would seem. Because a system's outputs are a function of the system as a whole, however, assuming even a moderate level of complexity, there need be no definitive expression of any particular component of a given system. As Davidson himself puts it describing judgements based on the intentional attitudes: 'Every judgement is made in light of all the reasons in this sense, that it is made in the presence of, and is conditioned by, that totality' (1970/1980, p. 40). The original vague notion, that any thought a creature might entertain must be expressible by that creature, may be transmogrified, then, into the idea that thoughts, indeed intentional states generally, necessarily affect the operation of the system of which they are a part. The effects may have obvious and direct behavioural repercussions

– as when we speak our minds – or they may be mediated, indirect, and behaviourally ambiguous.

## 8. TALK

Where does this leave us with respect to Davidson's fundamental idea that language and thought are conceptually connected? I have allowed that Crusoe, and even Spot, might evidence thought non-linguistically. Surely this puts me at odds with Davidson.

Let us recall, briefly, Davidson's conjecture. Language is required for thought because only a creature with a capacity to interpret utterances could possess the concept of thought, and only a creature possessing the concept of thought could think. If we focus on interpretation, however, and not on articulated sentences, we may come to doubt the necessity of specifically linguistic talents. What is important is that a thinking creature possess a battery of interpretative capacities of the sort we rely on in coming to understand the utterances of others. This *may* mean that a creature capable of thought must in some sense instantiate a theory of meaning. Perhaps, however, we can allow that the possession of such a theory is a matter of being in a position to identify, distinguish, and correlate representations with representations.

The remaining question is whether nonlinguistic representation could possess the requisite definiteness required by the intensional test. Here, I turn to C. B. Martin (1987) for help. Martin inveighs against 'the persistent mystique of language'.

Nonlinguistic activity at its more sophisticated and structured levels has a remarkable pattern of parallels to that of linguistic activity. It is a matter of degree, but when an agent shows enough of this pattern of parallels, this structured network of procedures can be called 'proto-language'. (1987, p. 277)

Proto-language, on this view, is not 'a kind of language as sign language *is* a kind of language' (p. 278). It is, rather, 'a structured rule-governed network of semantic, procedural activity prior to and basic to linguistic activity, having an almost totally unnoticed and surprising pattern of parallels to language itself' (p. 278). The semantic resources of natural languages could have, it seems, non-linguistic, procedural analogues in the everyday activities – overt and covert – of intelligent agents. If Martin is right about this, then reference, quantification, modality, tense, and the rest are shown thereby not to be language-dependent. That is, we can find roles for such things in systems lacking a means of expressing them linguistically.

The point is perhaps best made by way of an example. The logical complexity of subjunctive conditionals and counterfactuals has, by some, been taken to lend support to the notion that the realisation of such things requires a distinctively linguistic medium. It seems possible, however, to imagine cases in which this is not so.

A native has noticed that when fish eat things they can be found in the stomach of the fish. He has also noticed that they eat different things at different times. When he catches a fish, he opens its stomach to see what it has been feeding on, so that he can use it as bait.

On one unsuccessful day's fishing he notices an approaching storm that looks like spoiling the fishing for a long time. Frustrated, he intends not to return to the fishing hole until the weather changes. He picks up his fishing gear and starts for the cave. He happens to frighten a mink eating a fish. His curiosity overtaking him, he opens the stomach to see what the fish had eaten and takes out some grasshoppers. This is a procedural action whose projected outcome is information about the past. It *also* has the point of finding out what *would* have helped him to catch fish if he had used it as bait. (p. 287)

Have we turned our backs on Davidson altogether, then? Davidson's conjecture is that there is a conceptual connection between thought and language. It now seems that this is unlikely. If this is so, have I then produced a refutation of Davidson's thesis and gone back on my earlier claim that 'the picture Davidson sketches is on the whole apt'? I seem to be arguing that Davidson is right in supposing that thinkers must be members of some speech community, except that they do not; and that he is right in holding that thought requires language, except that it does not.

I have suggested already that Davidson's appeal to 'speech communities' is consistent with there being solitary thinkers. I now suggest that the prospect of creatures animated by thoughts in the absence of a natural language is consistent with Davidson's reasoning *up to* its dénouement. What is required for thought is a sophisticated array of capacities, including interpretive capacities. Perhaps such capacities could be had only by a creature who possessed the concepts of representation, of an objective world, and of alternative possibilities of representation. My suggestion is that we can perfectly well agree with all this, and much more, yet stop just this side

224

of Davidson's claim that these concepts and their associated capacities are impossible in the absence of language. Davidson could be dead wrong about *that* without missing by much.

The point is easy to overlook if one underestimates how much remains. In requiring that, in order to entertain thoughts, a creature must possess the sorts of capacity sketched here, we are requiring a great deal. It is partly an empirical question, but it could easily turn out that the class of thinkers picked out by reference to these capacities is coextensive with the class picked out, as Davidson would have it, by reference to linguistic ability. Thus, it could easily turn out that any creature capable of the sort of procedural sophistication envisaged by Martin would thereby be a creature with a capacity for language. Were that so, we should have a tidy connection between thought and linguistic capacity. Perhaps that is all Davidson's argument requires.

A final word. I have taken huge liberties in interpreting Davidson as I have. It is more than just possible that I have diverted the thrust of his thesis. If that is so, however, I have at least identified an interesting thesis, one that leads us to a striking conclusion. I am tempted to think it is the thesis Davidson *should* have defended.

# 7

# *The nature of true minds*

## 1. THE STANDING OF INTENTIONALITY

On one reading of the commonsense notion of agency, agents'
behaviour is influenced causally by their intentional attitudes – their
beliefs, desires, intentions, fears, and hopes. The attitudes, on this
reading, affect behaviour according to their intentional content.
Clara's believing that Hesperus twinkles is distinct from her believing that Phosphorus twinkles. The difference would be reflected in
the divergent roles these beliefs would have in Clara's psychological
economy and, ultimately, in what Clara might say and do. This
notion of agency is central, not only in our informal, everyday
thinking about ourselves and our fellows; it underlies as well our
best efforts to understand intelligent behaviour systematically: Psychology and the social sciences take agency for granted.

What others take for granted, philosophers ponder. Often these
ponderings are all but unintelligible to those whose domain is under scrutiny. So it is with commentaries on the intentional attitudes. Although psychologists and social scientists undoubtedly
worry from time to time about the status of such things, these
worries are, for the most part, very different from those occupying
philosophers. The matter raises deep questions about the place of
philosophy vis à vis other disciplines, questions about which I have
nothing original to say. Nowadays the orthodox line is that philosophy is descriptive, not legislative. Yet a plethora of books,
articles, symposia, and conferences devoted to the prospects of
psychology – and, by extension, the social sciences – suggests
otherwise. Philosophers argue that psychology must be solipsistic,
that it must be syntactic, that it ought – or ought not – to abandon
reference to agents' intentional characteristics altogether. This
*looks,* at least, prescriptive.

226

Significantly, when we take the trouble to examine the psychological literature, we find, not the single-minded austerity urged by many philosophers, but theories brimming with talk about a wide range of intentional states and processes. This, of course, may be a mistake, even a deep mistake, but it is unlikely that philosophers are in an especially strong position to establish that it is. We should, I think, do well to view with suspicion philosophical theses that advance conceptions of psychology wildly at odds with the actual practices of psychologists.

I have urged that certain philosophical worries about the status of the intentional attitudes are unfounded. We can suppose that intentional characteristics supervene on 'more basic' features of agents, even that such characteristics are 'broadly supervenient', dependent on agents' circumstances, and still allow that our access to our own states of mind is epistemically distinctive, and that those same states of mind might have a causal part in the production of behaviour. This falls somewhat short of a proof that there are or must be intentional attitudes or even that, if the intentional attitudes exist, they do in fact influence behaviour causally. I would not know how to go about constructing such a proof. The matter is, so far as I can tell, in no small measure empirical. We must, perhaps, be satisfied with the conclusion that there are, at present, no very good philosophical or empirical reasons to doubt the existence and efficacy of the intentional attitudes, hence to pull back from the ordinary conception of agency. To go further, we should have to leave philosophy behind and indulge in largely unconstrained empirical speculation.

Why should anyone doubt the reality of the intentional attitudes? Why indeed. In another context, G. E. Moore contended that sceptical arguments purporting to undermine the possibility of knowledge about the world around us must fail. It is in the nature of things that the sceptic's premises are bound to be less certain for us than the denial of the sceptical conclusion (Moore 1922, p. 228). Something analogous is perhaps appropriate in the present case. Our encounter with intentional items, like our encounter with objects populating the 'external world', is immediate and impressive. Those who wish to call such things into question bear a distinctly nontrivial burden of proof.

Not everyone would agree. Those who speak disparagingly of folk psychology contend that the intentional attitudes, to be worthy of respect, must be shown to have a place in a healthy cognitive science, a discipline continuous with neurobiology and physics. The intentional idiom, they contend, is dependent on the theoretical framework of folk psychology in the way the terminology of folk medicine is dependent on an analogous folk theory. In abandoning the theory we abandon the categories it supports. Folk theories may prove occasionally serviceable. Their success, however, is due, not to their having got things right, but to their having stumbled on generalisations supported by deeper truths, the articulation of which awaits the development of more respectable theories. A certain herbal mixture may cure a rash. This is not because it contains the right proportion of *yin* and *yang*, but because the mixture has a particular chemical composition that destroys rash-causing bacteria. Similarly, I may predict that you will behave in a certain way by appealing to beliefs, desires, and intentions I take you to have. My prediction may prove correct, though not because I am right about your beliefs, desires, and intentions, and the connection these bear to your behaviour, but because of neural happenings beyond my ken.

This appeal to the theory dependence of postulated entities would be an impressive one were we convinced in advance that the intentional attitudes are nothing more than posits of a floundering folk theory. It is not obvious, however, that we must accept this way of framing the issue. We might admit that modern-day psychology has been, on the whole, something of a disappointment. We might grant, as well, if only for the sake of the argument, that its disappointing character is a consequence of a misguided attempt to turn our ordinary ways of speaking about one another into a rigorous science on the model of physics or astronomy. To reject the existence of the intentional attitudes by way of rejecting these efforts, however, is rather like rejecting the existence of lightning on the grounds that lightning was for a time thought to be embodied in bolts hurled by Zeus. There is no Zeus, hence no bolts hurled by Zeus, hence no lightning. Scepticism concerning the prospects of modern-day intentionalistic psychology by itself warrants neither the abandonment of ordinary intentional categories nor the rejection of ordinary – 'folk' – modes of explanation.

Eliminativist arguments, whatever their ultimate merit, do at least force us to examine commitments concerning which we should otherwise remain complacent. My strategy has been to focus on reasons we have for thinking that a 'naturalistic' picture of our world can perfectly well accommodate intentional characteristics and, with these, our ordinary conception of agency. The conception of intentionality I have sought to make room for is a broadly 'realist' one. The intentional attitudes are, or certainly seem to be, genuine constituents of the world on a par with tables, trees, and $H_2O$ molecules. If intentional characteristics exist, they would continue to exist, even if they featured in no empirical theory, indeed even – although, in light of considerations advanced in Chapter 6, this may need qualification – if there were no language in which to describe them.

A conception of this sort could be attacked from two directions. On the one hand, its realist aspect may be accepted and reasons offered for doubting that a proper inventory of the world would include anything resembling the intentional attitudes as we presently conceive them. This is the route taken by 'error theorists', eliminativist detractors of folk psychology. On the other hand, a realist construal of the attitudes might be called into question by those embracing an antirealist notion of mentality. Antirealists make intentional content depend on some constructive activity or other: theorising, interpreting, or describing, for instance. My harbouring the belief that $p$, then, might be thought to require that I be described or interpreted in a certain way. Were I exactly as I am, though not embedded in a particular community of theorisers, describers, or interpreters, I could not be said to hold the belief that $p$.

Both eliminativism and antirealism might be thought to draw support from the view, now widely shared, that the content of the intentional attitudes is fixed, not by the intrinsic features of agents, but by their circumstances. We have seen, however, that the external fixing of intentional content need not turn the intentional attitudes into shadowy constructs. Indeed, an out-and-out antirealism about such things verges on incoherence. If my thought's having a certain content requires that it be described, interpreted, theorised about in a certain way, how are we to understand *these* activities except intentionally. A describer, theoriser, or interpreter must think about, designate, or refer to what he describes, theorises about, or interprets. Such activities either require some further act of interpretation or they do not. If they do, then a regress looms. If they do not, then we are owed an explanation of how we are to take them. The regress can be blocked, perhaps, by opting for a broader

229

antirealism, one that encompasses, not merely the intentional attitudes, but the nonintentional world as well.[1] This seems to be what Putnam has in mind in advancing the view that 'the mind and the world jointly make up the mind and the world. (Or, to make the metaphor even more Hegelian, the Universe makes up the Universe – with minds – collectively – playing a special role in the making up.)' (1981, p. xi).

An antirealism of this sort represents the culmination of a difficult chain of reasoning, the evaluation of which falls well outside the intended scope of this volume. It is futile, of course, to attempt the refutation of such doctrines by constructing head-on counterexamples: Berkeley's immaterialism survived unscathed Dr. Johnson's brisk stone kicking. Nevertheless, there is something to the Johnsonian style of response. Antirealism represents more a failure of nerve than a bold theoretical advance. The antirealist manoeuvre insinuates itself whenever we cannot find a place in the natural world for a given class of entity. We go antirealist about values, for instance, only *after* having convinced ourselves that there is no plausible story to tell that places values 'out there'. We go antirealist about colours, only *after* we have decided that no 'objective' physical characteristic of objects fits our idea of what colours must be.[2] In general, antirealisms might be thought to represent a conceptual last resort.

My suggestion has been that, in the case of intentionality, other options remain open and viable. We can regard the intentional characteristics of agents as being realised by physical constituents of those agents, where the realising of $\alpha$'s by $\beta$'s is a matter of $\alpha$-exemplifications being constituted by $\beta$-exemplifications. A view of this sort can be rendered consistent with externalist conceptions of intentionality if we allow the exemplifying of intentional characteristics to depend on the historical circumstances of agents. Two agents, then, might exhibit comparable neurological characteristics without possessing the identical intentional characteristics. This

---

1 The regress might be blocked, as well, by embracing a kind of coherentism: I owe my intentional characteristics to your interpretive efforts, you owe yours to mine. It is possible – though, as I argue in Chapter 6, unlikely – that this is what Davidson envisages in associating thought and language.

2 Doubtless, some antirealists are born, not made, some prefer antirealist solutions to problems when others are available. Such preferences, I am supposing, are, in a certain sense, philosophically perverse.

could happen if the history of those agents, hence the history of their neurological 'tropes', differed in certain ways.

In opening the door to externalism in this way, it might appear that we have closed it to the possibility of mental causation. It is this thought, perhaps, that does most to motivate a range of eliminativist and antirealist manoeuvrings. It is no good being told that the intentional attitudes *exist*, but that they are causally inert. One need not be a functionalist to suppose that there is a vital conceptual connection between the character of particular representational states and their having *roles* in the system to which they belong. If we exclude these roles by rendering intentional characteristics causally inert, we have effectively excluded those characteristics.

Could this be right? Could it be, as I have suggested, something on the order of a conceptual truth that representational states have roles in the system to which they belong? Is it somehow unthinkable that we might discover representations that were systemically inert? Imagine a species of tree, for instance, that, owing to some unlikely biological accident, sprouted snapshots of its surroundings instead of ordinary leaves, but that these served only the function that leaves serve on ordinary trees.[3] Here, we apparently have representational entities that, qua representational, play no role in the system to which they belong.

Certainly the point of making photographs is typically representational. But even when it is not, even when photographs are made inadvertently, the result might seem obviously to be the production of a representational entity. The matter, however, is more complicated than the example suggests. A photograph, I think, like the fossil impression of a fern in an ancient rock, a tree's rings, and the water level in my neighbor's birdbath is indeed informative or potentially informative. The features of such things covary nonaccidentally with the features of objects or states of affairs concerning which they might be said to afford information. Because of these informational characteristics, such things might come to function as representations. Their *being* representations, however, is a matter of their being *deployed* as representations, their having a role in a system that exploits their representational character.

Agents' intentional characteristics, in one respect then, have a causal element built in. Representational states necessarily have a

3 An example of this sort was suggested to me by Alfred Mele.

role in the operation of the system to which they belong. They have this role partly in virtue of their representational character, and they are representational states partly in virtue of their having this role. This is so for simple systems like thermostats that contain at most first-order representations, and for more complex systems like human beings who enjoy a capacity for second- as well as first-order representations.

This sounds plausible, perhaps, so long as we remain close to home, so long as we ignore the possibility of physically similar systems that, because of differences in circumstances or causal history, might be thought to differ with respect to their intentional characteristics. The operation of systems intrinsically alike in pertinent physical respects, given the autonomy of the physical domain and given relevantly similar background conditions, must be physically indistinguishable. How then is it possible to regard representational – intentional – characteristics as 'making a difference' to the behaviour of any system?

The causal standing of mental characteristics, I have insisted, does not turn on our finding evidence of 'downward causation'. The presence of an intentional characteristic in a system does not add a causal element not available already in the system's purely physical components. Rather, agents' intentional attitudes are realised in those agents' physical constitutions, and it is via these physical realisations that they possess whatever causal relevance we might reasonably take them to possess.

The requirement that intentional features subserve some role in the system to which they belong, a role that reflects their intentional character, imposes nontrivial constraints on the structure, constitution, and behaviour of such systems. One result is that the operation of systems with the requisite structure and complexity depends on, and is partly explicable by reference to, their intentional features. These systems are such that, among other things, were they to lack these features, they would behave differently. Excluding cases of overdetermination, when an intentional characteristic, $M$, is realised in a system, $S$, then, it can be true of $S$ that had $M$ *not* been realised in $S$, $S$ would now be operating differently. In imaginatively 'slicing off' or subtracting from $S$ the historical and contextual factors we should need to subtract in order to eliminate the mental characteristic, $M$, we should alter $S$'s history in such a way as to alter $S$'s current physical character. In such cases, were the mental characteristic, $M$, not exemplified by $S$, $S$'s physical condition, and consequently $S$'s behaviour, would differ as well.

Twin Earth cases suggest that it is conceivable, even nomologically possible, that another system, $S^*$, might be indistinguishable from $S$ with respect to its intrinsic physical characteristics, yet fail to realise $M$. The moral, however, is not that $M$ lacks causal standing, but that $M$ is not coextensive – conceptually or nomologically – with certain intrinsic physical properties exemplified by agents. $M$ might nevertheless possess all the causal authority we could reasonably expect of a supervenient characteristic. $M$'s exemplification is constituted by the exemplification of some unproblematic physical characteristic, and there is a web of systematic, projectible truths holding for agents exemplifying $M$, truths that support counterfactual and subjunctive conditional claims of the form: Had this agent not possessed $M$ he would not now be behaving as he is behaving. These truths are grounded in unremarkable facts about the agent and his circumstances.

All this suggests a picture of intentional characteristics as constituents of the physical world, constituents the presence of which is necessitated by the character of 'more basic' constituents. A picture of this sort is at odds with conceptions that place intentional characteristics outside the natural order. Some externalists, for instance, put considerable weight on the social dimension of language and thought: Thought is possible only within a social, linguistic context. We have seen that there is a way of understanding views of this sort that is both consistent with the supervenience hypothesis – agents' intentional characteristics supervene on their nonintentional, physical characteristics – and with Davidson's claim that agents' possession of intentional characteristics is inseparable from their possession of capacities of the sort associated with the use and interpretation of language. Emphasis on social factors can, however, lead to further, more dubious claims as to the irreducibly institutional character of intentionality. The truth of the matter is that intentional characteristics call for complex structured capacities. These may occur outside of any linguistic or social setting. Nevertheless, the capacities in question are of a sort that, while they could be possessed by a solitary intelligent agent, may find their natural expression in a social and linguistic milieu.

What we must avoid, I think, is the notion that intentional characteristics might somehow 'float free' of the physical world. If

233

there are any intentional characteristics, they supervene on ordinary physical characteristics, and their exemplifications are constituted by the exemplifications of those physical characteristics. This does not mean that intentional characteristics are definable in terms of, or are nothing but, physical characteristics. It does mean, however, that intentional characteristics can be counted on to have physical realisations and these are explainable, potentially at least, in physical terms.

Even if we were convinced that intentional items depend on agents' social circumstances, those circumstances themselves might be taken to depend ultimately on distributions of assorted nonintentional, nonsocial, physical characteristics. The alternative is a radical form of dualism, one that raises as many questions as it answers. My suggestion is that, in honouring the traditional conception of agency, we need not be forced to choose between a dualism of this sort and some dreary eliminativist scheme.

## 2. PHILOSOPHY AND COGNITIVE SCIENCE

What is called for, it would seem, is the recognition that the sorts of problem confronted here require for their solution a wider range of resources than are traditionally available in philosophy. In this respect, Quine is right: Philosophy must be seen as continuous with the empirical sciences. The philosophy of mind, no less than epistemology, must in this sense take the naturalistic turn.

A fetching image, perhaps, but what exactly does it mean? Not, I think, that philosophers should give up 'doing philosophy'. The practice of philosophy is, from our current point of view, ineliminable. In embracing naturalism, we are doing no more than acknowledging the status quo. The philosophy of mind has always had an interest in empirical studies of brains and behaviour, and those studies have always been influenced by prevailing philosophical conceptions of mind. Indeed, philosophy and psychology were wedded until the mid-nineteenth century when psychology filed for divorce. Textbooks in the history of psychology exhibit a certain ambivalence about the affair. It is exhilarating, on the one hand, to trace one's roots to Plato and Aristotle. On the other hand, the association serves as a reminder that, in comparison to physics, say, or geology, or medicine, theoretical progress in psychology has been something less than spectacular. It is tempting to suppose

234

that this discouraging track record might be blamed, at least in some measure, on the presence of unexamined and disreputable philosophical presumptions lingering close to the heart of the enterprise. The invisibility of such presumptions is insured by their being universally embraced.

Even if we imagine that this is so, however, that philosophy continues to exert beneath the surface a corrupting influence on psychological theorising, we should beware of simplistic attempts to dissociate the disciplines. Such a strategy inevitably results in the repression of materials that may continue to make themselves felt, though in ways that thwart detection. In his introduction to a recent edition of James's *Principles of Psychology*, George Miller alludes to philosophical skeletons populating psychologists' closets:

> Today . . . young American psychologists . . . are educated to think of psychology as a discipline independent of philosophy, with its own problems and methods. Even when wrestling with questions that also concern philosophers, psychologists are likely to work alone, apparently on the assumption that you can ignore the skeletons so long as you don't open the closet. . . . But sometimes the bones rattle.[4]

Quite so. Still, we ought to regard with equal suspicion those who suppose that philosophers might step in and take on a consulting role helping psychologists put their houses conceptually in order. If the thought of philosophers being given the cold shoulder by psychologists is mildly disturbing, the prospect of their being heeded is surely terrifying.

Philosophy and psychology, as disciplinary matrices, are alike in many ways. Both encompass a variety of divergent traditions, problem areas, and research programmes, each with its own theoretical priorities, manipulative techniques, and standards of taste. So long as we work exclusively in our particular niche, diversity is patent. When we peer across the disciplinary divide, in contrast, disagreement and controversy are no longer salient. All of us find it difficult to explain our work and its significance to outsiders. Philosophers, for instance, are apt to be brought up short when asked how *philosophers* regard some particular topic. It is not that we lack opinions, of course, it is that we share so few. We resist being lumped into schools, even, recognising that points of stability and agreement are mostly overwhelmed by expanses of controversy.

4 From Miller's introduction to James (1890/1983, p. xi).

It is easy to lose perspective, however, when one is consulted by investigators representing other disciplines. Philosophers, here in the United States anyway, are not used to being taken seriously. When urged by nonphilosophers to pronounce on some philosophical topic, then, we are apt to be infused with a sense of authority that is at once unfamiliar and titillating. We are flattered. We imagine that our words may make a difference. Very quickly, however, exhilaration gives way to anxiety. We realise that our standing is precarious, that we possess only so much intellectual capital. It is crucial, then, that, when asked, we say The Right Thing.

The Right Thing, unsurprisingly, turns out be something with what we judge to have appropriate scientific standing. Here we encounter a difficulty. For in psychology, no less than in philosophy, theories are everywhere. As outsiders, however, we philosophers are in the enviable position of being free to disregard doubt and diversity. Our lack of empirical commitment enables us to fasten on whatever strikes us as most promising. This same lack of commitment, however, renders us powerfully susceptible to trends and fads the origins of which may include forgotten or ignored philosophical elements. There is a tendency to latch onto whatever is *comme il faut* and treat it as definitive. Our view of the territory may, as a result, be wildly skewed. Worse, by pretending in this way that psychologists speak with one voice, we invite others to suppose that our own philosophical proclivities are entirely innocent. We put to rest doubts voiced by colleagues in our own discipline by invoking empirical lore; and we gain standing among psychologists by taking care always to ride the crest of the latest wave.

Perhaps others have observed, as I have, hard-nosed philosophers, paragons of rigor and caution, swallowing seemingly outrageous claims advanced by fellow philosophers when these are presented as issuing somehow from the laboratory. The gap between the favoured philosophical thesis and the empirical theory taken to corroborate it – let alone the familiar gap between experimental findings and empirical theory – is often breathtaking. We philosophers, however, may find our critical faculties disarmed when confronted by claims given empirical billing. My suspicion is that psychologists experience a corresponding loss of nerve when they cross over into philosophical territory. Inevitably, such breakdowns threaten to blunt our usefulness to one another. We give just

236

at those points where we might remain firm, and, where flexibility is called for, we stiffen.

I mention all this by way of suggesting that official cooperation among philosophers, cognitive psychologists, neurobiologists, and others under the banner of cognitive science is not an unmixed blessing. Dangers and disutilities are apt to be hidden or disguised. Philosophers, perhaps, are most at risk. Psychological theories, by incorporating covert philosophical commitments, may in effect return these to philosophy by the back door. We philosophers, I have suggested, are far too uncritical of pronouncements we take to be empirically founded. The upshot is that philosophical theories, even those thought to be discredited, may be recycled, returned to philosophy as part of the theoretical baggage unreflectively toted by psychologists. We have convinced ourselves that when philosophers endeavour to constrain psychological theorising a priori, the blind lead the blind. When we take the naturalistic turn, philosophers and psychologists may exchange places – but in important respects the blind *still* lead the blind.

Despite the tenor of these remarks, I am not recommending that philosophers and cognitive psychologists retreat behind disciplinary barricades.[5] I want only to emphasise the complexity of a situation the complexity of which often goes unremarked and thereby to call attention to a few of the inevitable pitfalls attendant on programs of interdisciplinary integration. A naturalistic approach to the philosophy of mind is to be distinguished, as it sometimes is not, from cheerleading on behalf of the empirical sciences. There remains much to do philosophically, although it would be naïve to imagine that philosophical investigation could be conducted in a vacuum.

## 3. CONCLUDING REMARK

The upshot may seem disappointing. We are left, as it were, at our starting point. Intentionality has been defended, but not explained. Its physical basis has been reaffirmed, but no physicalistic reduction propounded. The status of intentional items as phenomena in their own right, items in need of theoretical accommodation as opposed

5 Philosophy is not autonomous, but – and this is rarely noted – neither is psychology or neurobiology autonomous with respect to philosophy.

to mere explanatory fabrications, has been emphasised, though the place of such items in a world of particles, forces, and neural goings-on has not been precisely characterised.

The aim, however, has not been to launch yet another theory of intentionality. I have set out, instead, to show that externalism, whatever its merits or liabilities, poses no immediate threat to the standing of the intentional attitudes, nor, by extension, to our ordinary conception of agency. Nonphilosophers will perhaps regard the exercise as frivolous, a characteristically philosophical attempt to establish the obvious. What is obvious, however, is no more than what can be comfortably taken for granted. Recent attacks on intentionality have, at the very least, reminded us that nothing is immune to examination, doubt, and alteration. Doubts are to be faced, not brushed aside. Faced, they may be mastered; ignored, they behave as repressed materials generally do, influencing us in unwholesome ways.

# Bibliography

Alston, W. P. 1971. Varieties of Privileged Access. *American Philosophical Quarterly*, 8: 223–41.

Anderson, J. R. 1985. *Cognitive Psychology and Its Implications*. 2d ed. New York: W. H. Freeman.

Anscombe, G. E. M. 1957. *Intention*. Oxford: Basil Blackwell.

———— 1971. *An Introduction to Wittgenstein's Tractatus*. 4th ed. London: Hutchinson.

Aristotle. *Nicomachean Ethics*. In W. D. Ross, ed., *The Works of Aristotle*, vol. 9. Oxford: Clarendon Press, 1915.

Armstrong, D. M. 1973. *Belief, Truth, and Knowledge*. Cambridge: Cambridge University Press.

Baker, L. R. 1987. *Saving Belief*. Princeton: Princeton University Press.

Beach, F. A., D. O. Hebb, C. T. Morgan, and H. W. Nissen, eds. 1960. *The Neuropsychology of Lashley*. New York: McGraw-Hill.

Beckermann, A., H. Flohr, and J. Kim, eds. 1992. *Emergence or Reduction? Essays on the Prospects of Nonreductive Physicalism*. Berlin: De Gruyter.

Bem, D. 1972. Self-Perception Theory. *Advances in Experimental Social Psychology*, 6: 1–62.

Bennett, J. 1964. *Rationality*. London: Routledge and Kegan Paul. Reprint. Indianapolis: Hackett, 1989.

———— 1976. *Linguistic Behaviour*. Cambridge: Cambridge University Press. Reprint. Indianapolis: Hackett, 1990.

———— 1985. Critical Notice: *Inquiries into Truth and Interpretation*. *Mind*, 94: 601–26.

Blackburn, S. 1984. *Spreading the Word*. Oxford: Clarendon Press.

Block, N., ed. 1980. *Readings in the Philosophy of Psychology*, vol. 1. Cambridge, Mass.: Harvard University Press.

Boyd, R. 1980. Materialism without Reductionism: What Physicalism Does Not Entail. In Block 1980: 67–106.

Broad, C. D. 1925/1960. *The Mind and Its Place in Nature*. Patterson, N.J.: Littlefield Adams.

Burge, T. 1979. Individualism and the Mental. *Midwest Studies in Philosophy*, 4: 73–121.

———— 1986. Individualism and Psychology. *Philosophical Review*, 45: 3–45.

———— 1988. Individuation and Self-Knowledge. *Journal of Philosophy*, 85: 649–63.

239

Churchland, P. M. 1979. *Scientific Realism and the Plasticity of Mind*. Cambridge: Cambridge University Press.

1981. Eliminative Materialism and the Propositional Attitudes. *Journal of Philosophy*, 78: 67–90.

1985. Reduction, Qualia, and the Direct Introspection of Brain States. *Journal of Philosophy*, 82: 8–28.

Churchland, P. S. 1986. *Neurophilosophy*. Cambridge, Mass.: MIT Press.

Cotman, C. W., and J. W. McGaugh. 1980. *Behavioural Neuroscience*. New York: Academic Press.

Cummins, R. 1983. *The Nature of Psychological Explanation*. Cambridge, Mass.: MIT Press.

Davidson, D. 1963/1980. Actions, Reasons, and Causes. *Journal of Philosophy*, 60: 685–700. Reprinted in Davidson 1980.

1970/1980. Mental Events. In Foster and Swanson 1970: 79–101. Reprinted in Davidson 1980.

1973/1980. The Material Mind. In Suppes, Henkin, Moisil, and Joja 1973: 709–22. Reprinted in Davidson 1980.

1973/1984. Radical Interpretation. *Dialectica*, 27: 313–28. Reprinted in Davidson 1984.

1975/1984. Thought and Talk. In Guttenplan 1975: 7–23. Reprinted in Davidson 1984.

1980. *Essays on Actions and Events*. Oxford: Clarendon Press.

1982/1985. Rational Animals. *Dialectica*, 36: 317–27. Reprinted in LePore and McLaughlin 1985.

1984. *Inquiries into Truth and Interpretation*. Oxford: Clarendon Press.

1985. Replies to Essays X–XII. In Vermazen and Hintikka 1985: 242–52.

1986. A Coherence Theory of Truth and Knowledge. In Le Pore 1986: 307–19.

1987. Knowing One's Own Mind. *Proceedings and Address of the American Philosophical Association*, 60: 441–58.

1992. Thinking Causes. In Heil and Mele 1992.

Dennett, D. 1987. *The Intentional Stance*. Cambridge, Mass.: MIT Press.

Descartes, R. 1642/1986. *Meditations on First Philosophy*. Translated by J. Cottingham. Cambridge: Cambridge University Press.

Dray, W. H. 1957. *Laws and Explanation in History*. Oxford: Clarendon Press.

Dretske, F. I. 1981. *Knowledge and the Flow of Information*. Cambridge, Mass.: MIT Press.

1988. *Explaining Behavior: Reasons in a World of Causes*. Cambridge, Mass.: MIT Press.

Feigl, H., and M. Scriven, eds. 1956. *Minnesota Studies in the Philosophy of Science*, 1 (*The Foundations of Science and the Concepts of Psychology and Psychoanalysis*). Minneapolis: University of Minnesota Press.

Fish, S. 1980. *Is There a Text in This Class?* Cambridge, Mass.: Harvard University Press.

1989. *Doing What Comes Naturally*. Durham, N.C.: Duke University Press.

Fodor, J. 1975. *The Language of Thought.* New York: T. Y. Crowell.

    1980/1981. Methodological Solipsism Considered as a Research Strategy in Cognitive Psychology. *Behavioral and Brain Sciences*, 3: 63–73. Reprinted in Fodor 1981.

    1981. *Representations: Essays in the Foundations of Cognitive Science.* Cambridge, Mass.: MIT Press.

    1987. *Psychosemantics.* Cambridge, Mass.: MIT Press.

    1991. A Modal Argument for Narrow Content. *Journal of Philosophy*, 88: 5–26.

Foster, L., and J. W. Swanson, eds. 1980. *Experience and Theory.* Amherst, Mass.: University of Massachusetts Press.

Gazzaniga, M. S. 1970. *The Bisected Brain.* New York: Appleton-Century-Crofts.

Georgalis, N. 1990. No Access for the Externalist: Discussion of Heil's 'Privileged Access'. *Mind*, 99: 101–8.

Goldman, A. I. 1970. *A Theory of Human Action.* Princeton: Princeton University Press.

Goodman, N. 1965. *Fact, Fiction, and Forecast.* Indianapolis: Bobbs-Merrill.

Grice, H. 1957. Meaning. *Philosophical Review*, 66: 377–88.

Grimes, T. 1988. The Myth of Supervenience. *Pacific Philosophical Quarterly*, 69: 152–60.

Gunderson, K., ed. 1975. *Minnesota Studies in the Philosophy of Science*, 12 (*Language, Mind, and Knowledge*). Minneapolis: University of Minnesota Press.

Guttenplan, S., ed. 1975. *Mind and Language.* Oxford: Clarendon Press.

Hamlyn, D. W. 1990. *In and Out of the Black Box: On the Philosophy of Cognition.* Oxford: Basil Blackwell.

Hare, R. 1952. *The Language of Morals.* Oxford: Clarendon Press.

    1984. Supervenience. *Proceedings of the Aristotelian Society* (Supl. vol. 58): 1–16.

Haugeland, J. 1981. Semantic Engines: An Introduction to Mind Design. In *Mind Design: Philosophy, Psychology, Artificial Intelligence.* Cambridge, Mass.: MIT Press.

    1982. Weak Supervenience. *American Philosophical Quarterly*, 19: 93–103.

Heil, J. 1982. What Does the Mind's Eye Look At? *Journal of Mind and Behavior*, 3: 143–49.

    1983. *Perception and Cognition.* Berkeley: University of California Press.

    1987. Are We Brains in a Vat? Top Philosopher Says 'No'. *Canadian Journal of Philosophy*, 17: 427–36.

    1988. The Epistemic Route to Anti-Realism. *The Australian Journal of Philosophy*, 66: 161–73.

Heil, J., and A. Mele, eds. 1991. *Mental Causation.* Oxford: Clarendon Press.

Hellman, G., and F. Thompson. 1975. Physicalism, Ontology, Determination, and Reduction. *Journal of Philosophy*, 73: 551–64.

Hellman, G. 1992. Supervenience/Determination a Two-way Street? Yes, But One of the Ways is the *Wrong Way! Journal of Philosophy*, 89: 42–47.

Honderich, T. 1988. *A Theory of Determinism: The Mind, Neuroscience, and Life-Hopes*. Oxford: Clarendon Press.

Horgan, T. 1982. Supervenience and Microphysics. *Pacific Philosophical Quarterly*, 63: 29–43.

Hubel, D. H., and T. N. Wiesel. 1979. Brain Mechanisms of Vision. *Scientific American*, 241: 150–62.

Hume, D. 1739/1964. *A Treatise of Human Nature*. Edited by L. A. Selby-Bigge. Oxford: Clarendon Press.

Huxley, T. 1917. *Method and Results*. New York: D. Appleton.

James, W. 1890/1983. *The Principles of Psychology*. Edited by G. A. Miller. Cambridge, Mass.: Harvard University Press.

Kertesz, A., ed. 1983. *Localization in Neurophysiology*. New York: Academic Press.

Kim, J. 1966. On the Psycho-Physical Identity Theory. *American Philosophical Quarterly*, 3: 227–35.

1973. Causation, Nomic Subsumption, and the Concept of Event. *Journal of Philosophy*, 70: 217–36.

1978. Supervenience and Nomological Incommensurables. *American Philosophical Quarterly*, 15: 149–56.

1979. Causality, Identity, and Supervenience in the Mind-Body Problem. *Midwest Studies in Philosophy*, 4: 31–49.

1982. Psychophysical Supervenience. *Philosophical Studies*, 41: 51–70.

1984a. Concepts of Supervenience. *Philosophy and Phenomenological Research*, 45: 153–76.

1984b. Epiphenomenal and Supervenient Causation. *Midwest Studies in Philosophy*, 9: 257–70.

1987. 'Strong' and 'Global' Supervenience Revisited. *Philosophy and Phenomenological Research*, 48: 315–26.

1989a. Mechanism, Purpose, and Explanatory Exclusion. *Philosophical Perspectives*, 3: 77–108.

1989b. The Myth of Nonreductive Materialism. *Proceedings and Addresses of the American Philosophical Association*, 63: 31–47.

1990. Supervenience as a Philosophical Concept. *Metaphilosophy*, 12: 1–27.

1992. 'Downward Causation' in Emergentism and Nonreductive Physicalism. In Beckermann, Flohr, and Kim 1992: 119–38.

Klagge, J. 1988. Supervenience: Ontological and Ascriptive. *Australasian Journal of Philosophy*, 66: 461–70.

Kosslyn, S., S. Pinker, G. Smith, and S. Schwartz. 1979. The Demystification of Mental Imagery. *Behavioral and Brain Sciences*, 2: 535–48.

Lashley, K. S. 1950. In Search of the Engram. Society of Experimental Biology Symposium No. 4: *Physiological Mechanisms in Animal Behaviour*. Cambridge: Cambridge University Press. Reprinted in Beach et al. 1960.

Leon, M. 1988. Realism, Scepticism (and Empiricism). *Metaphilosophy*, 19: 143–57.

Le Pore, E., ed. 1986. *Truth and Interpretation: Perspectives on the Philosophy of Donald Davidson*. Oxford: Basil Blackwell.

Le Pore, E., and B. Loewer. 1987. Mind Matters. *Journal of Philosophy*, 84: 630–42.

　1989. More on Making Mind Matter. *Philosophical Topics*, 17: 175–91.

Le Pore, E., and B. McLaughlin, eds. 1985. *Actions and Events: Perspectives on the Philosophy of Donald Davidson*. Oxford: Basil Blackwell.

Lewis, D. 1983a. New Work for a Theory of Universals. *Australasian Journal of Philosophy*, 61: 343–77.

　1983b. *Philosophical Papers*, vol. 1. New York: Oxford University Press.

Linneberg, E. H. 1967. *Biological Foundations of Language*. New York: John Wiley and Sons.

Locke, J. 1690/1978. *An Essay Concerning Human Understanding*. Edited by P. H. Nidditch. Oxford: Clarendon Press.

Lombard, L. 1986. *Events: A Metaphysical Study*. London: Routledge and Kegan Paul.

Luria, A. R. 1973. *The Working Brain: An Introduction to Neuropsychology*. Translated by B. Haigh. Harmondsworth: Allen Lane.

Macdonald, C. 1989. *Mind-Body Identity Theories*. London: Routledge and Kegan Paul.

McGinn, C. 1989. *Mental Content*. Oxford: Basil Blackwell.

Mackie, J. L. 1974. *The Cement of the Universe: A Study of Causation*. Oxford: Clarendon Press.

McKinsey, M. 1991. Anti-Individualism and Privileged Access. *Analysis*, 51: 9–16.

McLaughlin, B. 1989. Type Epiphenomenalism, Type Dualism, and the Causal Priority of the Physical. *Philosophical Perspectives*, 3: 109–35.

　1992. The Rise and Fall of British Emergentism. In Beckermann, Flohr, and Kim 1992: 49–93.

Malcolm, N. 1968. The Conceivability of Mechanism. *Philosophical Review*, 77: 45–72.

Martin, C. B. 1987. Proto-Language. *Australasian Journal of Philosophy*, 65: 277–89.

Martin, C. B, and K. Pfeifer. 1986. Intentionality and the Non-Psychological. *Philosophy and Phenomenological Research*, 46: 531–54.

Meehl, P., and W. Sellars. 1956. The Concept of Emergence. In Feigl and Scriven 1956: 239–52.

Melden, A. I. 1961. *Free Action*. London: Routledge and Kegan Paul.

Mele, A. R. 1992. *Springs of Action: Understanding Intentional Behavior*. New York: Oxford University Press.

Miller, R. 1990. Supervenience Is a Two-Way Street. *Journal of Philosophy*, 87: 695–701.

Millikan, R. G. 1984. *Language, Thought, and Other Biological Categories*. Cambridge, Mass.: MIT Press.

　1989. Biosemantics. *Journal of Philosophy*, 86: 281–97.

Moore, G. E. 1903/1968. *Principia Ethica*. Cambridge: Cambridge University Press.

　1922. *Philosophical Studies*. London: Routledge and Kegan Paul.

Morgan, L. 1923. *Emergent Evolution*. London: Williams and Northgate.

Morrison, J. 1977. Two Unresolved Difficulties in the Line and the Cave. *Phronesis*, 22: 212–31.

Nagel, E. 1961. *The Structure of Science: Problems in the Logic of Scientific Explanation.* New York: Harcourt, Brace, and World.

Noonan, H. W. 1992. Object Dependent Thoughts–A Case of Superficial Necessity but Deep Contingency. In Heil and Mele 1992.

Oakley, D. A., ed. 1985. *Brain and Mind.* London: Metheuen.

Penfield, W. 1967. *The Excitable Cortex in Conscious Man.* Liverpool: Liverpool University Press.

Pepper, S. C. 1926. Emergence. *Journal of Philosophy*, 23: 241–45.

Pereboom, D., and H. Kornblith. 1991. The Metaphysics of Irreducibility. *Philosophical Studies*, 61: 131–51.

Peters, R. S. 1958. *The Concept of Motivation.* London: Routledge and Kegan Paul.

Petrie, B. 1987. Global Supervenience and Reduction. *Philosophy and Phenomenological Research*, 48: 119–30.

Post, J. 1987. *The Faces of Existence: An Essay in Nonreductive Metaphysics.* Ithaca: Cornell University Press.

1991. *Metaphysics: A Contemporary Introduction.* New York: Paragon House.

Premack, D. 1986. *Gavagai! Or the Future History of the Animal Language Controversy.* Cambridge, Mass.: MIT Press.

Putnam, H. 1975a/1975b. The Meaning of 'Meaning'. In Gunderson 1975.

1975b. *Mind, Language, and Reality: Philosophical Papers*, vol. 2. Cambridge: Cambridge University Press.

1981. *Reason, Truth, and History.* Cambridge: Cambridge University Press.

Quine, W. V. 1960. *Word and Object.* Cambridge, Mass.: MIT Press.

Ramsey, F. 1978. *Foundations: Essays in Philosophy, Logic, Mathematics, and Economics.* Edited by D. H. Mellor. London: Routledge and Kegan Paul.

Ryle, G. 1949. *The Concept of Mind.* London: Hutchinson.

Schiffer, S. 1991. *Ceteris Paribus* Laws. *Mind*, 100: 1–17.

Seager, W. 1988. Weak Supervenience and Materialism. *Philosophy and Phenomenological Research*, 48: 697–709.

Searle, J. 1980. Minds, Brains, and Programs. *Behavioral and Brain Sciences*, 3: 417–24.

1983. *Intentionality.* Cambridge: Cambridge University Press.

Smart, J. J. C. 1959. Sensations and Brain-Processes. *Philosophical Review*, 68: 141–56.

Sosa, E. 1992. Abilities, Concepts, and Externalism. In Heil and Mele 1992.

Sperry, R. W. 1952. Neurology and the Mind-Brain Problem. *American Scientist*, 40: 291–312.

Stich, S. 1978. Autonomous Psychology and the Belief-Desire Thesis. *The Monist*, 61: 573–91.

1983. *From Folk Psychology to Cognitive Science: The Case against Belief.* Cambridge, Mass.: MIT Press.

244

Suppes, P., L. Henkin, G. Moisil, and A. Joja, eds. 1973. *Proceedings of the Fourth International Congress for Logic, Methodology, and Philosophy of Science* (Bucharest, 1971). Amsterdam: North Holland.

Van Cleve, J. 1990a. Mind-Dust or Magic? Panpsychism versus Emergence. *Philosophical Perspectives*, 4: 215–26.

1990b. Supervenience and Closure. *Philosophical Studies*, 58: 225–38.

Van Gulick, R. 1988. A Functionalist Plea for Self- Consciousness. *Philosophical Review*, 97: 149–81.

Vermazen, B., and M. B. Hintikka, eds. 1985. *Essays on Davidson on Actions and Events*. Oxford: Clarendon Press.

von Frisch, K. 1950/1971. *Bees: Their Vision, Chemical Senses, and Language*. Rev. ed. Ithaca: Cornell University Press.

Vonnegut, K. 1973. *Breakfast of Champions*. New York: Dell.

Williams, B. 1978. *Descartes: The Project of Pure Inquiry*. Harmondsworth: Penguin Books.

Williams, D. 1966. *Principles of Empirical Realism*. Springfield: Charles Thomas.

Wittgenstein, L. 1921/1960. *Tractatus Logico-Philosophicus*. Translated by D. F. Pears and B. F. McGuinness. London: Routledge and Kegan Paul.

1953/1968. *Philosophical Investigations*. Translated by G. E. M. Anscombe. Oxford: Basil Blackwell.

1958. *The Blue and Brown Books*. Oxford: Basil Blackwell.

1974. *Philosophical Grammar*. Edited by R. Rees. Translated by A. Kenny. Oxford: Basil Blackwell.

Young, J. Z. 1987. *Philosophy and the Brain*. Oxford: Oxford University Press.

# Index

246

248

| DATE DUE | BORROWER'S NAME |
|---|---|
|  |  |
|  |  |
|  |  |
|  |  |